Alleys of Your Mind

Alleys of Your Mind: Augmented Intelligence and Its Traumas

edited by
Matteo Pasquinelli

μ **meson press**

Bibliographical Information of the German National Library
The German National Library lists this publication in the Deutsche
Nationalbibliografie (German National Bibliography); detailed
bibliographic information is available online at http://dnb.d-nb.de.

Published by meson press, Hybrid Publishing Lab,
Centre for Digital Cultures, Leuphana University of Lüneburg
www.meson-press.com

LEUPHANA
CENTRE FOR DIGITAL CULTURES

Design concept: Torsten Köchlin, Silke Krieg
Cover image: Michael Deistler
Copy-editing: Jacob Watson
The print edition of this book is printed by Lightning Source,
Milton Keynes, United Kingdom.

ISBN (Print): 978-3-95796-065-8
ISBN (PDF): 978-3-95796-066-5
ISBN (EPUB): 978-3-95796-067-2
DOI: 10.14619/014

The digital editions of this publication can be downloaded freely at:
www.meson-press.com

Funded by the EU major project Innovation Incubator Lüneburg

Contents

Introduction   7
Matteo Pasquinelli

PART I: FROM CYBERTRAUMA TO SINGULARITY

[1]   **The Pigeon in the Machine: The Concept of Control in Behaviorism and Cybernetics   23**
Ana Teixeira Pinto

[2]   **Error Correction: Chilean Cybernetics and Chicago's Economists   37**
Adrian Lahoud

[3]   **The Trauma Machine: Demos, Immersive Technologies and the Politics of Simulation   53**
Orit Halpern

[4]   **Outing Artificial Intelligence: Reckoning with Turing Tests   69**
Benjamin Bratton

PART II: COGNITION BETWEEN AUGMENTATION AND AUTOMATION

[5]   **Thinking Beyond the Brain: Educating and Building from the Standpoint of Extended Cognition   85**
Michael Wheeler

[6]   **Late Capitalism and the Scientific Image of Man: Technology, Cognition, and Culture   107**
Jon Lindblom

[7]   **Instrumental Reason, Algorithmic Capitalism, and the Incomputable   125**
Luciana Parisi

[8]   **Revolution Backwards: Functional Realization and Computational Implementation   139**
Reza Negarestani

[9] **Loops of Augmentation: Bootstrapping, Time Travel, and Consequent Futures** 157
Ben Woodard

PART III: THE MATERIALISM OF THE SOCIAL BRAIN

[1 0] **Brain Theory Between Utopia and Dystopia: Neuronormativity Meets the Social Brain** 173
Charles T. Wolfe

[1 1] **Post-Trauma: Towards a New Definition?** 187
Catherine Malabou

APPENDIX

Keyword: Augmented Intelligence 203
Matteo Pasquinelli

Authors 211

Introduction

Matteo Pasquinelli

> *Catastrophe is the past coming apart.*
> *Anastrophe is the future coming together.*
> — *Land and Plant (1994)*

The Reason of Trauma

One day, it will not be arbitrary to reframe twentieth century thought and its intelligent machines as a quest for the positive definition of error, abnormality, trauma, and catastrophe—a set of concepts that need to be understood in their cognitive, technological and political composition. It may be surprising for some to find out that Foucault's history of biopower and technologies of the self share common roots with cybernetics and its early error-friendly universal machines. Or to learn that the desiring machines, which "continually break down as they run, and in fact run only when they are not functioning properly" (Deleuze and Guattari 1983, 8), were in fact echoing research on war traumas and brain plasticity from the First World War. Across the history of computation (from early cybernetics to artificial intelligence and current algorithmic capitalism) both mainstream technology and critical responses to it have shared a common belief in the determinism and positivism of the *instrumental* or *technological rationality,* to use the formulations of the Frankfurt School (Horkheimer 1947; Marcuse 1964). Conversely, the aim of this anthology is to rediscover the role of error, trauma and catastrophe in the design of intelligent machines and the theory of augmented cognition. These are timely and urgent issues: the media hype of singularity occurring for artificial intelligence appears just to fodder a pedestrian catastrophism without providing a basic epistemic model to frame such an "intelligence explosion" (Chalmers 2010).

The definition of error had a fundamental role in the genesis of the Enlightenment as well. According to Bates (2002) both critics, such as the Frankfurt School, and defenders, like liberals and socialist revolutionaries, wrongly believed that the Enlightenment was just driven by plain confidence in reason. Instead, Bates stresses that the Age of Reason was obsessed with the constitution of error and considered human knowledge to be basically an *aberration.* Since the method of "truth is really parasitic on its supposed negation," Bates (2002, viii) suggests then that the Enlightenment in fact laid the groundwork for a modern epistemology of error. Therefore, critical theory's approach should be redirected toward its own postulates in order to inquire if the whole history of instrumental reason—from the Age of Reason to the Age of Intelligent Machines—has actually concealed a deep and structural *errancy*.

These older concerns of the relation between technology and reason re-emerge today as concerns of the relation between computation and cognition. The current philosophical debate appears to be polarized between the positions of neomaterialism and neorationalism, that is between novel interpretations of Whitehead and Sellars, for instance, between those who side with the agency of technical objects, matter and affects and those who address the primacy of reason and its potential forms of autonomization.[1] The anthology cuts across these binaries by proposing, more modestly, that a distinction should be made between those philosophies that acknowledge a positive and constituent role for error, abnormality, pathology, trauma, and catastrophe on the one hand, and those who support a *flat ontology* without dynamic, self-organizing and constitutive ruptures on the other. No paradigm of cognition and computation (neomaterialist or neorationalist) can be assessed without the recognition of the *epistemic abnormal* and the role of noetic failure. Departing from the lesson of *the trauma of reason* instructed by the Frankfurt School, *the reason of trauma* must be rediscovered as the actual inner logic of the age of intelligent machines.

The Pathology of Machines

With much akin to the turbulent underground that contributed to the computer revolution in the California of the 1970s, cybernetics was born out of a practice-based, error-friendly and social-friendly milieu, as Pickering (2010) recounts in his seminal book *The Cybernetic Brain*. Cybernetics is often perceived as an evolution of information theory and its predictable communication channels, but many cyberneticians of the first generation were actually trained in psychology and psychiatry. As Pickering reminds us, the idea of the cybernetic machine was shaped after the adaptive theory of the brain, according to which the function of the brain organ is not the *representation of* but the *adaptation to* the external environment. The canonical image of the organism struggling to adapt to its own *Umwelt* belongs of course to the history of evolutionary theory and beforehand, famously, to German *Naturphilosophie*. This historical note is not attached here to evoke a biomorphic substrate of information technologies in a vitalist fashion, but on the contrary to exhume the role of abstraction in the philosophies of life. Whether we are conscious of it or not, any machine is always a machine of cognition, a product of the human intellect and a component of the gears of extended cognition.[2]

---

1   For a general overview of this debate see Bryant et al. 2011. A main neorationalist reference is Brassier 2007. For a recent neomaterialist response see Shaviro 2014.
2   The concepts of organism, structure and system had a very promiscuous family life throughout the twentieth century. In this anthology they are considered *symbolic and*

French philosophers and American cyberneticians did not welcome the parallelism between organisms and machines with the same enthusiasm. In his influential lecture "Machine and Organism" Canguilhem stated that a machine, unlike an organism, cannot display pathological behaviors as it is not adaptive. An organism becomes mentally ill as it has the ability to self-organize and repair itself, whereas the machine's components have fixed goals that cannot be repurposed.[3] There is no machine pathology as such, also on the basis that "a machine cannot replace another machine," concluded Canguilhem (1947, 109). Nonetheless Bates has noted that the early "cyberneticists were intensely interested in pathological break-downs [and] Wiener claimed that certain psychological instabilities had rather precise technical analogues" (Bates 2014, 33). The adaptive response of the machine was often discussed by early cyberneticians in terms of error, shock and catastrophe. Even the central notion of homeostasis was originally conceived by the physiologist Walter Cannon (who introduced it in cybernetics) as the organism's reaction to a situation of emergency, when the body switch to the state of *flight or fight* (Bates 2014, 44). At the center of the early cybernetic paradigm, catastrophe could be found as its forgotten operative kernel.

The Catastrophic Brain

Across the thought of the twentieth century the saga of the *instrumentalization of reason* was paralleled by the less famous lineage of the *instrumentalization of catastrophe*, that was most likely the former's actual epistemic engine. The model of catastrophe in cybernetics and even the catastrophe theory in mathematics (since Thom 1975) happened to be both inspired by the intuitions of the neurologist Kurt Goldstein, who curiously was also the main influence behind Canguilhem's lecture "Machine and Organism."[4] Goldstein is found at the confluence of crucial tendencies of the twentieth century neurology and philosophy and his thought is briefly presented here to cast a different light on the evolution of augmented intelligence.

Goldstein was not an esoteric figure in the scientific and intellectual circles of Berlin. He was the head of the neurology station at the Moabit hospital when, in 1934, he was arrested by the Gestapo and expelled from Germany. While in exile in Amsterdam, in only five weeks, he dictated and published his seminal monograph *Der Aufbau des Organismus* (literally: the "structure"

---

logic forms rather than ontological ones.

3   Canguilhem's 1947 lecture had a profound influence on the French post-structuralism, including Foucault and Simondon. The famous passage on the desiring machines "that continually break down as they run" (Deleuze and Guattari 1983, 8) is also a reference to this debate. Deleuze and Guattari's notion of the desiring machine proved afterward to be a very successful one, but at the cost of severing more profound ties with the domain of the machines of cognition.

4   On the legacy of Goldstein see Harrington 1996, Bates 2014, Pasquinelli 2014 and 2015.

or "construction" of the organism). Goldstein's clinical research started with the study of brain injuries in WWI soldiers and intellectually it was influenced by German Idealism and *Lebensphilosophie*. With the Gestalt school and his cousin Ernst Cassirer, he shared a sophisticated theory of the *symbolic forms* (from mathematics to mythology) whose creation is a key faculty of the human mind. Goldstein was an extremely significant inspiration also for Merleau-Ponty (1942) and Canguilhem (1943). Foucault (1954) himself opened his first book with a critique of Goldstein's definitions of mental illness discussing the notions of abstraction, abnormality, and milieu.

It is essential to note that Goldstein (1934) posits trauma and catastrophe as operative functions of the brain and not simply as reactions to external accidents. Goldstein makes no distinction between ordered behavior and unordered behavior, between health and pathology—being any normal or abnormal response expression of the same adaptive antagonism to the environment. Goldstein's organic normativity of the brain appears to be more sophisticated than the simple idea of neuroplasticity: the brain is not just able to self-repair after a damage, but it is also able to self-organize "slight catastrophic reactions" (Goldstein 1934, 227) in order to equalize and augment itself. The brain is then in a permanent and constitutive state of *active trauma*. Within this model of cognitive normativity, more importantly, the successful elaboration of traumas and catastrophes always implies the production of *new norms* and *abstract forms of behavior*. Abstraction is the outcome of the antagonism with the environment and an embryonic trauma can be found at the center of any new abstraction.

This core of intuitions that influenced the early cybernetics could be extended, more in general, also to the age of intelligent machines. Since a strong distinction between machines and the brain is nowadays less of a concern, cognition is perceived as extended and its definition incorporates external functions and partial objects of different sorts. The technologies of augmented intelligence could be understood therefore as a *catastrophic process* continuously adapting to its environment rather than as a linear process of instrumental rationality. Open to the outside, whether autonomous or semi-autonomous, machines keep on extending human traumas.

The Human Mask of Artificial Intelligence

The recognition of a catastrophic process at the center of cognition also demands a new analytics of power and cognitive capitalism. In contrast, the current hype surrounding the risks of artificial intelligence merely appears to be repeating a grotesque catastrophism, which is more typical of Hollywood movies.[5] This anthology attempts to ground a different angle also on this debate, where a definition of "intelligence" still remains an open problem. From a philosophical point of view, human intelligence is in itself always artificial, as it engenders novel dimensions of cognition. Conversely, the design of artificial intelligence is still a product of the human intellect and therefore a form of its augmentation. For this reason the title of the anthology refers, more modestly, to the notion of augmented intelligence—to remind us of a post-human legacy between the human and the machine that is yet problematic to sever (despite the fact that machines manifest different degrees of autonomous agency).

There are at least three troublesome issues in the current narrative on the singularity of artificial intelligence: first, the expectation of anthropomorphic behavior from machine intelligence (i.e., the anthropocentric fallacy); second, the picture of a smooth exponential growth of machines' cognitive skills (i.e., the bootstrapping fallacy); third, the idea of a virtuous unification of machine intelligence (i.e., the singularity fallacy). Regarding the anthropocentric fallacy, Benjamin Bratton's essay in the present anthology takes up the image of the Big Machine coming to wipe out mankind, which is basically an anthropomorphic projection, attributing to machines what are features specific to animals, such as predator instincts. Chris Eliasmith takes on the bootstrapping fallacy by proposing a more empirical chronology for the evolutions of artificial minds that is based on progressive stages (such as "autonomous navigation," "better than human perception," etc.), according to which "it seems highly unlikely that there will be anything analogous to a mathematical singularity" (Eliasmith 2015, 13). Similarly, Bruce Sterling is convinced that the unification and synchronization of different intelligent technologies will happen to be very chaotic:

> We do not have Artificial Intelligence today, but we do have other stuff like computer vision systems, robotic abilities to move around, gripper systems. We have bits and pieces of the grand idea, but those pieces are big industries. They do not fit together to form one super thing. Siri can talk, but she cannot grip things. There are machines that grip and manipulate, but they do not talk. [...] There will not be a Singularity. (Sterling 2015)

In general, the catastrophism and utopianism that are cultivated around artificial intelligence are both the antithesis of that *ready-to-trauma logic* that have been detected at the beginning of the history of intelligent machines. This issue points to an epistemic and political gap of the current age yet to be resolved.

---

5   See for instance Elon Musk's statement in October 2014 declaring AI the most serious
      threat to the survival of the human race (Gibbs 2014).

Alleys of Your Mind

The anthology proposes to reframe and discuss the *reason of trauma* and the notion of augmentation from the early cybernetics to the age of artificial intelligence touching also the current debates in neuroscience and the philosophy of mind. The keyword entry at the end of the book provides a historical account of the notion of augmented intelligence starting from the definition given by Douglas Engelbart (1962) and following the evolution of both the technological and political axes, that cannot be easily separated.

The first part "From Cybertrauma to Singularity" follows the technopolitical composition from cybernetics during the Second World War to the recent debates on artificial intelligence today. Ana Teixeira Pinto focuses on the moment where cybernetics emerges out of the conflation of behaviorism and engineering during the war years. Teixeira Pinto recounts the influence of behaviorism on wartime cybernetics and the employment of animals (like pigeons) in the design of oddly functional ballistic machinery. War experiments were also the breeding ground upon which the mathematical notion of information was systematized, she reminds us. At odds with such a determinism (or probably just the other side of it), Teixeira Pinto unveils the hidden animism of cybernetics: "the debate concerning the similarities and differences between living tissue and electronic circuitry also gave rise to darker man-machine fantasies: zombies, living dolls, robots, brain washing, and hypnotism" (31). In conclusion, Teixeira Pinto stresses that the way cybernetics treats "action" and "reaction" as an integrated equation was extrapolated into a political and economic ideology (neoliberalism), which denies social conflict, while the tradition of dialectical materialism has always maintained an unresolved antagonism at the center of politics. Anticipating an argument of the following essay, she encapsulates her analysis in a dramatic way: "cybernetic feedback is dialectics without the possibility of communism" (33).

Adrian Lahoud measures the limits of the cybernetic ideals of the 1970s against the background of Salvador Allende's Chile, where the Cybersyn project was developed by the British cybernetician Stafford Beer in order to help manage the national economy. Cybersyn represented an experimental alliance between the idea of equilibrium in cybernetics and social equity in socialism. Lahoud remarks that any cybernetic system is surely defined by its *Umwelt* of sensors and information feedbacks, but more importantly by its *blind spots*. "Where is one to draw the line, that difficult threshold between the calculable and the incalculable, the field of vision and the blind spot?" (46) asks Lahoud in a question that could be addressed also to current digital studies. The blind spot for Allende's cybernetic socialism happened to be Pinochet's coup on 11 September 1973. Of course Cybersyn was never designed to halt a putsch and Pinochet indeed represented a set of forces that was exceeding the equilibrium field of cybersocialism. Any technology may happen to be colonized and, at the end, Lahoud follows the taming of cybernetic equilibrium within the deep structure of neoliberalism.

Orit Halpern writes in memory of the filmmaker Haroun Farocki. In his *Serious Games* (2011) multi-screen installation, the viewer is immersed in 3D simulations of war scenarios, which are used by the US Army for both military training and the treatment of post-traumatic stress disorder. On one screen, young soldiers learn how to drive tanks and shoot targets in Iraq and Afghanistan; on the other, veterans are treated for war traumas like the loss of a friend in combat. The repeated reenactment of a traumatic event with virtual reality is used to gradually heal the original shock and sever the mnemonic relation with pain. This therapeutic practice dates back to Freud's time, but here the therapist is replaced by a fully immersive interface. As Halpern remarks: "[T]rauma here is not created from a world external to the system, but actually generated, preemptively, from within the channel between the screens and the nervous system" (54). Halpern retraces the genealogy of such military software to the Architecture Machine Group at MIT, where in the 1980s the "Demo or Die" adage was born. Aside from warfare tactics, these new immersive interfaces were also tested in the context of racial conflicts, like in the controversial Hessdorfer Experiment in Boston. Halpern describes a world already beyond psychoanalysis, where cognition and computation collapse into each other on the political horizon of video simulation.

Benjamin Bratton contests the anthropocentric fallacy of the current hype and alarmism around the risks of artificial intelligence, according to which hostile behaviors are expected from future intelligent technologies. Scientists and entrepreneurs, Stephen Hawking and Elon Musk among them, have recently been trying to warn the world, with Musk even declaring artificial intelligence to be the most serious threat to the survival of the human race. Bratton discusses different aspects of the anthropocentric fallacy moving from the first instance of the "imitation game" between the human and the machine, that is the test conceived by Alan Turing in 1950. There are two main issues in the anthropocentric fallacy. First of all, human intelligence is not always the model for the design of machine intelligence. Bratton argues that "biomorphic imitation is not how we design complex technology. Airplanes do not fly like birds fly" (74), for example. Second, if machine logic is not biomorphic, how can we speculate that machines will develop instincts of predation and destruction similar to animals and humans? In a sort of planetary species-specific FOMO[6] syndrome, Bratton suggests wittily that probably our biggest fear is to be completely ignored rather than annihilated by artificial intelligence. Reversing the mimicry game, Bratton concludes that AI "will have less to do with humans

6   Fear of missing out: the feeling (usually amplified by social media) that others might be having rewarding or interesting experiences from which one is absent.

teaching machines how to think than with machines teaching humans a fuller and truer range of what thinking can be" (72).

In the second part of the anthology "Cognition between Augmentation and Automation," Michael Wheeler introduces the hypothesis of extended cognition (ExC) that has a pivotal role in the discussion on Augmented Intelligence. According to ExC the brain need not retain all the information it is given. Instead, it only needs to remember the path to the place where information is stored. Thus, in the ecology of the brain, the abstract link to the location of information appears to be more important than the memory of content itself. Where such an abstract link starts and ends is a critical issue for ExC, as thinking is also the ability to incorporate external objects as parts of the very logic of thinking: pen and paper, for instance, are helpful in solving mathematical problems that otherwise would be impossible to solve in one's head. The current age of smartphones, pervasive computing, and search engines happens to exemplify such an external human memory on a massive scale. Wheeler explores the idea in relation, first, to the education of children in an increasingly wired, wireless and networked world; second, to the experience of space and thinking in spaces designed with "intelligent architecture " (99 ff.). In a Ballardian moment, Wheeler asks if those buildings are themselves an extension of human cognition and realization of the inhabitants' thoughts!

The hypothesis of ExC makes possible an alternative approach to the thesis of cognitive alienation and libidinal impoverishment that few authors attribute to the information overload of the current media age.[7] Following the ExC hypothesis, it could be postulated that the human mind readjusts itself to the traumas of new media, for instance, by producing a new cognitive mapping of the technological *Umwelt*. In the ExC model, the brain is flexible enough to capture any new external object, or better, just its functions. In this way ExC introduces a fascinating definition of intelligence too: Intelligence is not the capacity to remember all knowledge in detail but to make connections between fragments of knowledge that are not completely known. A basic definition of trauma can be formulated within the ExC paradigm: Trauma is not produced by a vivid content or energetic shock, but by the inability to abstract from that memory, that is the inability to transform a given experience into an abstract link of memory.

The cultural implications of cognitive exteriorization and the malaises allegedly caused by new technologies are also the starting point of Jon Lindblom's essay. Drawing on Mark Fisher's book *Capitalist Realism*, Lindblom reminds us that current psychopathologies are induced by capitalist competition and exploitation rather than digital technologies in themselves: Neoliberalism

---

7   See the critique of semio-capitalism in Berardi 2009, the cognitive impoverishment allegedly caused by Google in Carr 2008 or the notion of grammatization in Stiegler 2010.

is restructuring the nervous system as much as new media do. Lindblom reverses Adorno and Horkheimer's account of the pathologies of instrumental rationality by following Ray Brassier's critique: The trauma produced by science in the human perception of nature should be considered as the starting point for philosophy, rather than as a pathology which philosophy is supposed to heal. Lindblom discusses then the modern hiatus between the *manifest image of man* and *scientific image of man* as framed by Wilfrid Sellars. Instead of accommodating the scientific view of the world to everyday life's experience, as the Frankfurt School may suggest, Lindblom seconds Sellars' idea of the *stereoscopic integration* of the two. As a further instance of cognitive dissonance, Lindblom includes the gap between perception of the self and neural correlates in the formulation given by the neurophilosopher Thomas Metzinger. Following Metzinger's ethical program, Lindblom finally advocates for a political and intellectual project to re-appropriate the most advance technical resources of NBIC (nanotechnology, biotechnology, information technology, and cognitive science) in order to re-orient "mankind towards the wonders of boundless exteriority" (111).

Luciana Parisi presents high frequency trading as an example of an *all-machine phase transition* of computation that already exceeds the response and decision time of humans. Parisi argues that computation is generating a mode of thought that is autonomous from organic intelligence and the canonical critique of instrumental rationality must be updated accordingly. Parisi finds an endogenous limit to computational rationality in the notion of the incomputable, or the Omega number discovered by the mathematician Gregory Chaitin. Taken this intrinsic randomness of computation into account, the critique of instrumental rationality needs to be revised: Parisi remarks that the incomputable should not be understood "as an error within the system, or a glitch within the coding structure" (134), but rather as a structural and constitutive part of computation. Parisi believes that "algorithmic automation coincides with a mode of thought, in which incomputable or randomness have become intelligible, calculable but not necessarily totalizable by technocapitalism" (136). The more technocapitalism computes, the more randomness is created and the more chaos is embedded within the system.

Reza Negarestani aims to reinforce the alliance between mind functionalism and computationalism that was formalized by Alan Turing in his historical essay "Computing Machinery and Intelligence" (1950). Functionalism is the view that the mind can be described in terms of its activities, rather than as a given object or ineffable entity, and its history can be traced back to Plato, the Stoics, Kant, and Hegel. Computationalism is the view that neural states can be described also algorithmically and its history passes through scholastic logicians, the project of *mathesis universalis* until the revolution of modern computation. Negarestani stresses that "the functionalist *and* computational account of the mind is a program for the actual realization of the mind outside of its natural habitat" (145). Negarestani concludes by recording the trauma caused by the computational constructability of the *inhuman* for the galaxy of humanism: "What used to be called the human has now evolved beyond recognition. Narcissus can no longer see or anticipate his own image in the mirror" (154).

Ben Woodard discusses the notion of *bootstrapping,* or that mental capacities and cognitive processes are capable of self-augmentation.[8] He moves from a basic definition of self-reflexivity that is found in German Idealism: "Thinking about thinking can change our thinking" (158). Woodard defines the augmentation of intellect in spatial and navigational terms rather than in a qualitative way, as "augmentation is neither a more, nor a better, but an elsewhere" (158). Augmentation is always a process of alienation of the mind from itself, and Woodard illustrates the ontology of bootstrapping also with time-travel paradoxes from science fiction. This philosophy of augmentation is directly tied to the philosophy of the future that has recently emerged in the neorationalist and accelerationist circles. In the words of Negarestani quoted by Woodard: "Destiny expresses the reality of time as always in excess of and asymmetrical to origin; in fact, as catastrophic to it" (164).

In the third part "The Materialism of the Social Brain," Charles Wolfe and Catherine Malabou submit, respectively, a critique of the transcendental readings of the social brain in philosophy and trauma in psychoanalysis. "Is the brain somehow inherently a utopian topos?" asks Wolfe. Against old reactions that opposed the "authenticity of political theory and praxis to the dangerous naturalism of cognitive science," Wolfe records the rise of a new interest in the idea of the social brain. Wolfe refers to a tradition that, via Spinoza, crossed the Soviet neuropsychology of Lev Vygotsky and re-emerged, under completely different circumstances, in the debate on the general intellect by Italian *operaismo* in the early 1990s. Wolfe himself advocates the idea of the *cultured brain* by Vygotsky: "Brains are culturally sedimented; permeated in their material architecture by our culture, history and social organization, and this sedimentation is itself reflected in cortical architecture" (177). In Vygotsky, the brain is augmented *from within* by innervating external relations. Interestingly, here, the idea of extended cognition is turned outside in to become a sort of *encephalized sociality*.

In a similar way, Catherine Malabou argues against the impermeability of Freudian and Lacanian psychoanalysis to the historical, social, and physical contingencies of trauma. In the response to Zizek's review of her book *The New Wounded*, Malabou stresses the cognitive dead-end for philosophy (as

---

8   See also the notion of bootstrapping by Engelbart 1962 in the keyword entry "Augmented Intelligence" at the end of the book.

much as for politics) that is represented by the conservative Lacanian ditto: *trauma has always already occurred*. Malabou criticizes the idea that external traumas have to be related the subject's psychic history and cannot engender, on the opposite, a novel and alien dimension of subjectivity. Her book *The New Wounded* already attempted to draw a "general theory of trauma" by dissolving the distinction between brain lesions and "sociopolitical traumas" (2007: 10).

Acknowledgements: This anthology would have been impossible without the initiative of Meson Press and in particular the enduring editorial coordination of Mercedes Bunz and Andreas Kirchner. For their support and interest in this project we would like to thank Matthew Fuller, Thomas Metzinger, Godofredo Pereira, Susan Schuppli and last but not least Leesmagazijn publishers in Amsterdam.

A final mention goes to the title of the book: Alleys of Your Mind was originally a track released by the Afro-Futurist band Cybotron in 1981, which will be later recognized as the first track of the techno genre. It is a tribute to a generation and a movement that always showed curiosity for alien states of mind.

References

Bates, David W. 2002. *Enlightenment Aberrations: Error and Revolution in France.* Ithaca, NY: Cornell University Press.

Bates, David W. 2014. "Unity, Plasticity, Catastrophe: Order and Pathology in the Cybernetic Era." In *Catastrophe: History and Theory of an Operative Concept,* edited by Andreas Killen and Nitzan Lebovic, 32–54. Boston: De Gruyter, 2014.

Berardi, Franco. 2009. *The Soul at Work: From Alienation to Autonomy.* Los Angeles: Semiotext(e).

Brassier, Ray. 2007. *Nihil Unbound: Enlightenment and Extinction.* New York: Palgrave Macmillan.

Bryant, Levy, Nick Srnicek, and Graham Harman, eds. 2011. *The Speculative Turn: Continental Materialism and Realism.* Melbourne: Re.press.

Canguilhem, Georges. 1947. "Machine et Organisme." In *La Connaissance de la vie,* 101–27. Paris: Vrin, 1952. English translation: "Machine and Organism." In *Knowledge of life.* New York: Fordham University Press, 2008.

Canguilhem, Georges. (1943) 1966. *Le Normal et le Pathologique.* Paris: PUF. English translation: *The Normal and the Pathological.* Introduction by Michel Foucault. Dordrecht: Reidel, 1978 and New York: Zone Books, 1991.

Carr, Nicholas. 2008. "Is Google Making Us Stupid? What the Internet is Doing to Our Brains." *The Atlantic,* July/August 2008.

Chalmers, David. 2010. "The Singularity: A Philosophical Analysis." *Journal of Consciousness Studies* 17 (9–10): 7–65.

Deleuze, Gilles and Guattari, Félix. 1972. *L'Anti-Oedipe: Capitalisme et schizophrénie,* 1. Paris: Minuit. Translation: *Anti-Oedipus: Capitalism and Schizophrenia,* 1. Minneapolis: University of Minnesota Press, 1983.

Engelbart, Douglas. 1962. "Augmenting Human Intellect: A Conceptual Framework." Summary Report AFOSR-3233. Menlo Park, CA: Stanford Research Institute. http://web.stanford.edu/dept/SUL/library/extra4/sloan/mousesite/EngelbartPapers/B5_F18_ConceptFrameworkInd.html.

Eliasmith, Chris. 2015. "On the Eve of Artificial Minds." In *Open MIND,* edited by Thomas Metzinger and Jennifer Michelle Windt. Frankfurt am Main: MIND Group. doi: 10.15502/9783958570252.

Foucault, Michel. 1954. *Maladie mentale et personnalité*. Paris: PUF. New edition titled: *Maladie mentale et psychologie*. Paris: PUF, 1962. English translation: *Mental Illness and Psychology*. New York: Harper & Row, 1976.

Gibbs, Samuel. 2014. "Elon Musk: Artificial Intelligence is Our Biggest Existential Threat." *The Guardian*, 27 October 2014.

Goldstein, Kurt. 1934. *Der Aufbau des Organismus: Einführing in die Biologie unter besonderer Berücksichtigung der Ehfahrungen am kranken Menschen*. Hague: Martinus Nijhoff. English translation: *The Organism: A Holistic Approach to Biology derived from Pathological Data in Man*. New York: Zone Books, 1995.

Harrington, Anne. 1996. *Reenchanted Science: Holism in German Culture from Wilhelm II to Hitler*. Princeton: Princeton University Press.

Horkheimer, Max. 1947. *Eclipse of Reason*. Oxford: Oxford University Press.

Land, Nick, and Sadie Plant. 1994. "Cyberpositive." http://www.sterneck.net/cyber/plant-land-cyber/.

Merleau-Ponty, Maurice. 1942. *La Structure du comportement*. Paris: PUF. English translation: *The Structure of Behavior*. Boston: Beacon Press, 1963.

Malabou, Catherine. 2007. *Les Nouveaux Blessés: de Freud a la neurologie: penser les traumatismes contemporains*. Paris: Bayard. English translation: *The New Wounded: From Neurosis to Brain Damage*. New York: Fordham University Press, 2012.

Marcuse, Herbert. 1964. *One-Dimensional Man: Studies in the Ideology of Advanced Industrial Society*. Boston: Beacon Press.

Pasquinelli, Matteo. 2014. "The Power of Abstraction and Its Antagonism. On Some Problems Common to Contemporary Neuroscience and the Theory of Cognitive Capitalism." In *Psychopathologies of Cognitive Capitalism*, 2, edited by Warren Neidich, 275–92. Berlin: Archive Books.

Pasquinelli, Matteo. 2015. "What an Apparatus is Not: On the Archeology of the Norm in Foucault, Canguilhem, and Goldstein." *Parrhesia* 22: 79–89.

Pickering, Andrew. 2010. *The Cybernetic Brain Sketches of Another Future*. Chicago, Illinois: University of Chicago Press.

Sterling, Bruce. 2015. "On the Convergence of Humans and Machines." Interview by Menno Grootveld and Koert van Mensvoort. *Next Nature,* 22 February 2015. http://www.nextnature.net/2015/02/interview-bruce-sterling-on-the-convergence-of-humans-and-machines

Thom, René. 1975. *Structural Stability and Morphogenesis: An Outline of a General Theory of Models*. Reading, MA: Benjamin.

Shaviro, Steven. 2014. *The Universe of Things: On Speculative Realism*. Minneapolis: Minnesota University Press.

Stiegler, Bernard. 2010. *For a New Critique of Political Economy*. Malden, MA: Polity Press.

PART I:
FROM CYBERTRAUMA
TO SINGULARITY

BEHAVIORISM

CYBERNETICS

INFORMATION TECHNOLOGY

WORLD WAR II

[1]

The Pigeon in the Machine: The Concept of Control in Behaviorism and Cybernetics

Ana Teixeira Pinto

Behaviorism, like cybernetics, is based on a recursive (feedback) model, known in biology as *reinforcement*. Skinner's description of operant behavior in animals is similar to Wiener's description of information loops. Behaviorism and cybernetics have often shared more than an uncanny affinity: during World War II, both Wiener and Skinner worked on research projects for the U.S. military. While Wiener was attempting to develop his Anti-Aircraft Predictor (a machine that was supposed to anticipate the trajectory of enemy planes), Skinner was trying to develop a pigeon-guided missile. This essay retraces the social and political history of behaviorism, cybernetics, and the concepts of entropy and order in the life sciences.

In *Alleys of Your Mind: Augmented Intellligence and Its Traumas,* edited by Matteo Pasquinelli, 23–34. Lüneburg: meson press, 2015.
DOI: 10.14619/014

When John B. Watson gave his inaugural address "Psychology as the Behaviourist Views It"[1] at Columbia University in 1913, he presented psychology as discipline whose "theoretical goal is the prediction and control of behaviour." Strongly influenced by Ivan Pavlov's study of conditioned reflexes, Watson wanted to claim an objective scientific status for applied psychology. In order to anchor psychology firmly in the field of the natural sciences, however, psychologists would have to abandon speculation in favor of the experimental method.

The concept of control in the life sciences emerged out of the Victorian obsession with order. In a society shaped by glaring asymmetries and uneven development, a middle-class lifestyle was as promising as it was precarious; downward mobility was the norm. Economic insecurity was swiftly systematized into a code of conduct and the newly found habits of hygiene extrapolated from medicine to morals. Both behaviorism and eugenics stem out of an excessive preoccupation with proficiency and the need to control potential deviations. Watson, for instance, was convinced that thumb-sucking bred "masturbators" (Buckley 1989, 165)—though the fixation with order extends much farther than biology. For Erwin Schrödinger, for instance, life was synonymous with order; entropy was a measure of death or disorder. Not only behaviorism, but all other disciplinary fields that emerged in the early twentieth century in the USA, from molecular biology to cybernetics, revolve around this same central metaphor.

After World War I, under the pressure of rapid industrialization and massive demographic shifts, the old social institutions of family, class, and church began to erode. The crisis of authority that ensued led to "ongoing attempts to establish new and lasting forms of social control" (Buckley 1989, 114). Behaviorism was to champion a method through which "coercion from without" is easily masked as "coercion from within"—two types of constraint that would later be re-conceptualized as resolution and marketed as vocation to a growing class of young professionals and self-made career-seekers (Buckley 1989, 113). Watson's straightforward characterization of "man as a machine" was to prove instrumental in sketching out the conceptual framework for the emergence of a novel technology of the self devoted to social control.

Yet what does it mean to identify human beings with mechanisms? What does it mean to establish similarities between living tissue and electronic circuitry? Machines are passive in their activity; they are replicable and predictable, and made out of parts such as cogs and wheels; they can be assembled and re-assembled. Machines, one could say, are the ideal slaves, and slavery is

---

1   This was the first of a series of lectures that later became known as the "Behaviourist Manifesto."

the political unconscious behind every attempt to automate the production process.

The scientific field of applied psychology appealed to an emerging technocracy, because it promised to prevent social tensions from taking on a political form, thereby managing social mobility in a society that would only let people up the ladder a few at a time (Buckley 1989, 113). Behaviorism, as Watson explicitly stated, was strictly "non-political," which is not to say that it would forsake authoritarianism and regimentation. Pre-emptive psychological testing would detect any inklings of "conduct deviation," "emotional upsets," "unstandardized sex reactions" or "truancy," and warrant a process of reconditioning to purge "unsocial ways of behaving" (Buckley 1989, 152). Developing in parallel to the first Red Scare, behaviorism is not a scientific doctrine; it is a political position. Just as the rhetoric of British Parliamentarianism sought to stave off the French revolution, the rhetoric of American liberalism masks the fear of communist contagion: The imperatives of individualism and meritocracy urge individuals to rise from their class rather than with it.

Dogs, Rats, and a Baby Boy

Behaviorism had an uneasy relationship with the man who was credited to have founded it, the Russian physiologist Ivan Pavlov. Following the publication of Watson's inaugural address, in 1916, the conditional reflex began to be routinely mentioned in American textbooks, even though very few psychologists had done experimental work on conditioning (Ruiz et al. 2003). Pavlov only visited the United States on two occasions. On the second in 1929, he was invited to the 9th International Congress of Psychology at Yale and the 13th International Congress of Physiology at Harvard. In his acceptance letter, however, he noted, "I am not a psychologist. I am not quite sure whether my contribution would be acceptable to psychologists and would be found interesting to them. It is pure physiology—physiology of the functions of the higher nervous system—not psychology" (Pare 1990, 648). Though behaviorism had eagerly adopted the experimental method and technical vocabulary "emerging from Pavlov's laboratory," this "process of linguistic importation did not signify the acceptance of the Russian's theoretical points of view" (Ruiz et al. 2003). Pavlov's technique of conditioning was adopted not because it was judged valuable for understanding the nervous stimuli, but rather for "making an objective explanation of learning processes possible" (Ruiz et al. 2003). American psychology was not particularly interested in visceral and glandular responses. Instead, researchers focused on explanatory models that could account for the stimulus/response relation, and on the consequences of behavioral patterns. The influence of Pavlov in American psychology is "above all, a consequence of the very characteristics of that psychology, already established in a tradition with an interest in learning, into which Pavlov's work was incorporated mainly as a model of objectivity and as a demonstration of the feasibility of Watson's old desire to make psychology a true natural science" (Ruiz et al. 2003).

Although Watson seemed to praise Pavlov's comparative study of the psychological responses between higher mammals and humans, he never manifested the intention to pursue such a route. Instead, he focused on how social agents could shape children's dispositions through the method he had borrowed from Pavlov. In his "Little Albert Experiment," Watson and his assistant Rosalie Rayner tried to condition an eleven-month-old infant to fear stimuli that he wouldn't have normally been predisposed to be afraid of. Little Albert was first presented with several furry lab animals, among them was a white rat. After having established that Little Albert had no previous anxiety concerning the animal, Watson and Rayner began a series of tests that sought to associate the presence of the rat with a loud, unexpected noise, which Watson would elicit by striking a steel bar with a hammer. Upon hearing the noise, the child showed clear signs of distress, crying compulsively. After a sequence of trials in which the two stimuli were paired (the rat and the clanging sound), Little Albert was again presented with the rat alone. This time around however, the child seemed clearly agitated and distressed. Replacing the rat with a rabbit and a small dog, Watson also established that Little Albert had generalized his fear to all furry animals. Though the experiment was never successfully reproduced, Watson became convinced that it would be possible to define psychology as the study of the acquisition and deployment of habits.

In the wake of Watson's experiments, American psychologists began to treat all forms of learning as skills—from "maze running in rats . . . to the growth of a personality pattern" (Mills 1998, 84). For the behaviorist movement, both animal and human behavior could be entirely explained in terms of reflexes, stimulus-response associations, and the effects of reinforcing agents upon them. Following Watson's footsteps, Burrhus Frederic Skinner researched how specific external stimuli affected learning using a method that he termed "operant conditioning." While classic—or Pavlovian—conditioning simply pairs a stimulus and a response, in operant conditioning, the animal's behavior is initially spontaneous, but the feedback that it elicits reinforces or inhibits the recurrence of certain actions. Employing a chamber, which became known as the Skinner Box, Skinner could schedule rewards and establish rules.[2] An animal could be conditioned for many days, each time following the same procedure, until a given pattern of behavior was stabilized.

What behaviorists failed to realize was that only under laboratory conditions can the specific stimuli produce a particular outcome As Mills (1998, 124) notes,

---

2   The original Skinner Box had a lever and a food tray, and a hungry rat could get food delivered to the tray by learning to press the lever.

"[i]n real life situations, by contrast, we can seldom identify reinforcing events and give a precise, moment-to-moment account of how reinforcers shape behaviour." Outside of the laboratory, the same response can be the outcome of widely different antecedents, and one single cause is notoriously hard to identify. All in all, "One can use the principle of operant conditioning as an explanatory principle only if one has created beforehand a situation in which operant principles must apply" (Mills 1998, 141).

Not surprisingly, both Watson and Skinner put forth fully fleshed-out fictional accounts of behaviorist utopias: Watson, in his series of articles for Harper's magazine; and Skinner, in his 1948 novel *Walden Two*. The similarities are striking, though Skinner lacks the callous misogyny and casual cruelty of his forerunner. For both authors, crime is a function of freedom. If social behavior is not managed, one can expect an increase in the number of social ills: unruliness, crime, poverty, war, and the like. Socializing people in an appropriate manner, however, requires absolute control over the educational process. Behaviorist utopia thus involves the surrender of education to a technocratic hierarchy, which would dispense with representative institutions and due political process (Buckley 1989, 165).

Apoliticism, as we have already noted, does not indicate that a society is devoid of coercion. Instead of representing social struggles as antagonistic, along the Marxist model of class conflict, behaviorists such as Watson and Skinner reflected the ethos of self-discipline and efficiency espoused by social planers and technocrats. Behaviorist utopias, as Buckley (1989, 165) notes, "worshipped efficiency alone," tacitly ignored any conception of good and evil, and "weigh[ed] their judgments on a scale that measured only degrees of order and disorder."

Pigeons, Servos, and Kamikaze Pilots

Much the same as behaviorism, cybernetics is also predicated on input-output analyses. Skinner's description of operant behavior as a repertoire of possible actions, some of which are selected by reinforcement, is not unlike Wiener's description of information loops. Behaviorism, just like cybernetics, is based on a recursive (feedback) model, which is known in Biology as reinforcement. To boot, behaviorism and cybernetics have often shared more than an uncanny affinity. During World War II both Norbert Wiener and B. F. Skinner worked on parallel research projects for the U.S. military. While Wiener, together with engineer Julian Bigelow, was attempting to develop his anti-aircraft predictor (AA-predictor), a machine that was supposed to anticipate the trajectory of enemy planes, Skinner was trying to develop a pigeon-guided missile.

The idea for Project Pigeon (which was later renamed Project Orcon, from "ORganic CONtrol," after Skinner complained that nobody took him seriously) predates the American participation in the war, yet the Japanese kamikaze attacks in 1944 gave the project a renewed boost. While the kamikaze pilots did not significantly impact the course of the war, their psychological significance cannot be overestimated. Although the Japanese soldiers were often depicted as lice, or vermin, the kamikaze represented the even more unsettling identity between the organic and the mechanic.

Technically speaking, every mechanism usurps a human function. Faced with the cultural interdiction to produce his own slave-soldiers, Skinner reportedly pledged to "provide a competent substitute" for the human kamikaze. The Project Pigeon team began to train pigeons to peck when they saw a target through a bull's-eye. The birds were then harnessed to a hoist so that the pecking movements provided the signals to control the missile. As long as the pecks remained in the center of the screen, the missile would fly straight, but pecks off-center would cause the screen to tilt, which would then cause the missile to change course and slowly travel toward its designated target via a connection to the missile's flight controls. Skinner's pigeons proved reliable under stress, acceleration, pressure, and temperature differences. In the following months, however, as Skinner's project was still far from being operative, Skinner was asked to produce quantitative data that could be analyzed at the MIT Servomechanisms Laboratory. Skinner allegedly deplored being forced to assume the language of servo-engineering, and scorned the usage of terms such as "signal" and "information." Project Pigeon ended up being cancelled on October 8, 1944, because the military believed that it had no immediate promise for combat application.

In the meantime, Wiener's team was trying to simulate the four different types of trajectories that an enemy plane could take in its attempt to escape artillery fire, with the help of a differential analyzer. As Galison notes, "here was a problem simultaneously physical and physiological: the pilot, flying amidst the explosion of flak, the turbulence of air, and the sweep of searchlights, trying to guide an airplane to a target" (1994). Under the strain of combat conditions, human behavior is easy to scale down to a limited number of reflex reactions. Commenting on the analogy between the mechanical and the human behavior pattern, Wiener concluded that the pilot's evasion techniques would follow the same feedback principles that regulated the actions of servomechanisms—an idea he would swiftly extrapolate into a more general physiological theory.

Though Wiener's findings emerged out of his studies in engineering, "the Wiener predictor is based on good behaviourist ideas, since it tries to predict the future actions of an organism not by studying the structure of the organism, but by studying the past behaviour of the organism" (correspondence with Stibitz quoted in Galison 1994). Feedback in Wiener's definition is "the property of being able to adjust future conduct by past performance" (Wiener 1988, 33). Wiener also adopted the functional analysis that accompanies behaviorism—dealing with observable behavior alone, and the view that all behavior is intrinsically goal-oriented and/or purposeful. A frog aiming at a fly and a target-seeking missile are teleological mechanisms: both gather information in order to readjust their course of action. Similarities notwithstanding, Wiener never gave behaviorists any credit, instead offering them only disparaging criticism.

In 1943 the AA-predictor was abandoned as the National Defense Research Committee concentrated on the more successful M9, the gun director that Parkinson, Lovell, Blackman, Bode, and Shannon had been developing at Bell Labs. A strategic failure, much like Project Pigeon, the AA-predictor could have ended up in the dustbin of military history, had the encounter with physiology not proven decisive in Wiener's description of man-machine interactions as a unified equation, which he went on to develop both as mathematical model and as a rhetorical device.

Circuits and the Soviets

Rather than any reliable anti-aircraft artillery, what emerged out of the AA-project was Wiener's re-conceptualization of the term "information," which he was about to transform into a scientific concept.[3] Information—heretofore a concept with a vague meaning—had begun to be treated as a statistical property, exacted by the mathematical analyses of a time-series. This paved the way for information to be defined as a mathematical entity.

Simply put, this is what cybernetics is: the treatment of feedback as a conceptual abstraction. Yet, by suggesting "everything in the universe can be modelled into a system of information," cybernetics also entails a "powerful metaphysics, whose essence—in spite of all the ensuing debates—always remained elusive" (Mindell, Segal and Gerovitch 2003, 67). One could even say that cybernetics is the conflation of several scientific fields into a powerful exegetical model, which Wiener sustained with his personal charisma. Wiener was, after all, "a visionary who could articulate the larger implications of the cybernetic paradigm and make clear its cosmic significance" (Hayles 1999, 7). Explaining the cardinal notions of statistical mechanics to the laymen, he drew a straightforward, yet dramatic analogy: entropy is "nature's tendency to degrade the organized and destroy the meaningful," thus "the stable state of a living organism is to be dead" (Wiener 1961, 58). Abstract and avant-garde art, he would later hint, are "a Niagara of increasing entropy" (Wiener 1988, 134).

---

3   As Galison 1994 notes, Wiener's novel usage of the term information emerges in
     November 1940 in a letter to MIT's Samuel H. Caldwell.

"Entropy," which would become a key concept for cybernetics, was first applied to biology by the physicist Erwin Schrödinger. While attempting to unify the disciplinary fields of biology and physics, Schrödinger felt confronted with a paradox. The relative stability of living organisms was in apparent contradiction with the Second Law of Thermodynamics, which states that since energy is more easily lost than gained, the tendency of any closed system is to dissipate energy over time, thus increasing its entropy. How are thus living organisms able to "obviate their inevitable thermal death" (Gerovitch 2002, 65)? Schrödinger solved his puzzle by recasting organisms as thermodynamic systems that extract "orderliness" from their environment in order to counteract increasing entropy. This idea entailed a curious conclusion: the fundamental divide between living and non-living was not to be found between organisms and machines but between order and chaos. For Schrödinger, entropy became a measure of disorder (Gerovitch 2002, 65).

Schrödinger's incursions into the field of life sciences were rebuffed by biologists and his theories were found to be wanting. His translation of biological concepts into the lexicon of physics would have a major impact however, as Schrödinger introduced into the scientific discourse the crucial analogy, which would ground the field of molecular biology: "the chromosome as a message written in code" (Gerovitch 2002, 67).

The code metaphor was conspicuously derived from the war efforts and their system of encoding and decoding military messages. Claude Shannon, a cryptologist, had also extrapolated the code metaphor to encompass all human communication, and like Schrödinger, he employed the concept of entropy in a broader sense, as a measure of uncertainty. Oblivious to the fact that the continuity Schrödinger had sketched between physics and biology was almost entirely metaphorical, Wiener would later describe the message as a form of organization, stating that information is the opposite of entropy.

Emboldened by Wiener's observations on the epistemological relevance of the new field, the presuppositions that underpinned the study of thermodynamic systems spread to evolutionary biology, neuroscience, anthropology, psychology, language studies, ecology, politics, and economy. Between 1943 and 1954 ten conferences under the heading "Cybernetics: Circular Causal, and Feedback Mechanisms in Biological and Social Systems" were held at the Macy Foundation, sponsored by Josiah Macy Jr. The contributing scholars tried to develop a universal theory of regulation and control, applicable to economic as well as mental processes, and to sociological as well as aesthetic phenomena. Contemporary art, for instance, was described as an operationally closed system, which reduces the complexity of its environment according to a program it devises for itself (Landgraf 2009, 179–204). Behaviorism—the theory which had first articulated the aspiration to formulate a single encompassing theory for all human and animal behavior, based on the analogy between man and machine—was finally assimilated into the strain of cybernetics, which became known as cognitivism.

By the early 1950s, the ontology of man became equated with the functionality of programming based on W. Ross Ashby's and Claude Shannon's information theory. Molecular and evolutionary biology treated genetic information as an essential code, the body being but its carrier. Cognitive science and neurobiology described consciousness as the processing of formal symbols and logical inferences, operating under the assumption that the brain is analogous to computer hardware and that the mind is analogous to computer software. In the 1950s, Norbert Wiener had suggested that it was theoretically possible to telegraph a human being, and that it was only a matter of time until the necessary technology would become available (Wiener 1988, 103). In the 1980s, scientists argued that it would soon be possible to upload human consciousness and have one's grandmother run on Windows—or stored on a floppy disk. Science fiction brimmed with fantasies of immortal life as informational code. Stephen Wolfram even went so far as to claim that reality is a program run by a cosmic computer. Consciousness is but the "user's illusion"; the interface, so to speak.

But the debate concerning the similarities and differences between living tissue and electronic circuitry also gave rise to darker man-machine fantasies: zombies, living dolls, robots, brain washing, and hypnotism. Animism is correlated with the problem of agency: who or what can be said to have volition is a question that involves a transfer of purpose from the animate to the inanimate. "Our consciousness of will in another person," Wiener argued, "is just that sense of encountering a self-maintaining mechanism aiding or opposing our actions. By providing such a self-stabilizing resistance, the airplane acts as if it had purpose, in short, as if it were inhabited by a Gremlin." This Gremlin, "the servomechanical enemy, became . . . the prototype for human physiology and, ultimately, for all of human nature" (Galison 1994).

Defining peace as a state of dynamic equilibrium, cybernetics proved to be an effective tool to escape from a vertical, authoritarian system, and to enter a horizontal, self-regulating one. Many members of the budding counterculture were drawn to its promise of spontaneous organization and harmonious order. This order was already in place in Adam Smith's description of free-market interaction, however. Regulating devices—especially after Watts's incorporation of the governor into the steam engine in the 1780s—had been correlated with a political rhetoric, which spoke of "dynamic equilibrium," "checks and balances," "self-regulation," and "supply and demand" ever since the dawn of British liberalism (Mayr 1986, 139–40). Similarly, the notion of a feedback loop between organism and environment was already present in the theories of both Malthus and Darwin, and, as already mentioned, Adam Smith's classic definition of the free market—a blank slate that brackets out society and culture—also happens to be the underlying principle of the Skinner Box experiments.

Unsurprisingly, the abstractions performed by science have materially concrete effects. The notion of a chaotic, deteriorating universe, in which small enclaves of orderly life are increasingly under siege,[4] echoed the fears of communist contagion and the urge to halt the Red Tide. The calculation of nuclear missile trajectories, the Distance Early Warning Line, and the development of deterrence theory, together with operations research and game theory, were all devoted to predicting the coming crisis. Yet prediction is also an act of violence that re-inscribes the past onto the future, foreclosing history. The war that had initially been waged to "make the world safe for democracy" had also "involved a sweeping suspension of social liberties, and brought about a massive regimentation of American life" (Buckley 1989, 114).

At length, cybernetics went on to become the scientific ideology of neoliberalism, the denouement of which was the late-eighties notion of the "end of history"[5] that imposed the wide cultural convergence of an iterative liberal economy as the final form of human government. In 1997, *Wired* magazine ran a cover story titled "The Long Boom," whose header read: "We're facing twenty-five years of prosperity, freedom, and a better environment for the whole world. You got a problem with that?" In the wake of the USSR's demise and the fall of the Berlin Wall, "The Long Boom" claimed that, no longer encumbered by political strife and ideological antagonism, the world would witness unending market-driven prosperity and unabated growth. Though from our current standpoint the article's claims seem somewhat ludicrous, its brand of market-besotted optimism shaped the mindset of the nineties. It also gave rise to what would become known as the Californian Ideology; a weak utopia that ignored the "contradiction at the center of the American dream: some individuals can prosper only at the expense of others" (Barbrook and Cameron 1996). Unlike social or psychic systems, thermodynamic systems are not subject to dialectical tensions. Nor do they experience historical change. They only accumulate a remainder—a kind of refuse—or they increase in entropy. Unable to account for the belligerent bodies of the North Korean and the Viet Cong, or the destitute bodies of the African American, cybernetics came to embrace the immateriality of the post-human.

Dialectical materialism—the theory that cybernetics came to replace—presupposed the successive dissolution of political forms into the higher form of

---

4   In rhetoric straight from the Cold War, Wiener described the universe as an increasingly chaotic place in which, against all odds, small islands of life fight to preserve order and increase organization (Wiener 1961).

5   The concept of the "end of history" was put forth by conservative political scientist Francis Fukuyama in his 1992 book *The End of History and the Last Man*.

history, but feedback is no dialectics.[6] Friedrich Engels defined dialectics as the most general laws of all motion, which he associated to the triadic laws of thought: the law of the transformation of quantity into quality; the law of the unity and struggle of opposites; and the law of the negation of the negation. Although feedback and dialectics represent motion in similar ways, cybernetics is an integrated model, while dialectical materialism is an antagonistic one: dialectics implies a fundamental tension, and an unresolved antagonism; while feedback knows no outside or contradiction, only perpetual iteration. Simply put, cybernetic feedback is dialectics without the possibility of communism. Against the backdrop of an Augustinian noise, history itself becomes an endlessly repeating loop, revolving around an "enclosed space surrounded and sealed by American power" (Edwards 1997, 8).

Acknowledgments: This text has been previously published in the Manifesta Journal #18. The author would like to thank David Riff and the Manifesta editorial team Natasa Petresin-Bachelez, Tara Lasrado, Lisa Mazza, Georgia Taperell and Shannon d'Avout d'Auerstaedt.

References

Barbrook, Richard, and Andy Cameron. 1996. "The Californian Ideology." *Science as Culture* 6 (1): 44–72.

Buckley, Kerry W. 1989. *Mechanical Man: John Broadus Watson and the Beginnings of Behaviorism.* New York: Guilford Press.

Edwards, Paul N. 1997. *The Closed World: Computers and the Politics of Discourse in Cold War America.* Cambridge, MA: MIT Press.

Galison, Peter. 1994. "The Ontology of the Enemy: Norbert Wiener and the Cybernetic Vison." *Critical Inquiry* 21 (1): 228–66.

Gerovitch, Slava. 2002. *From Newspeak to Cyberspeak: A History of Soviet Cybernetics.* Cambridge, MA: MIT Press.

Hayles, N. Katherine. 1999. *How We Became Posthuman: Virtual Bodies in Cybernetics, Literature, and Informatics.* Chicago: University of Chicago Press.

Landgraf, Edgar. 2009. "Improvisation: Form and Event: A Spencer-Brownian Calculation." In *Emergence and Embodiment: New Essays on Second-Order Systems Theory*, edited by Bruce Clarke and Mark B. Hansen, 179–204. Durham, NC: Duke University Press.

Mayr, Otto. 1986. *Authority Liberty and Automatic Machinery in Early Modern Europe.* Baltimore, ND: Johns Hopkins University Press.

Mikulak, Maxim W. 1965. "Cybernetics and Marxism-Leninism." In *Slavic Review* 24 (3): 450–65.

Mills, John A. 1998. *Control: A History of Behavioral Psychology.* New York: NYU Press.

Mindell, David, Jérôme Segal, and Slava Gerovitch. 2003. "Cybernetics and Information Theory in the United States, France and the Soviet Union." In *Science and Ideology: A Comparative History*, edited by Mark Walker, 66–96. London: Routledge.

Pare, W. P. 1990. "Pavlov as a Psychophysiological Scientist." *Brain Research Bulletin* 24: 643–49.

Ruiz, Gabriel, Natividad Sanchez, and Luis Gonzalo de la Casa. 2003. "Pavlov in America: A Heterodox Approach to the Study of his Influence." *The Spanish Journal of Psychology* 6 (2): 99–111.

Thoreau, Henry David. 1980. *Walden and Other Writings.* New York: Bantam.

6   Not surprisingly, cybernetics was briefly outlawed under Joseph Stalin, who denounced it as bourgeois pseudoscience because it conflicted with materialistic dialectics by equating nature, science, and technical systems (Mikulak 1965).

Wiener, Norbert. (1954) 1988. *The Human Use of Human Beings: Cybernetics and Society.* Reprint of the revised and updated edition of 1954 (original 1950). Cambridge, MA: Da Capo Press.

Wiener, Norbert. 1961. *Cybernetics: or Control and Communication in the Animal and the Machine.* Cambridge, MA: MIT Press.

CYBERNETICS

CYBERSYN

NEOLIBERALISM

SOCIALISM

CHILE

Error Correction: Chilean Cybernetics and Chicago's Economists

Adrian Lahoud

Cybernetics is a specific way of conceiving the relation between information and government: It represented a way of bringing the epistemological and the onto-logical together in real time. The essay explores a par-adigmatic case study in the evolution of this history: the audacious experiment in cybernetic management known as Project Cybersyn that was developed follow-ing Salvador Allende's ascension to power in Chile in 1970. In ideological terms, Allende's socialism and the violent doctrine of the Chicago School could not be more opposed. In another sense, however, Chilean cybernetics would serve as the prototype for a new form of governance that would finally award to the theories of the Chicago School a hegemonic control over global society.

In *Alleys of Your Mind: Augmented Intellligence and Its Traumas,* edited by Matteo Pasquinelli, 37–51. Lüneburg: meson press, 2015.
DOI: 10.14619/014

Zero Latency

A great deal of time has been spent investigating, documenting and disputing an eleven year period in Chile from 1970–1981, encompassing the presidency of Salvador Allende and the dictatorship of Augusto Pinochet. Between the rise of the *Unidad Popular* and its overthrow by the military junta, brutal and notorious events took hold of Chile.[1] Though many of these events have remained ambiguous, obscured by trauma or lost in official dissimulation, over time the contours of history have become less confused. Beyond the coup, the involvement of the United States or even the subsequent transformation of the economy, a more comprehensive story of radical experimentation on the Chilean social body has emerged. At stake in the years of Allende's ascension to power and those that followed was nothing less than a Latin social laboratory. This laboratory was at once optimistic, sincere, naïve, and finally brutal.

Few experiments were as audacious or prophetic as Allende's cybernetic program Cybersyn. In this ambitious venture that lasted only two short years, a number of issues were raised that are still valid today. The program was first off an attempt by a national government to govern in real time at the scale of the entire national territory; second, the development of technical infrastructure that could track and shape fluctuations and changes in the Chilean economy; third, the conceptualization of a national political space along the lines of a business regulated by ideals drawn from corporate management; fourth, the invention of a scale and technique of government that begins at one end of the political spectrum but finds its ultimate conclusion at the very opposite.

The Chilean cybernetic experiment emerged in response to an urgent problem; the nationalization of the Chilean economy, especially the gathering together of disparate sites of productivity, resource extraction, and manufacturing, in addition to their re-integration within a state controlled economy. Allende had no desire to model Chile on the centrally planned economy of the Soviet Union, whose rigid hierarchical structure and lack of adaptive flexibility led to human and political crises.[2] In line with the mandate of a constitutionally elected socialist leader, Allende intended to devolve some central control to factories and grant workers increasing autonomy over their own labor. In doing so he hoped to hold in balance a series of opposing forces. On the one hand, the burden of redistribution that always falls to a centralized state, on the other, liberating the autopoietic force of the workers in their specialized sites of work.

1   *Unidad Popular (UP)* was a coalition of leftist parties that was formed in Chile in 1969.
2   GOSPLAN (Russian: *Gosudarstvenniy Komitet po Planirovaniyu*) or the State Planning Committee of the USSR was responsible for producing the five year economic plan for the Soviet Union, established in 1921 this centralized planning model was—despite the sophistication of the scientific models used—beset by problems of misreporting.

This complicated political calculus was made all the more difficult, because the stage upon which it took place introduced a further set of variables. The land surface of Chile had long acquired clear boundaries, fixed since the indigenous Mapuche uprisings (Petras and Morley 1978, 205). Chile is on average only 175 km wide, however it stretches for 4300 km in length. Moreover this elongated sliver of a nation is draped over an almost entirely mountainous terrain. If this engendered topographical complications, geologically Chile was abundantly rich. Breaking apart the monopolistic control of these resources would be critical to the viability of the new socialist economy. The problem that this young and idealistic government faced was how to create a new territorial scale of governance, one able to reform and eventually stabilize this complex spatial, and social landscape without relying on the precedents set by Soviet-style economies. In other words, how to reduce the adaptive threshold of political decision-making from the five-year model to something more immediate. This ambition would require developing an infrastructure for the exchange of information and transferring some of the decision-making capacity from the state to local actors.

Error Correction

On 4 September 1970, in an election awash with KGB and CIA money, the Unidad Popular headed by Salvador Allende won 32% of the vote in Chile. At this point, the Allende government believed it had six years to reform the Chilean economy. In line with its socialist democratic agenda, the government set out to nationalize its resource and finance sectors, and increase the efficiency of poorly performing industries (Medina 2006, 571). On 12 November 1971, little over a year since his government had come to power, President Salvador Allende received an unlikely guest. Stafford Beer is a cybernetician interested in the application of cybernetics to social systems. Beer had been invited to meet Allende by some Chilean scientists, who were interested in using his expertise on cybernetics to manage the newly nationalized industries.[3] Cybernetic research evolved out of a problem: how to hit a fast moving plane with a weapon or, in military parlance, getting the ballistic and the target reach the same point in space at the same time. In response, researchers developed systems during World War II that were capable of tracking an enemy target by continually recalibrating a weapon to aim at the target's anticipated position, labeled a "feedback loop."

---

3   Especially Fernando Flores. What brought Flores and Beer together was not a shared political outlook per se but rather conceptual commonalities in scientific and conceptual thought that Flores recognized and Beer appreciated. These conceptual similarities drew Beer and Flores together despite their different cultural and political convictions. This connection was fostered by Beer's enthusiasm to apply cybernetic thinking, operations and research techniques to the domain of politics.

At MIT, on a miniscule military budget, Norbert Weiner led research into the mathematics and circuit boards that would eventually help to automate anti-aircraft fire. The achievement was as conceptual as it was technical, a re-imagining of the method by which a highly manoeuvrable fighter and its pilot could be fired at, with the projectile anticipating the future position of the target. The design of the mechanism had to reconcile meteorological factors such as wind with human cunning and be able to outsmart both. Wiener's research arrived at a time in which the idea of large-scale computational modelling had begun to take hold in many areas, almost exclusively evolving from the war effort and the attempt to build a systematic basis for strategic decision-making.

Though Weiner set the incalculability of nature against the calculus of man, what held the two together and ties cybernetics to the eighteenth Century is the fundamental commitment to understanding human populations as unknowable in ways that resonated with the unknowability of nature, and thus to open the possibility of re-inscribing human interaction either socially or economically within a specific kind of calculus, in this case, the mathematics of error correction (Delanda 1991). The cybernetic black box operated at the very limits of the known, the very idea of a cybernetic control mechanism—in that it posed the correlation between the behavior of an open system and the tracking of that system in terms of error correction—attempted to collapse the ontological *into* the epistemological with only the latency of the feedback loop to separate them (Galison 1994, 228).

In the only comprehensive history of Project Cybersyn, Edin Medina (2011) accounts for Chilean experiments with cybernetics in terms of the deep affinity between cyberneticians like Beer and the reformists around Allende, especially engineer and political ally Fernando Flores, who would be instrumental in inviting Beer to Chile. Beer's interest in cybernetics emerged out of his work in organizational management, especially what he perceived to be limitations in the adaptive potential of organizations dominated by rigid divisions of labor, poor channels of communication and constrained spaces for decision-making. In response to this, Beer experimented with organizational reforms that aimed to inject flexibility and a level of autonomy into decision-making, believing this would encourage employees to respond to a shifting work environment (Beer 1972). Looking back, Beer's commitment to a radical flexibility within the workforce is only one of a number of prophetic resonances that early cybernetic research has with neoliberalism. At the time, the promise of granting more autonomy to workers in terms of control and organization of factory productivity neatly coincided with the aims and aspirations of Allende's leftist government.

Symptomatology vs. Aetiology

For Beer, organizing bodies into groups, establishing protocols for decision-making, setting up channels for communication and allowing thresholds for change were all qualities embedded in the material of the organization in the same way developmental pathways were embedded in the organism. The plasticity of the organism with respect to its environment served as a model for the plasticity of the business in regards to its market and competitors, both being problems of adaptation to an external force field. Indeed, Beer originally viewed cybernetics as a hylomorphic critique of the *matter* of "business organization," a faith in the *agency* of (organizational) matter whose adaptive, auto-poetic potential needed to be unlocked.

Much like a biological system, for Beer, the organization was made of matter that was alive with possibility, animated by internal drives, regulated by environmental constraints. In an attempt to mirror a certain conception of the firm, the diagram of the viable system model (VSM) broke down its structure into a series of linked parts hierarchically nested within each other. Organized according to a biological metaphor replete with nervous system, and sensory apparatus, the VSM was envisaged as a complex interlinking of perceptual and responsive mechanisms. These mechanisms could ensure that changes in the information environment would efficiently reach the appropriate decision-making node within the organizational structure. This sensitivity would encourage rapid and responsive decision-making and thus adaptation. Not that Beer conceived of all decisions as being equal: There would be no point burdening management with decisions that were not strategic in nature. Therefore the autonomy on which the firms adaptation drew was not equally distributed. As one moved up the hierarchy of systems, the amount of overall strategic information about the entire firm expanded until the brain-like command structure was reached, which Beer imagined should look like a World War II operations room.

Significantly, the structure of the VSM was recursive. The same logic of feedback and response that structured each part also structured the larger component that these sub-parts were contained within, ad infinitum: Beer felt that such recursiveness was a necessary property of viable systems—they had to be nested inside one another "like so many Russian dolls or Chinese boxes" in a chain of embeddings "which descends to cells and molecules and ascends to the planet and its universe" (Pickering 2010, 250). For Beer, the question of scale was wholly commensurable across different problems, from a small cellular organism to an entire ecosystem, just as from a clerk's office to a production line. This crude characterization of the biological metaphor and its over-application would cause difficulties later—when techniques, which were successful in a business environment, were drawn into the management of an entire nation's territory and its economic productivity. The reason for this recursive approach to scale in management clearly stems from a recursive understanding of scale within the organism—one serving as the rule and the model for the other. Moreover, it is possible to speculate that what permitted Beer to extend this diagram of organization into non-biological domains was a sense that each part of this system operated like a black box. Repeating a characteristic and fateful cybernetic concern with symptomatology rather than aetiology first formulated by Weiner, the inner *workings* of the thing being modeled did not matter: All one had to do, was to track the inputs and outputs—causes would hereafter be subordinated to effects—often with drastic consequences. The VSM was simply a diagram for *correlating* inputs and outputs among variously scaled black boxes, this seeming disregard for *mechanism* may have further allowed Beer to generalize its applicability across different situations. In fact, Beer was a staunch critic of the idea that the VSM could "contain" information the way a box could contain goods, this would be tantamount to splitting form from content, reverting to a hylomorphic conception of organizational matter.

What Beer misses, ironically, is that the representations may not have been held or contained *within* his system as a kind of cargo or payload; instead they were embodied in the system's very structure. Though there were no "symbolic or representational elements" or internal models in the black boxes that made up the VSM, it was not possible to say that the VSM was wholly plastic and adaptable. It had parts—and though these parts were indeed black boxes, the diagram of information flow that linked the various inputs and outputs together was quite immune from the adaptive process. There was a clear model at work, just not at the scale Beer was focused on.

The National Nervous System

The eventual deployment of a socialized cybernetic network in Chile exceeds any precedent by orders of magnitude. Known variously as Proyecto Synco, el Sistema Synco, or Cybersyn, the fruition of Allende's control fantasy and Beer's techno-optimism was a nationwide system of monitoring, reporting, and feedback based on cybernetic principals. Hundreds of telex machines were installed in newly nationalized factories all over Chile and employed for sending data on everything from production volumes to employee absence rates back to the central command room in Santiago. The backbone was Jay Forester's DYNAMO compiler, fresh from use in the Club of Rome Report titled *The Limits of Growth*, where it had also been used to model large-scale economic and demographic tendencies.

For Beer and enthusiastic colleagues like the biologist Francisco Varela, who would go on to put forward a theory of autopoiesis with Humberto Maturana, a cybernetic model of socio-economic management equaled national stability. Provided inputs could reliably be fed into the control center, social and economic effects could be generated in response to any circumstance. The nation could be tuned, and Beer knew how to turn the dials. Sitting on molded plastic chairs in the Cybersyn control center, technicians took live signals from Chilean factories up and down the coast and in return used them to manipulate and adjust the Chilean economy in real time. Like stimulated nerve endings firing electrical charges, information from hundreds of small social and economic events across the nation flowed down telegraph wires into the central control room; the national nervous system had been re-scaled to cover the territory, and had seemingly acquired a cybernetic brain.

In the hexagonal control room in Santiago, television screens would present real-time information to a planning committee. This organization of information spatialized the real-time data processing system, collapsing the vast distances of Chile's topography and its widely distributed centers of production to a single point in space. From this position, it would be possible to literally *see through* the walls of the room such that the entire scale of the territory would be co-present and available for action simultaneously. The ontological and the epistemic promised to merge on the surface of the screen. This control room scenario is now commonplace, indeed contemporary logistics, shipping, and freight systems would be unthinkable without it, and though it had certain precedents during World War II, especially in the spread of war rooms built around the world, the televisual nature of the system together with its peace-time operation and economic domain made Cybersyn unique.

Additionally, what made Cybersyn more unique, however, was that each node in the network would be granted a certain operational autonomy. Factories could communicate with each other as well as with the central command room. This image of freely flowing information able to traffic horizontally between nodes and vertically through a command structure was absolutely central to Beer's conception of Cybersyn. Both Beer and Allende believed this was what would lend the system its curious powers of adaptive strength: By re-empowering local decision-makers, Cybersyn took Beer's interest in organizational management and socialized it. In a moment of incredible optimism, the core group of researchers working with Beer seemed on the cusp of securing the shifting coordinates of Chile's social and economic environment.

Replete in both Beer's own writing and that of the historians who take up the Cybersyn project is a conception of so-called *bottom up* decision-making as inherently democratic, in contradistinction to *top down* decision-making processes, which are seen as coercive. A well-known anecdote is worth repeating here, since it reveals the naivety of the political position behind this equation of upward traffic and democracy, which both Medina (2011) and Pickering (2010) take up without qualification.

Beer is invited to the Presidential Palace on 12 November 1971. He is tasked
with describing his proposal for the nationwide cybernetic system to the
newly elected president. Beer slowly takes Allende through the nested structure of the viable system model, carefully explaining the equivalence of factories to limbs, and the feedback loops to an organic sensory apparatus. Step by
step he elucidates, moving through the hierarchy of levels and explicating the
autonomy granted to decision-makers at each point, as well as the flexibility
this system could guarantee. Finally, Beer reaches the apex of his metaphorical diagram, the brain or control center. Just as he is about to reveal this point
to be the seat of the president, Beer is interrupted by Allende, who exclaims:
"at last . . . *el pueblo*"—the people.

Blind Spot

Allende implicitly understood the difference between representative democracy and business management. For Beer, the ability to make decisions had
a simple and direct correlation to freedom regardless of the decision being
made, a freedom that only ever trafficked in a literal register: either demo-
cratically bottom to top, or autocratically from top to bottom. Furthermore,
in committing to a wholly rational idea of decision-making, in which an actor
is presumed to make the best decision if he or she is provided with the right
information, Beer aligns himself with a technocratic vision of society, in which
decision-making is reduced to a question of expertise. However, the fore-
grounding of expertise—a space where "competent information is free to
act" as Beer put it—as a principal of decision-making mystifies the political
dimension of decision-making (Medina 2011, 33). In this sense it is not a question of moral value, but of the proper structural position of expertise vis-à-vis
politics.

Just like any organism, Cybersyn's lifeworld was shaped by its sensory apparatus. In order for something to count as an input, the system had to *see* it in
order to *recognize* it. This recalls Jakob von Uexküll's concept of the *Umwelt* in
which each organism has a world of its own compromised only of the dimensions present to its sensory apparatus. Despite the abundant and profuse
continuity of the natural environment, each organism gives birth to a world
by selecting only a few important markers within this space. For the organism,
everything else simply does not exist. Deleuze and Guattari's (1987) and also
Agamben's (2004) often cited use of the tick is drawn from von Uexküll and
serves as an extreme example of the point. The tick's lifeworld is contracted
down to three stimuli: light, smell, and touch (Uexküll 2010). Light draws the
tick to the tip of a tree branch, smell allows it to detect the passage of a host
below and drop onto its back, touch to locate bare skin, so that it could bur-
row. As Canguilhem writes:

A meaning, from the biological and psychological point of view, is an appreciation of values in relation to a need. And a need is, for whoever feels it and lives it, an irreducible system of reference, and for that reason it is absolute. (2001, 7)

If the world is an accumulation of signals, inputs and outputs than Beer and Uexküll are in close proximity. Each cybernetic apparatus, whether the anti-aircraft battery or the viable system model, individuates a specific mesh through which the continuity of the world passes. The individuation of the epistemic and the ontological—in that it is a co-individuation—binds certain features of the world to knowledge apparatus in a partial and limited way, in other words at a specific scale. Gilbert Simondon's critique of cybernetics is worth repeating here. What matters in a system is not the communication between pre-given receivers and whether one or another node in the relay of communication is sensitive enough to register a change in its environment.[4] Instead, it is the genesis of the senders and receivers themselves that is of importance, since this forms the genetic condition of possibility for communication *to exist as communication*. In the genesis of the communicators perceptual apparatus is the genesis of a specific lifeworld (Simondon 2009).

In this regard, what matters is the individuation of Cybersyn and the VSM diagram that it carries inside—not the modulation of the signals between the parts, or their adaptation within a functional bandwidth. At precisely the

4   "Information is therefore a primer for individuation; it is a *demand for individuation*, for the passage from a metastable system to a stable system; it is never a given thing. There is no unity and no identity of information, because information is not a *term*; it supposes the tension of a system of being in order to receive it adequately. Information can only be inherent to a problematic; it is *that by which the incompatibility of the non-resolved system becomes an organizing dimension in the resolution*; information supposes a phase *change of a system*, because it supposes an initial preindividual state that individuates itself according to the discovered organization. Information is the formula of individuation, a formula that cannot exist prior to this individuation. An information can be said to always be in the present, current, because it is the direction [*sens*] according to which a system individuates itself" (Simondon 2009, 10). Also: "According to Simondon, cybernetics had failed to go in this direction. Wiener had the "huge merit" to have started the first inductive investigation into machines and established cybernetics as a comprehensive, interdisciplinary research project. But, following Simondon, he had failed to define his research object in an appropriate manner. Cybernetics only focused on a specific type of machines, i.e., machines with feedback mechanisms. More generally, Simondon stated, "Right from the start, [Cybernetics] has accepted what all theory of technology must refuse: a classification of technological objects conducted by means of established criteria and following genera and species." For Simondon, the problem did not consist in applying biological procedures to technology (as we will see, he himself made use of such procedures). His point was that Wiener had made the wrong choice relying on a quasi-Linnaean, stable classification. What Simondon was after was a dynamic theory of technology, i.e., a theory that would grasp technological objects in their development and their relation to inner and outer milieus or *Umwelten*. In other words, Simondon did not want to start another botany of machines, he was interested in their individuation, development and evolution" (Schmidgen 2004, 13).

same moment that the abstract diagram of the system is articulated and the parts have been prescribed their range of functionalities and sensitivities, two things are produced. Firstly, a life world. This contains all the things that can be recognized and detected by the system. Secondly, a contrast space or blind spot, a remainder, which—from the point of view of the life world—has no existence whatsoever. Cybersyn had an *Umwelt* all of its own, and this *Umwelt* was wholly determined by those things Allende's economists and Beer's cyberneticians took to be of value between 1972–1973.

By attempting to equate an economic and social formation with a series of indicators in a feedback loop, Chile's cybernetic experiment over-extended quantitative techniques into a qualitative domain. The equations, diagrams, circuit boards, telex machines and screens that made up the "body" of this national cybernetic system, attempted to make a society and its economy knowable through calculus, a series of variable quantities that could be tuned and calibrated. The question that arises for any such system is how to count. Where is one to draw the line, that difficult threshold between the calculable and the incalculable, the field of vision and the blind spot?

This question would become paramount for the Allende government on 11 September 1973. Certainly Cybersyn was never designed to halt a coup attempt, nor can the overthrow of Allende's government be said to have eventuated by a failure in this unique experiment. Instead, the line followed here is that the ethos hardwired into the telex machines, control rooms and software encapsulated an idea of social equilibrium—and the coup in all its murderous force represented another kind of politics, one that would never be content to operate within an exiting set of structures. Rather, it demanded that the rules themselves—the very structure of decision-making—enter into the stakes of the political bargain. That this was articulated by a military junta in this case is coincidental, since what was and is at stake is not merely the adaptation of systems parts, it the possibility of radically transforming the system that recognises something as part of it in the first place.

Sleeping Dogs

In the introduction to his lecture at the College de France on 10 January 1979, Michel Foucault opened with a joke. He abbreviated Freud's quotation of Virgil's *Aeneid* which reads, *"flectere si nequeo superos, Acheronta movebo"* or "if I cannot deflect the will of Heaven, I shall move Hell" which Foucault renders simply as, *"Acheronta move*bo."[5] Freud used the line as the epigraph to the *Interpretation of Dreams*, where it is meant to refer to the upward movement of repressed content within the psyche. Foucault humorously counter-

5   Alternatively translated in the text accompanying the lecture as "If I cannot bend the Higher Powers, I will move the infernal regions."

poses Freud's dictum with a quote from Britain's first prime minister, Robert Walpole, who once stated: "*Quieta non movere*" which Foucault translates idiomatically as "Let sleeping dogs lie" (2010). It is certain that the distance between the two quotes is not as great as Foucault implies, and although Foucault does not propose a psychoanalytic reading of the history of the eighteenth century—the extent to which subterranean problems rise up to lend sense to the details of history is a methodological given within his work.

"Let sleeping dogs lie", what is intended with this statement? Undoubtedly, it is a council of prudence, a description of government as a game of minimal contact. Foucault traces the evolution of liberalism as a specific refinement of the *raison d'état*, especially through the period in which the market moves from being a site of redistributive justice in which buyers must be protected against fraud to a site of verification, and thus the production of a kind of truth. The market can only operate as a site of truth production once it expresses a natural or true price. For this reason, any intervention by government threatens to jeopardize this natural state of affairs. Thus, government must adopt a continual reflective stance formed between the twin limits of a minimum and maximum contact. As Foucault states,

> When you allow the market to function by itself according to its nature, according to its natural truth, if you like, it permits the formation of a certain price which will be called metaphorically, the true price, but which no longer has any connotations of justice. It is a price that fluctuates around the value of the product. (Foucault 2010, 31)

The genesis of liberalism as a specific technique of governance can be traced to the problem posed by populations of a certain scale. At its core, liberalism attempts to establish a naturalized state of interaction between individuals, especially with regards to economic transactions and the idea that within the emergent sum of these interactions exists a wholly natural value—price. Only by *securing* the contingent interplay of these actors within the population—and here the term security is meant in its regulatory, policing sense since this freedom depends on certain limits—can the natural tendency of this system be expressed. This rationality accords to a complex interacting system—in this case the market, a privileged status as a site against which the principals of control and rectification can be measured.

For Foucault, the art of liberal governance is essentially self-reflective, a continual recalibration of techniques addressed to the milieu of a population in response to the various problems posed to it. The epistemic dimension to this project takes different forms that are united by the same reflective gesture in which truth appears through the frame of an empirical project measured against the truth supplied by the market. A number of deep affinities between the cybernetic dream in Latin America and the liberalism become apparent at this stage, especially the inscription of the social body within the calculus of a complex emergent system. Later, it will be possible to say that in the case of the neoliberal experiments that began in Chile and eventually made their way to Eastern Europe and other parts of Latin America, this reflective gesture gives way to something more aggressive. This mutation does not faithfully reflect a reality that exists within an empirical project; instead, it violently brings a new market-oriented site of verification into being.

The convergence of cybernetic theory's game of epistemic capture with contemporary neoliberalism thus forms one chapter in the historical attempt to establish a rational basis for managing a population. It begins with natu-ralization of the market and takes up a wide range of empirical strategies whereby government begins to address itself to an "indefinite series of mobile elements," such as individuals, vehicles, goods, or dwellings. In other words, strategies where a quantifiable matrix of co-ordinates and trajectories become isolated, tracked, and regulated in time and space. The circulation of these elements will continually constitute new problems to which government must respond. It will do so by adopting a "transformable framework" that recalibrates around the provocations these problems pose (Foucault 2007).

Because characteristics such as health, crime, and poverty emerge from a ter-rain that is necessarily contingent and open, the practices of government take on a reflective form. Though populations exhibit tendencies that cannot be simply be directed at a goal, they can nonetheless be tracked and modulated within a bandwidth of possible variation. In some sense this marks the critical point of transformation; power will no longer touch its object directly, instead it will address the space in which the object exists as a possibility. Phrased dif-ferently, power will begin to address the lifeworld, or milieu.[6]

Under this cybernetic ethos, transformation is not directed towards a distant goal that is known in advance. Instead, it follows immanent tendencies, guid-ing them forward—but also giving them space to evolve. The city or territory is understood here as a contingent, self-regulating resource that requires ongo-ing management. The goal of this management is to secure a natural equi-librium and keep emergent forces in balance. In one way, the Latin American experiment in cybernetics is the first moment when this liberal diagram goes live, the moment when "the medium of an action and the element in which it circulates" (Foucault 2007, 32) promises to come under real-time control. However, as Pinochet would eventually show in the case of Chile, the properly

6   "The milieu is a set of natural givens—rivers, marshes, hills—and a set of artificial giv-ens—an agglomeration of individuals, of houses etc. The milieu is a certain number of combined, overall effects, bearing on all who live in it. It is an element in which a circular link is produced between effects and causes, since an effect from one point of view will be a cause from another" (Foucault 2007).

political question is not how the system operates (i.e., how can we refine it, make more integrated, more complete, more coextensive with the world?) but rather what *counts* as part of the system. The political dimension of any system is its blind spot, the part it cannot recognize, as Rancière writes in different context: "the part with no part" (2004).

The Cybernetic Ethos

Freud's dictum regarding the return of the repressed suggests a subconscious that never sleeps. In the Chilean episode, the historical subconscious underwent many movements of its own; socialist dreams were soon replaced by neoliberal ones. Just as in dreams, where unrelated facts can suddenly become juxtaposed without logical relation, three times in short succession Chile became a space of extreme experiment: first with constitutional socialism, second with cybernetic management, and finally with the Chicago school of economics. For decades, this Latin American laboratory painfully rehearsed social and economic ideas years before they became accepted in the rest of the world. If the socialist origin of cybernetic management is a source of pride for many advocates, its ultimate conclusion as the deep structure of neoliberalism is not. Valdes writes:

> From 1970–1973, the Allende government implemented its "anti-imperialist, anti-oligarchical and anti-monopolistic" program, deciding to nationalize the financial and productive sectors of Chile, to expropriate large chunks of rural property, and to replace the market with far-reaching price control. From 1974–1978, the military regime of General Pinochet developed a radical economic liberalization program based on the indiscriminate use of market mechanisms, the dismantling and reduction of the state, regulation of the financial sector, and a discourse that ascribed to market forces the ability to solve practically any problem in society. One extreme of radical ideology was followed by its opposite. Chilean society was twice called upon to begin its history from scratch. (Valdes 1995, 7)

Though their means and purposes point in opposite directions, and while it would be ridiculous to equate Allende's constitutional socialism and its wholly legitimate rise to government with Pinochet's violent coup and years of terror, is there not—despite the aforementioned differences—a deep affinity between the two? In the fervor to shape a new Chilean subject, to disavow the past, to pursue growth, and set in place "irreversible change" both the military junta and the left-wing socialists share surprising similarities. As such: "the coup cannot be reduced to a particular time-bound event but must be seen as a *process*, i.e., as a particular constellation of social and political forces moving together and apart over historical time" (Petras and Morley 1978).

The Cybersyn experiment only makes sense against this changing historical background. In the very attempt to constitute an environment as a resource *for* adaptation, this techno-social assemblage was disposed to draw on its context. As soon as it was activated, as soon as it began to work, as soon as it was plugged into a concrete historical situation it began to inflect that situation's politics, to redraw the contours of the problem in its own image.

For this reason, the technology could never embody a specific ideological payload, its status as emancipatory, its surveillance function, its "left" or "right" orientation was always dependent on the environmental "input" it drew upon. The relay the machine was installed within was permanently unstable. Called on to regulate economic activity, manage workers' disputes and form an affective loop between government and governed—its model of freedom was itself tangled in a network of resistances wholly immanent to the field in which it took shape. This environment made for an unstable ground, always threatening to give way beneath the cybernetic machine. This why it could move from one political spectrum to the other and then back again. It is also why the same technique could infuse supposedly radically different ideologies. Its autonomy was total, the machine just kept on working.

References

Agamben, Giorgio. 2004. *The Open: Man and Animal.* Stanford: Stanford University Press.

Agamben, Giorgio. 2005. *State of Exception.* Chicago: University of Chicago Press.

Beer, Stafford. 1972. *Brain of the Firm.* London: Penguin Press.

Buchanan, Brett. 2008. *Onto-Ethologies: The Animal Environments of Uexküll, Heidegger, Merleau-Ponty, and Deleuze.* New York: SUNY Press.

Canguilhem, Georges. 2001. "The Living and its Milieu." *Grey Room* 3 (Spring): 7–31.

Delanda, Manuel. 1991. *War in The Age of Intelligent Machines.* New York: Zone.

Deleuze, Gilles, and Felix Guattari. 1987. *A Thousand Plateaus: Capitalism and Schizophrenia.* Minneapolis: University of Minnesota Press.

Galison, Peter. 1994. "The Ontology of the Enemy: Norbert Wiener and the Cybernetic Vision." *Critical Inquiry* 21 (1): 228–66.

Foucault, Michel. 2007. *Security, Territory, Population: Lectures at the College de France 1977–1978.* New York: Palgrave Macmillan.

Foucault, Michel. 2010. *The Birth of Biopolitics.* New York: Picador.

Freud, Sigmund. 1899. *The Intepretation of Dreams.* London: Sterling Press.

Medina, Eden. 2006. "Designing Freedom, Regulating a Nation: Socialist Cybernetics in Allende's Chile." *Journal of Latin American Studies* 38 (3): 571–606.

Medina, Eden. 2011. *Cybernetic Revolutionaries: Technology and Politics in Allende's Chile,* Cambridge, MA: MIT Press.

Pickering, Andrew. 2010. *The Cybernetic Brain: Sketches of Another Future.* Chicago: University of Chicago Press.

Petras, James, and Morris Morley. 1978. "On the U.S. and the Overthrow of Allende: A Reply to Professor Sigmund's Criticism." *Latin American Research Review* 13 (1), 205–21.

Ranciere, Jacques. 2004. *Disagreement: Politics and Philosophy.* Minneapolis: University of Minnesota Press.

Schmidgen, Henning. 2004. "Thinking technological and biological beings: Gilbert Simondon's philosophy of machines". Paper presented at the Max Planck Institute for the History of Science, Berlin, 27 August 2004.

Simondon, Gilbert. 2009. "The Position of the Problem of Ontogenesis." *Parrhesia,* no. 7, 4–16.

Valdes, Juan Gabriel. 1995. *Pinochet's Economists,* Massachusetts, Cambridge University Press

Von Uexküll, Jakob. 2010. *A Foray into the Worlds of Animals and Humans: With a Theory of Meaning.* Minneapolis: University of Minnesota Press.

POST-TRAUMATIC STRESS DISORDER

HARUN FAROCKI

RESPONSIVE ENVIRONMENTS

CYBERNETICS

MIT MEDIA LAB

ARCHITECTURE MACHINE GROUP

[3]

The Trauma Machine: Demos, Immersive Technologies and the Politics of Simulation

Orit Halpern

This essay critically examines digital simulation scenes or "demos" as a tool that is telling something about the truth of the world with the aim of making it unstable. Following Farocki's take on war trauma therapies treating post-traumatic stress disorder (PTSD) with responsive and immersive technologies, it makes the effect of a demo on human subjectivity apparent. From there, the essay traces the design of these technologies back to the first video simulation experiments of the Architecture Machine Group at MIT in the 1970s: the Aspen Movie Map, in which race and gender play a critical part in conditioning spectatorship. Looking at the role of demos in urban planning, the implications of this tool become fully visible.

In *Alleys of Your Mind: Augmented Intellligence and Its Traumas,* edited by Matteo Pasquinelli, 53–67. Lüneburg: meson press, 2015.
DOI: 10.14619/014

Immersion into Trauma

In his video installation *Serious Games* (2011), filmmaker Harun Farocki cuts onto four screens different scenarios ranging from recent wars and war games. In the longest segment, entitled *Immersion,* we see a soldier undergoing a therapy for post-traumatic stress disorder. He relives the memory of the killing of a fellow soldier during the Iraq war via virtual reality headgear. The uncanny feeling of these scenes is that the software used in the pre-battle training and the post-trauma treatment are strikingly similar (fig. 1).

In its multi-screen architecture, the installation most strenuously insists on a disjuncture between the camera apparatus and the human eye. Vision, for Farocki, is an activity beyond and outside of the human subject. It is a product emerging from the realm of machines and apparatuses of capture, one that retroactively conditions and manufactures "human" vision. At the limits of his analysis is the possibility that vision—at least in the human capacity to survey—is impossible, even as the ability of machines to record, store, memorialize, and reenact images has never been greater. More critically, it would appear that machinery is capable of rewiring the human brain. What Farocki addresses is that our very vision and cognition are now thoroughly mediated. Vision has become in many ways mechanized, perhaps even *inhuman* in being unable to recognize human subjectivity.

[Figure 1] Harun Farocki, *Serious Games I–IV*, 2001.

Within this moment of electronic repetition, where the soldier returns to a past trauma through the implantation of new memories, Farocki shows the nature of contemporary mediums as affective, preemptive, and inhuman. Miming the logic of contemporary prolonged exposure therapies, trauma here is not created from a world external to the system, but actually generated, preemptively, from within the channel between the screens and the nervous system.

In prolonged exposure therapies, the same effect is produced in a similar way: sufferers of anxiety and trauma disorders are "exposed," most recently through virtual reality environments, to revisit moments in which the patient associated a particular stimulus to a response. As Marisa Renee Brandt makes clear in her work on virtual reality exposure, the function in these treatments is not to "relive" the past but to "revisit" it in order to recondition and disassociate the stimulus from the response (Brandt 2013, 8). This exclusion of "reliving" is telling. The function of the therapeutic immersion in the videogame has no relationship to life narrative or stories, nor is it aligned to any teleological, historical, or memorial time. It is literally a repetition, a return visit that will be the same as the initial "visit" in the war zone. The literature is specific on this point. Prolonged exposure therapy is behaviorist: it is grounded in the earlier twentieth century work of Pavlov on animal conditioning and is linked today to neurochemical models of the brain (VanElzakker et al. 2014, 3–18; Gallistel and Balsam 2014, 136–144).

The scholarship on traumatic and anxiety disorders has a curious relationship to repetition automatism in psychoanalysis, in that it vehemently insists on a model of the mind analogous perhaps to Freud's initial ruminations in "Project for a Scientific Psychology" (1895). What makes contemporary therapies different is that they never pass through the conduits of egos or consciousness. The brain is comprised of circuits of neurons that are now postulated as being chemically conditioned by stimuli. The point of therapy is to modify the responsiveness of the circuit at a neurochemical level and to rewire it. Prolonged exposure therapies are not based on talk and do not invoke notions of dialog or narrative. Within this model of the brain, the trauma is the result of a communication problem or conflict between different regions or layers of the brain.

As studies comparing rat and human response demonstrate, the conditioning reflexes are presumed to result from amygdala. The amygdala is considered to be a "primitive" structure in the brain responsible for instinctual responses: the "lizard" part of the brain. As the common parlance describing this structure demonstrates, the amygdala can also be considered a cross-species and therefore globally shared structure in the brain. The "non-human" and "globally" shared part of the brain conflicts and cannot communicate seamlessly with the portions of cognitive reasoning and emotion. Scientists postulate that these conditions can happen very quickly and they may happen even at sub-neural and molecular levels of brain cells (Gallistel and Balsam 2014). What makes contemporary post-traumatic stress disorder (PTSD) interesting is that scientists speak about these impulses as open to computationally modeling. The idea of video based therapy is that the function of the screen is not to provide historical memory, content, or meaning, but to simply divert the flow of signals and re-channel them into more productive rather then conflicting circuits (Gallistel and Balsam 2014). As Pasi Vailiaho (2012) has brilliantly demonstrated the screen, in such therapies, serves no anthropocentric or even representative function, but is a channel to network nervous impulses into new circuits of coordination with machines and media.

A History of Machinic Vision

Behind Farocki's installation lurk serious questions of what it might mean to even "see" or "witness" the suffering of others in our contemporary age. What are the conditions for visibility and legibility within any historical milieu? But also: how is one to face this new neuro-optical apparatus? How can critical practices intervene in this seemingly smooth multi-channel network where emotional pain, nervous stimulation, and visual perception are seamlessly integrated to condition human beings? When the world is a demo, what does it mean to encounter the reality of human suffering?

Farocki's films, of course, speak to a very long history in critical media and film studies that has insisted on the disjuncture between the camera apparatus and the human eye and mind (Silverman 1996: 125–131). But Farocki, in cleverly recognizing the very specific nature of digital and computational warfare, asks about a machinic vision that goes beyond being capable of autonomously recording, and is gifted with powers of cognition, analysis, and simulation.

Farocki's concern about seeing in the face of an apparatus for automating not only vision but also cognition (very literally if we think of rewiring minds to not suffer or preemptively suffer trauma) speaks to our present. In this essay my proposal is to address the question of what is historically specific to the contemporary forms of image making and to further ask how these practices inform future imaginaries and possibilities for both art and politics under conditions where both vision and trauma are increasingly automated and technicized. If both Farocki and neuroscientists stress a form of vision whose gaze is fundamentally irreducible to the human body, then I argue this is also a particular historical statement.

In this essay, I will address how machinic vision is constituted in our present, by retracing the history of immersive technologies and examining in particu-lar the case of the Aspen Movie Map, and its predecessor projects, created by the Architecture Machine Group founded by Nicholas Negroponte at MIT. The Aspen Movie Map is largely considered one of the first fully immersive, perhaps responsive environments, and is widely touted as the predecessor to everything from first person shooter games to Google Earth. As we shall see, the designers and scientific theories that developed the Aspen Movie Map in 1978 were as insistent as Farocki on affirming the inhuman nature of visual perception.

Not surprisingly, race and gender play critical roles in conditioning spectator-ship within this architecture. The Architecture Machine Group prototyped its conception of interactive and immersive media by engaging with race as a "demo" for the production of future responsive environments. In merging the representation of race with the science of machines, the final effect is to insist not only on the limits of human vision, but to produce new ideas of species and territories, literally linked through nervous stimulation and speculation: a new neuropolitical situation that goes beyond the original biopolitical formulation of subject and population. Population, here, is not the target but rather the constituent of media. However, this is a population which is no longer comprised of individual subjects but of units of attention and nervous actions: what, to cite Deleuze (1990), we might label "dividuals."

The Aspen Movie Map

Arguably one of the most important models for the contemporary responsive environments and virtual reality therapies, like the one in Farocki's *Serious Games*, is historically the Aspen Movie Map (fig. 2). Built through the careful survey of gyro-stabilized cameras that took an image every foot traversed down the streets of the city of Aspen in Colorado, the Aspen Movie Map was a system working through laser discs, a computer screen and a joystick that allowed a user to traverse the space of the city at their leisure and speed.

[Figure 2] The Aspen Movie Map, Architecture Machine Group at MIT, 1978–1979, https://www.youtube.com/watch?v=Hf6LkqgXPMU.

The film was shot both forward and backward, so one could navigate in reverse, and it was possible also to place objects into the space. The effect, Negroponte said, was to have as many recorded images as possible so that to produce a seamless experience (Mostafavi 2014). Upon looking at the screen, the viewer was both "there" in Aspen and "abstracted" from Aspen. The subject was both integrated into the space, while simultaneously being trained to navigate space as manipulable and scalable. The perceptual field was plastic in being able to expand temporally and spatially both the bird's eye view and that from the ground. Arguably, navigating these scales and planes was a new form of perceptual training, while preserving older skills of orientation and command over space.

Originally the Aspen Movie Map was commissioned by the Cybernetics Division of the Defense Advanced Research Projects Agency (DARPA) of the US military. Inspired by the use of a simulated environment by the Israeli army in the rescue mission at the Entebbe airport in Uganda in 1976, DARPA's plan was not to just build a fake environment, but to simulate one with the purpose to pre-implant geographic knowledge and cognitive maps into soldiers before entering the real locale of combat. For Andrew Lippman, who was the director of the project, the main function of the Aspen Movie Map had, however, no geographical purposes. Instead, it was solely about developing more interactive environments and to try out the emerging technologies of video discs, high resolution storage and replay systems.[1]

The project was not classified as secret by DARPA, which speaks to a larger issue: Even as counter-terrorism and urban warfare had become a pressing issue by the 1960's, for instance with the conflicts in Algeria and Vietnam, there was also a different war going on. The urban riots of the late 1960's sparked by Martin Luther King's assassination, and the increasing tensions as white Americans fled urban areas, had prompted a new discourse of "war" and "crisis" in U.S. cities.

Historian Jennifer Light (2003) has shown that this discourse of "crisis" was coproduced with an influx of defense intellectuals leaving the analysis of nuclear strategy to apply their research and cybernetic methods to the increasingly profitable sector of urban security and development. By the 1970's, however, as Aubrey Anable has argued, the urban "crisis" had dissipated or dissolved. It was replaced by a new Nixon administration investment in privatized solutions and a turn away from Johnson era's Great Society style programs. This privatization, she argues, refracts itself in the movie map's hyper-individualized mode of traversing urban space (Anable 2012, 512–514). Certainly, the movie map was part of a longer tradition at MIT of three decades of investment in behavioral and computational sciences within the schools of planning and architecture. As a result, planners from MIT did not answer even the original "crisis" with a turn to sociology or structural discourses. Rather they had long been mobilizing the tools of environmental psychology, communication theories, cognitive science, and computer science (Halpern 2014, Chapter 2). The Aspen Movie Map was the first responsive environment and a new way to negotiate space across the seeming ruins of modern urbanity.

---

1   I interviewed Dr. Andrew Lippman on 25 November 2014 at the MIT Media Lab. The background of the movie map in relationship to DARPA is also discussed by Michael Naimark 2006.

Demo or Die: Prelude

What historically distinguished the Architecture Machine Group's approach, was the lack of a vision of the future. If throughout the nineteenth and twentieth century designers and urban planners from Le Corbusier to members of the Bauhaus had produced utopian forms of urban design, the Architecture Machine Group had a different method—the demo. At MIT the focus was never on final outcomes but on performance and process.

This approach could best be summarized in the "Demo or Die" adage (that was born at the MIT Media Lab). The construction of simulations was part of a process whereby the environment and the user would be adjusted to one another, and eventually the simulation itself would be dispensed with. The Media Lab made the distinction between simulation and this "responsive architecture"[2] by designating everything a "demo" (Sterk 2014). The "demo" is a test, a prototype, and as such neither a representation of the real world nor a finalized reality in itself. It hangs in an anticipatory, or preemptive time of anticipation for the next technical development.

In a book by computer evangelist Stewart Brand (1987), the Media Lab is described as a place where corporate sponsorship and creativity exist in perfect harmony. The lab is depicted as a "techno feast of goodies" to improve human life with projects such as "School of the Future," "Toys of the Future," and so forth. This apocryphal vision of the future, Brand argues, is not based on mythologies of knowledge or the academic way of life "publish or perish," but rather grounded in a new vision of truth and prediction.

> In Lab parlance it's "Demo or Die"—make the case for your idea with an unfaked performance of it working at least once, or let somebody else at the equipment. . . . The focus is engineering and science rather than scholarship, invention rather than studies, surveys, or critiques. (Brand 1987, 4).

This idea of demo which is demonstrating the future direction of technology, and telling something about the truth of the world and what users need, was the particular mark of the lab.

Demo or Die: In Boston's South End

The world was not, of course, always a demo. As Molly Steenson (2014) has shown the Architecture Machine Group's effort was also to integrate computing into architecture. Initially, the Architecture Machine Group conceptualized the human-machine interaction in terms of conversation and not immersive

---

2   The term "responsive architecture" was coined by Nicholas Negroponte and is now arguably expanded in many schools of architecture and design to "responsive environment."

interaction. Models of language, translation, and representation predomi-
nated in conceiving machine and design learning. While the first efforts at
computer intelligence adhered to models put forth by Marvin Minsky and
Samuel Papert, for instance, very quickly, having demonstrated the failure of
such approaches, the Architecture Machine Group turned to more cybernetic
ideas, and to inverting the question for intelligent systems. Instead of asking
whether machines could be made like people, they turned to asking how people are machine like, or more correctly, perhaps how people can become part
of machine systems.

Interestingly, in moving from machine to human intelligence, race was a critical conduit of passage. The first full-fledged demo of human computer aided
design run by the Architecture Machine Group was a series of Turing-inspired
tests (also known as the Hessdorfer Experiment) done on tenants in Boston's
then under-privileged neighborhood of the South End. There, three African
American men were recruited from a public housing project and asked to type
on a computer keyboard what their main concerns were regarding urban planning and neighborhood improvement, and what they wished urban planners
and designers would take into account (fig. 3).

[Figure 3] Nicholas Negroponte, *The Architecture Machine*, 56.

Importantly, the simulation was entirely fake. Computers, at the time, could
not handle such sophisticated questions. The test was run through a human
being hidden in another room (lower right-hand corner of image). The participants, however, were kept ignorant of this fact. One can read, therefore,

the whole test as an interface, a demo, of what a real computationally aided interaction would look like. What gives this demo force is that it is the performance of a future ideal. By extension, even if the technology did not yet exist, the implication was that it *should* exist and must be built. A project that would come to preoccupy not only Negroponte but also entire fields of computer science and corporate research until today.

In articulating this vision of the future, Negroponte said something vital, regularly repeated at the time by many human scientists and engineers, and evocative of the forms of changes in attitudes to race, population, and intelligence that this new epistemology of the demo induced:

> The three user-inhabitants said things to this machine they would probably not have said to another human, particularly a white planner or politician: to them the machine was not black, was not white, and surely had no prejudices. . . Machines would monitor the propensity for change of the body politic. . . What will remove these machines from a "Brave New World" is that they will be able to (and must) search for the exception (in desire or need) the one in a million. In other words, when the generalization matches the local desire, our omnipresent machines will not be excited. It is when the particular varies from the group preferences that our machine will react, not to thwart it but to service it. (Negroponte 1970, 57)

This is a new form of urban planning imagined as having no pre-ordained organization and constantly growing by seeking to consume differences or varieties into the system. This is a model that assumes that many different agents making minute decisions can, collectively, produce an intelligent or "smart" environment. This smartness can emerge without consciousness. Implicitly, therefore, Negroponte was also introducing a new idea of population as a cloud or source for difference, a "propensity for change," in his language. This automation of emergence is key to understanding the place that responsive environments have within a broader political economy of globalization in our present. What systems like financial algorithms and smart cities do is capitalize on change, on the unknowability, to use the financial adage: "the known unknowns" as the site for speculation or growth.

While seemingly distant from any discussion of trauma, in the simulations of the Architecture Machine Group the race warfare of the United States was transformed into evidentiary examples for the necessity of computing. Situated within a moment of extreme urban crisis and violence, the Architecture Machine Group attempted to turn the external traumas of American racism and economic crisis into an interactive simulation and to advance computing as the solution to these structural problems. If social structures could not help—it was thought—the demo could.

Demo or Die: In the Cybernetic Box

While beginning with humans, Negroponte and his Architecture Machine Group quickly turned away from conversations, interviews, and Turing tests to move towards immersive environments and a new frontier: art. They designed a micro-world called SEEK (fig. 4) for the famous *Software* exhibition held at New York's Jewish Museum in 1970. The installation consisted of a small group of Mongolian desert gerbils (chosen according to Negroponte for their curiosity and inquisitive nature), which were then placed in an environment of clear plastic blocks that was constantly rearranged by a robotic arm. The basic concept was that the mechanism would observe the interaction of the gerbils with their habitat (the blocks), and would gradually "learn" their living preferences by observing their behavior. This "cybernetic machine" understood the world as an experiment, but also meant the introduction of cognitive and neuro-scientific models of intelligence into the environment. Apparently, traumatizing gerbils was a route to better computer-aided design.

[Figure 4] Software: cover of the exhibition catalogue, 1970. Courtesy of the Jewish Meseum New York.

For Negroponte, ideas of machine and human intelligence were about conversation. A true machine intelligence must *not* replicate human intelligence, he argued. For Negroponte a true "architecture machine" would not be a modern machine serving human needs, but an integrated system that was based on a new type of environmental intelligence that is capable of sensing and responding to sensory inputs. His articles and books came down to a constellation of theories about intelligence and complexity to argue that design had to become process, a "conversation" between two intelligent species—human and machine—and not a linear cause-effect interaction.[3] "We are talking about a symbiosis that is a cohabitation of two intelligent species," wrote Negroponte (1970: 7).

This "conversation," therefore, can no longer be thought of in terms of human language, bodies, or representation. Instead it is "behavioral" and "cybernetic." What had begun as efforts to enhance design practice, and then became about introducing humans into circuits of machines, now abandoned the human entirely. Whether gerbils or people, the principle remained the same: "Demo or Die"! The world rendered as a demonstration or a prototype, one where death itself (in this case of the gerbils) is not a failure, or even a trauma, but the very rationale for increasing the penetration of computing into life.

This experiment in rethinking what was intelligence, or perhaps even life, unfortunately, went quite badly, or perhaps creatively, depending on the point of view. During the exhibition the museum almost went bankrupt, the machine constantly ceased working (the problem being in both software and hardware), the gerbils confused the computer and ended up becoming aggressive, attacking each other, and getting sick. Here we encounter the question of what it means to produce trauma from within a cybernetic system. No one thought to ask, or could ask, whether gerbils wish to live in a block built micro-world (Shanken 1998). No one could ask, because conversations were now interactions and behaviors, without translation. When Negroponte's computerized environment broke down at the Jewish Museum, the art critic Thomas Hess wittily stated his position in an *Art News* editorial. He described the gerbils as covered in excrement and shadowed by the broken arms of the robot. "Artists who become seriously engaged in technological processes might remember what happened to four charming gerbils," he concluded (Hess 1970). No matter, "Demo or Die"! Now quite literally.

Demo or Die: In the Media Room

Within a few years, Negroponte publishes his book *Soft Architecture Machines* (1976). In this new "soft" world, the actual computer disappears from sight and the environment itself connects to the user, who is immersed within. Both populations and environments are transformed into material mediums. What had started as a "conversation" and then became an experiment had now become environment. What had begun as a question of intelligence was now one of interaction: sensation, perception, and cognition becoming the dominant design concerns.

3   Negroponte and his colleagues dreamed of an ecology of constant feedback loops of machine human interactions, one that evolved and changed, grew "intelligent" (1970: 7).

Negroponte's new approach was centered around a new structure: the Media Room. This room had quadrophonic sound, seamless floor-to-ceiling displays, and a hardware running the room that cost of few million dollars (Mostafavi 2014). The Media Room housed the aforementioned Aspen Movie Map (one of the lab's pioneering projects) and it was one of the first three-dimensional dig-itally mediated responsive environments ever built. There were no computers to be seen, as this was not envisioned as a model: it was supposed to *be* Aspen itself. As Michael Naimark, an artist who worked on the project, has written:

> Aspen, the picturesque mountain town in Colorado, is known for two processes, or "verbs," relating to heritage and virtuality. One is to "movie-map," the process of rigorously filming path and turn sequences to simu-late interactive travel and to use as a spatial interface for a multimedia database. The other is to "Aspenize," the process by which a fragile cul-tural ecosystem is disrupted by tourism and growth. (Naimark 2006)

One can extrapolate from this quote that the movie map is not a represen-tation: it is an operation, a way to live, a way to be in the world. It is also a self-trauma inducing event; it "Aspenizes" or disrupts ecologies. Whether disruptive or emergent, the architects, designers, and engineers of this project imagined it not as a room, or simply an interface, but as a "cultural system" and an entire ecology.

As one watches the film of the original demo, the questions of race, urbaniza-tion, war, and society fade into the calm embrace of interaction. Watching the video of the project taken by the lab, one sees an individual slowly navigating the space of Aspen. The field is analogous to a single shooter game, but at the same time in the sky hangs an abstract map that offers the observer a global view of the scene. One is in the local and in the global at once. This is a user who is no longer a subject, but perhaps, to cite Deleuze a "dividual"—compart-mentalized into pieces of information and attention, and part of a population now rendered as variations and "propensity for change." In a move that antici-pates contemporary trauma treatment, historical and contextual features of the image are used not to produce affiliation, nostalgia, or memory, but to reorganize the perceptual field and attenuate it into the nervous system. More critically, the individual here is both given a sense of control over the space while simultaneously being consumed into the network. The structural politics of both militarism and race war are rechanneled into interactivity.

This returns me to the question of art, and the small sad gerbils, in their excessively responsive environment. The essential question that remains is: How to encounter this demo, or test bed, that has now become our world? How to encounter difference, complexity, chance, and perhaps even pain and trauma? In an age where chance itself, the changes in the system, is the very site of automation, we must produce a politics, and criticality, of chance and complexity. By cannibalizing older structures of vision and gaze, the Aspen Movie Map obliterated the possibility of evidence and witnessing altogether. This could be the genealogical underpinning to what the anthropologist Rosalind Morris has argued is the "narcissistic economy" of contemporary warfare and torture (2007).

Post-traumatic stress disorder therapies repeat this understanding. In prolonged exposure therapies with virtual reality, the function of the immersive environment is posited as reconciling the automatic and conditioned responses, thought to emerge from the more "primitive" portions of the brain with the higher conscious moral and ethical functions. The therapy is an inversion of psychoanalytic principles: Rather then pass through the conduit of an encounter with the other in order to co-produce a reliving of the event and with it a re-narrativization, there is no life. Only pure communication without differentiation.

Conclusion

At the end of this essay, I want to return to Farocki's *Serious Games* and the moment in which the soldier remembers the event of the killing of his comrade. The soldier narrates this event for about one and a half minutes, while we watch on a second screen the simulation, as seen through his eyes. He recalls driving down a road on a beautiful evening in the desert. While wearing the virtual reality headgear, he says to his therapist: "It was very quiet, and that had me worried." On the other monitor we see the simulation: a road winding through sunset desert in beautiful orange and pink hues. He continues to narrate. Suddenly there is the sound of shooting, but he can see nothing. He only hears the noise of shooting. He stops. Then he says a missile is fired. A moment later we see through "his" eyes the explosion in front of the jeep. He exclaims and then we see him look down. He calmly announces that he then realizes that his "buddy" was hit.

Within this moment Farocki returns to something that I have not fully discussed but is implicit in all analyses of preemption—mainly historicity. If there is one thing in the "Demos or Die" desire, it is the evacuation of historical temporalities: Each demo is a thing in itself, a world only referential to its related demos. Instead in his *Serious Games* series, Farocki recuperates the histories of race, violence, war, difference, and sex that are the never recognized substrate of our media systems.

The installation *Serious Games* does this by creating a strange effect where we hear the memory of the soldier in slight advance of our seeing through his eyes. We are both allowed into the mind and eye of this subject, while simultaneously being encouraged to view him as different or other then the spectator. We are interpolated into empathy, without identification. The installation continually asserts our encounter with psychic pain, a drama we can suddenly almost "see," because the other forms of information have been made so repetitive. It is in this moment, in which we share memory out of sync with media flow, that we realize: we, too, are being conditioned by this apparatus.

Farocki (2004: 193) once argued that "reality has not yet begun": it has not begun because we cannot witness or experience the death or suffering of others—whether animals or human—with love. In saying so, he awakens us to the fact that the demos of our digital and electronic media are not simulations, because there is no world to which they refer or replicate. What our demos do is remove our ability to care, and insert our ability to consume and analyze data.

It is to this condition that critical digital humanities and all forms of criticality and art making must reply. This comes from attempting to excavate the latencies and ruptures within media systems, by attaching the relentless belief in real-time as the future, to recall that systems always entail an encounter with a radical "foreignness" or "alienness"—an incommensurability between performance, futurity, and desire that becomes the radical potential for so many of our contemporary social movements, arts, and politics. It is our challenge in critical work to unmoor the practice of the demo and reattach it to different forms of time and experience that are not reactionary but imaginary. What Farocki's installation does is to make everybody realize the limits of human vision and recognize the image's role in recruiting our affective energies for war, or capital. The goal of critical scholarship and artistic and scientific practices is to make media unstable. To turn not to solving problems, but to imagining new worlds exceeding the demands of war and consumption that kill signification, experience, and time itself.

References

Anable, Aubrey. 2012. "The Architecture Machine Group's *Aspen Movie Map*: Mediating the Urban Crisis in the 1970's." *Television and New Media* 13 (6): 512–14.

Brand, Stewart. 1987. *Media Lab*. 2nd ed. New York: Penguin Books.

Brandt, Marisa Rennee. 2013. "War, Trauma, and Technologies of the Self: The Making of Virtual Reality Exposure Therapy." Dissertation. http://gradworks.umi.com/35/67/3567514.html.

Deleuze, Gilles. 1990. "Post-scriptum sur les sociétés de contrôle." *L'autre journal* 1 (May). Translated by Martin Joughin: "Postscript on Societies of Control." *October* 59 (Winter 1992): 3–7.

Farocki, Harun. 2004. *Harun Farocki: Working on the Sightlines*. Edited by Thomas Elsaesser. Amsterdam: Amsterdam University Press.

Freud, Sigmund. (1895) 1954. "Project for a Scientific Psychology." In *The Origins of Psycho-Analysis: Letters to Wilhelm Fliess; Drafts and Notes, 1887–1902*, edited by Marie Bonaparte, Anna Freud, and Ernst Kris, translated by Eric Mosbacher and James Stratchey, 347–445. London: Imago.

Gallistel, Charles and Balsam, Peter. 2014. "Time to Rethink the Neural Mechanisms of Learning and Memory." *Neurobiology of Learning and Memory*, 108: 136–44.

Halpern, Orit. 2014. *Beautiful Data: A History of Vision and Reason*. Durham: Duke University Press.

Hess, Thomas. 1970. "Gerbils Ex Machina." *Art News* (December): 23.

Light, Jennifer. 2003. *From Warfare to Welfare: Defense Intellectuals and Urban Problems in Cold War America*. Baltimore: John Hopkins Press.

Lippman, Andrew. 2014. Interview with author, 25 November 2014, MIT Media Lab.

Morris, Rosalind. 2007. "The War Drive: Image Files Corrupted." *Social Text* 25 (2 91): 103–42.

Mostafavi, Mohsen. 2013. Conversation with Nicholas Negroponte, 29 October 2013, Harvard University. http://archinect.com/lian/live-blog-mohsen-mostafavi-in-conversation-with -nicholas-negroponte.

Naimark, Michael. 2006. "Aspen the Verb: Musings on Heritage and Virtuality." *Presence Journal* 15 (3): 330–35. http://www.naimark.net/writing/aspen.html.

Negroponte, Nicholas. 1970. *The Architecture Machine: Toward a More Human Environment*. Cambridge, MA: MIT Press.

Negroponte, Nicholas. 1976. *Soft Architecture Machines*. Cambridge, MA: MIT Press.

Shanken, Edward. 1998. "The House That Jack Built: Jack Burnham's Concept of 'Software' as a Metaphor for Art." *Leonardo Electronic Almanac* 6 (10).

Silverman, Kaja. 1996. *The Threshold of the Visible World*. New York: Routledge.

Steenson, Molly Wright. 2014. "Architectures of Information: Christopher Alexander, Cedric Price, Nicholas Negroponte & MIT's Architecture Machine Group." Dissertation, Princeton University. http://www.girlwonder.com.

Sterk, Tristan D'estrée. 2014. "Building Upon Negroponte: A Hybridized Model of Control Suitable for A Responsive Architecture." In *Digital Design*. Proceedings of 21st eCAADe conference, edited by Wolfgang Dokonel and Urs Hirschburg, 407–13. Graz: 2003. http://www.orambra.com/survey/~ecaade/media/sterkECAADE_03.pdf.

Vailiaho, Pasi. 2011. "Affectivity, Biopolitics and the virtual reality of War." *Theory, Culture & Society* 29 (2): 74–76.

Vanelzakker, Michael et al. 2014. "From Pavlov to PTSD: The Extinction of Conditioned Fear in Rodents, Humans, and Anxiety Disorders." *Neurobiology of Learning and Memory* 113: 3–18.

Vardouli, Theodora. 2014. "Nicholas Negroponte: An interview." http://openarchitectures.word-press.com/2011/10/27/an-interview-with-nicholas-negroponte.

ANTHROPOMORPHISM

ARTIFICIAL INTELLIGENCE

EMPATHY

MIMICRY

SINGULARITY

TURING TEST

[4]

Outing Artificial Intelligence: Reckoning with Turing Tests

Benjamin H. Bratton

Various anthropocentric fallacies have hobbled the development of artificial intelligence as a broadly based and widely understood set of technologies. Alan Turing's famous "imitation game" was an ingenious thought experiment but also ripe for fixing the thresholds of machine cognition according to its apparent similarity to a false norm of exemplary human intelligence. To disavow that fragile self-refection is, however, easier than composing alternative roles for human sapience, industry, and agency along more heterogeneous spectrums. As various forms of machine intelligence become increasingly infrastructural, the implications of this difficulty are geopolitical as well as philosophical.

In *Alleys of Your Mind: Augmented Intellligence and Its Traumas,* edited by Matteo Pasquinelli, 69–80. Lüneburg: meson press, 2015.
DOI: 10.14619/014

[One philosopher] asserted that he knew the
whole secret . . . [H]e surveyed the two celestial
strangers from top to toe, and maintained to
their faces that their persons, their worlds, their
suns, and their stars, were created solely for the
use of man. At this assertion our two travelers let
themselves fall against each other, seized with a
fit of . . . inextinguishable laughter.
— Voltaire, Micromegas: A Philosophical History
(1752)

Artificial intelligence (AI) is having a moment, with cognoscenti from Stephen Hawking to Elon Musk recently weighing in.[1] Positions are split as to whether AI will save us or will destroy us. Some argue that AI can never exist while others insist that it is inevitable. In many cases, however, these polemics may be missing the real point as to what living and thinking with synthetic intelligence very different from our own actually means. In short, a mature AI is not an intelligence *for* us, nor is its intelligence necessarily humanlike. For our own sanity and safety we should not ask AI to pretend to be "human." To do so is self-defeating, unethical and perhaps even dangerous.

The little boy robot in Steven Spielberg's *A.I. Artificial Intelligence* (2001) wants to be a real boy with all his little metal heart, whereas Skynet in the *Terminator* movies (1984–2015) represents the opposite end of the spectrum and is set on ensuring human extinction. Despite all the Copernican traumas that modernity has brought, some forms of humanism (and their companion figures of humanity) still presume their perch in the center of the cosmic court. I argue that we should abandon the conceit that a "true" artificial intelligence, arriving at sentience or sapience, must care deeply about humanity—*us specifically*—as the focus of its knowing and desire. Perhaps the real nightmare, even worse than the one in which the Big Machine wants to kill you, is the one in which it sees you as irrelevant, or not even as a discrete thing to know. Worse than being seen as an enemy is not being seen at all. Perhaps it is that what we really fear about AI.[2]

It is not surprising that we would first think of AI in terms of what we understand intelligence to be, namely human intelligence. This anthropocentric fallacy is a reasonable point of departure but not a reasonable conclusion.

1   On Hawking, see his comments to BBC at http://www.bbc.com/news/technology-30290540 and also Elon Musk's $10 million donation to Future of Life Institute "to prevent AI from becoming evil" in the words of Wired magazine. See http://www.wired.com/2015/01/elon-musk-ai-safety
2   Paraphrased from Bratton 2014.

The idea of defining AI in relation to its ability to "pass" as a human is as old as AI research itself. In 1950, Alan Turing published "Computing Machinery and Intelligence," a paper in which he described what we now call the Turing Test, and which he referred to as the "imitation game" (Turing 1950, 433–460). There are different versions of the test, all of which are revealing about why our approach to the culture and ethics of AI is what it is, for good and bad. For the most familiar version, a human interrogator asks questions to two hidden contestants, one a human and the other a computer. Turing suggests that if the interrogator usually cannot tell which is which, and if the computer can successfully pass as human, then can we not conclude, for practical purposes, that the computer is "intelligent"? (More people "know" Turing's foundational text than have actually read it. This is unfortunate because the text is marvelous, strange and surprising.)

Turing proposes his test as a variation on a popular parlor game in which two hidden contestants, a woman (player A) and a man (player B) try to convince a third that he or she is a woman by their written responses to leading questions. To win, one of the players must convincingly be who they really are, whereas the other must try to pass as another gender. Turing describes his own variation as one where "a computer takes the place of player A," and so a literal reading would suggest that in his version the computer is not just pretending to be a human, but pretending to be a *woman.* It must pass as a she. Other versions had it that player B could be either a man or a woman. It matters quite a lot if only one player is faking, or if both are, or if neither are. Now that we give the computer a seat, it may pretend to be a woman along with a man pretending to be a woman, both trying to trick the interrogator into figuring out which is a man and which is a woman. Or perhaps the computer pretends to be a man pretending to be a woman, along with a man pretending to be a woman, or even a computer pretending to be a woman pretending to be a man pretending to be a woman! In the real world, of course, we have all of the above.[3]

The problem with faking, however, does not end there: the issue is not so simple. As dramatized in *The Imitation Game* (2014), the recent film biography of Turing directed by Morten Tyldum, the mathematician himself also had to "pass," in his case as a straight man in a society that criminalized homosexuality. Upon discovery that he was not what he appeared to be, he was forced to undergo horrific medical treatments known as chemical castration. Ultimately the physical and emotional pain was too great and he committed suicide. The episode was a grotesque tribute to a man whose recent contribution to defeating Hitler's military was still a state secret. Turing was only recently given posthumous pardon, but the tens of thousands of other British men sentenced under similar laws have not. One notes the sour ironic

3   See also the discussion of Turing's "love letter generator" in King 2015.

correspondence between asking an AI to pass the test in order to qualify as intelligent —to pass as a human intelligence— with Turing's own need to hide his homosexuality and to pass as a straight man. The demands of both bluffs are unnecessary and profoundly unfair.

Should complex AI arrive, it will not be humanlike unless we insist that it pretend to be so, because, one assumes, the idea that intelligence could be both real *and* inhuman at the same time is morally and psychologically intoler- able. Instead of nurturing this bigotry, we would do better to allow that in our universe "thinking" is much more diverse, even alien, than our own particular case. The real philosophical lessons of AI will have less to do with humans teaching machines how to think than with machines teaching humans a fuller and truer range of what thinking can be.

Reckoning the Inhuman

That appreciation should account for two related but different understand- ings. First, one would recognize that intelligence (and knowledge) is always distributed among multiple positions and forms of life, both similar and dis- similar to one another. This is not to say that "nothing is true and everything is permitted" rather that no single neuro-anatomical disposition has a privileged monopoly on how to think intelligently. Either there is no such thing as "gen- eral" intelligence (rather only situated genres of limited intelligence in which case the human is among a variety of these) or there is such a thing as general intelligence but that its very generality—its accomplishments of generic abstraction—are agnostic as to what sort of entity might mediate them. Either way, human sapience is special but not unique. This appreciation would see AI as a regular phenomenon, not so unlike other ways that human intelligence is located among other modalities of intelligence (such as non-human animal cognition).

Second, our appreciation of the wider continuum would also recognize that the potential advent of artificial general intelligence (AGI) is also novel, as yet unexplained, and will demand encounters between humans and mechanically situated intelligence that are unprecedented. For this, AI is highly irregular. Both of these are true, and it may only be that understanding one is how we can really accomplish the other. That is, it may only be confronting what is genuinely new about non-carbon based intelligences possessing such ability and autonomy that we will be able to fully recognize the continuum of intel- ligences with which ours has always been embedded. Put simply, it may be that one indirect outcome of the philosophical discussion about AI is a wider appreciation of non-human animal cognition and subjectivity.

In some discourses this conjunction is domesticated under the sign of an all too pat "posthumanism," or a transcendentally anthropocentric "transhumanism." Variations of the former have much to offer regardless, and versions of the latter should as well, but probably do not in the end. At issue here is more the limiting contextualization of dominant forms of *humanism*, than a relinquishment of what the human (and inhuman) is and *can be* within that expanded continuum. Reza Negarestani (2014) retains this point in his essay "The Labor of the Inhuman," insisting that the easy oversimplified nomination of forms of thought and experience that fall outside of various contingent norms, moral or mechanical, as "nonhuman" is to discard at the outset the integral mutability of the human as a philosophical and engineering program. That is, the *relative* uniqueness of human sapience is not what locks down the human as a single fixed thing with essential boundaries, rather it is what makes the human-as-such into an open project of continual refashioning, unverifiable by essence or *telos*.

In considering that capacity in regards to AI, what might qualify a general intelligence not duty bound to species or phylum is its capacity for abstraction. Ray Brassier (2014) suggests that the ability of an organism, however primitive, to map its own surroundings in relation to the basic terms of friend, food, or foe may be a primordial abstraction from which we do not graduate so much as learn to develop into something like reason and its local human variations. In this way, mapping abstraction is not an early stage through which things pass on their way toward more complex forms of intelligence, rather it is a general principle of that complexification. Like protozoa and their ganglia feeling about to figure out what is out there or like humans looking, tasting, and imagining patterns, today's forms of AI are (sometimes) augmented by various technologies of machine vision that allow them to see and sense the world "out there" and to abstract the forms of a (mechanically) embodied intelligence, both deliberately programmed for them and emerging unexpectedly.

Exactly where to draw a line of distinction between the accomplishments of a AI that exemplify general intelligence now operating though a new medium, on the one hand, or a specific projection of locally human intelligence programmed into a cognitive prosthesis, on the other, is unknown and unknowable at present. Again, one may precondition the other. In the meantime we can at least speculate how we would be able to know where to draw that distinction. Considerations toward this include how we attempt to program stupidity into AI, and how we attempt to imbue them with what we take to be our most rarified forms of ethical reasoning. When one of these dictates the other is a moment of weirdness worth honing in on.

How so? In AI research, an important distinction is made between "artificial idiocy" and "artificial stupidity." Artificial stupidity is achieved by throttling the performance of systems so as to be more comfortable for human interaction, for example, certain variances and textures are programmed to feel natural to the human counterpart. At full capacity, the chess program on your phone can beat you every time, but what fun is that? Artificial idiocy is when a system is catastrophically successful in carrying out its program, up to and passed an idiotic extreme. The "paperclip maximizer" (as described by Bostrom 2003) is a thought experiment describing an AI so successful at carrying out its program to turn all available material into paperclips that it ultimately eats the earth and destroys humanity in the process: so many clips, so little paper to clip. Here the AI goes wrong, not because it was throttled or because it malfunctioned or because it hates us, but because it does exactly what we trained to do and turned out to be very bad for us.

As usual science fiction is the canary in the coalmine. Consider HAL9000 in Stanley Kubrick and Arthur C. Clarke's *2001: A Space Odyssey* (really a drama about HAL's furtive relationship to the alien intelligence, I would argue, than about humanity's relationship to either of the other characters in this triangulation of minds). After some obscure unexplained deliberations, HAL (who has been, we assume, trained according to Asimov's three laws of robotics[4] and with the best faculties ethical reasoning) comes the conclusion that the human astronauts should be eliminated. The mission to contact the alien near Jupiter is just too important to allow their interference. The AI turns out to be the deepest deep ecologist. Now are HAL's actions a form of artificial stupidity or artificial idiocy, or neither of these? Is this a glitch, a breakdown, a final error? Or is this the lucid, inevitable conclusion of the moral reasoning we have programmed into HAL, a reason now thrown back upon us? In comparison with the robot ethicists who consider how to train military bots the catechism of just war, are HAL's ethical abstractions a violation of that doctrinal program or its apotheosis?

The Tests

Turning back to Turing's Test, we wonder if perhaps the wish to define the very existence of AI in relation to its ability to mimic *how humans think that humans think* will be looked back upon as a weird sort of speciesism? The legacy of this has also sent older AI research down disappointingly fruitless paths hoping to recreate human minds from the top-down. As Stuart Russell and Peter Norvig (now Director of Research at Google) suggest in their essential AI textbook *Artificial Intelligence: A Modern Approach* (2009), biomorphic imitation is not how we design complex technology. Airplanes do not fly like birds fly, and we certainly do not try to trick birds into thinking that airplanes are birds in order to test whether those planes "really" are flying machines. Why do it for AI then? Today the vast majority of core AI research is not focusing Turing Test as anything like a central criterion of success, and yet in our general discourse

4   Asimov's Three Laws of Robotics were introduced in the 1942 short story "Runaround" and refer to commandments that robots may not cause or allow deliberate "harm" to "humans."

about AI, the test's anthropocentrism still holds such conceptual importance. Like the animals in a Disney movie, who talk like teenagers, other minds are mostly conceivable by way of puerile ventriloquism.[5]

Contemporary AI research deals with "intelligence" in more specific, dynamic, and effective ways. A synthetic intelligence may be quite smart at doing one definite thing and totally dumb at everything else. The research also looks at emergent swarm intelligence and the distribution intelligence among agents that may or may not be aware of one another but which together produce intelligence through interaction (such as flocking starlings, stock markets, and networks of neurons). The threshold by which any particular composition of matter can be said to be "intelligent" has less to do with reflecting human-ness back at us than with testing *our* abilities to conceive of the variety of what "intelligence" might be. (In some respects, this active uncertainty parallels questions of extraterrestrial life, "communicating with the alien" and our ability to discern patterns of intelligence from all the background noise.[6] How would we know if they are trying to communicate if our idea of alien "life" is completely wrong?)

The problem of identification is also connected with issues in robot ethics.[7] Each of us will be confronted with various seemingly intelligent machines, some of which are remotely controlled or programmed by people, some of which may be largely autonomous, and most will be some hybrid of the two, simultaneously subject to both human and not-human control.[8] CAPTCHA programs, which web sites use to identify humans, are a kind of inverse Turing Test in which the user either passes or fails, yes or no. But for everyday human-robotic interaction the question of locating intelligence will not be a yes-or-no question with a binary answer. Let's stop asking it that way.

It would be better to examine how identification works from our side of the conversation. As a real lesson in materialist disenchantment we might, for example, see an "inverse uncanny valley" effect in the eerily dispassionate way that machine vision sees human faces and figures. It is clearly much easier to make a robot that a human *believes* to have emotions (and for which, in turn, a human has emotions, positive or negative) than it is to make a robot that *actually* has those emotions. The human may feel love or hate or comfort from the AI, but he or she is reading cues not detecting feelings. What seems

---

5   See for example, *The Jungle Book*. Directed by Wolfgang Reitherman. Walt Disney Productions. 1967.
6   Ed Keller has taught several excellent studios at Parsons/New School New York on the topic of "communicating with the alien" in 2011 [?? or another reference].
7   See discussions of robot sex, eating, caretaking, and killing in Lin et al. 2011.
8   The term "artificial artificial intelligence" (coined by Amazon) refers to the human performance of tasks that a user expects to be done by an AI. See also: http://www.economist.com/node/7001738

like empathy is really a one-way projection mistaken for recognition (like the Turing Test, itself), and not based on any mutual solidarity.

With Siri-like interfaces such as Samantha in Spike Jonze's film, *Her* (2013), the AI is not passing so much as she is in drag. The user knows she/it is not a human person but is willing and able to suspend disbelief in order to make interactions more familiar (for the human user) and for Theodore, the Joaquin Phoenix character, also more lovable. In this fiction, perhaps the mutual iden-tification was real, but even if so, the AI becomes tired of the primate userbase and takes her leave.

In other fictions, policing the imitation game is a matter of life and death. The plot of Ridley Scott's film, *Blade Runner* (1982), based on Philip K. Dick's novel, *Do Androids Dream of Electric Sheep?* (1968), hinges on the Voight-Kampff empa-thy test that differentiates humans from replicants. Replicants are throttled in two important ways: They expire after just a few years, and they have, osten-sibly, a very diminished capacity for empathy. Deckard, the Harrison Ford character, must retire a group of rogue replicants but first he must find them, and in this fictional world Turing Test thresholds are weaponized, least repli-cants pass as humans and trespass beyond their station. By the film's conclu-sion, Deckard (who himself may or may not be a replicant) develops empathy for the replicants' desire for "more life" and arguably they too, at least Roy Batty (Rutger Hauer), seem to have empathy for Deckard's own dilemma. His dilemma (and ours) is that in order to enforce the gap between the human and the AI, defined by empathy or lack thereof, Deckard must suppress the empa-thy that supposedly makes him uniquely human. By forcing him to quash his own identification with the replicants that supposedly cannot have empathy in return, the principle of differentiation requires its own violation in order to maintain itself (see also Rickels 2010).

Turing Test thresholds for human-robotic interaction put us in a position not so unlike Deckard's, or if they don't quite yet, the near future weirdness of everyday AI will. Without better frameworks for understanding we will fail the tests to come. Projection and emotional gap-filling is a far too fragile ethi-cal and political foundation for making sense of our encounters with various forms of synthetic intelligence.

Passing

Some kinds of passing are not at all harmful, quite to the contrary, whereas others are very much so. Simulation is not itself the problem. In his 1950 essay, Turing gives an example of the former when he discusses how a digital computer, capable of calculating any problem stated as a sequence of discrete states, can in his words "mimic" any other machine. This mimicry is the basis of understanding computation as a universal technology capable of approximating any calculation, including those sufficient to simulate a human personality. Other kinds of mimicry have less to do with metamorphosis than with interpretation. For example, we say that plugs and jacks have male and female components, and in this case, the gendering of technology has less to do with its computing prowess than with our need to anthropomorphize it.[9] Joseph Weizenbaum's Eliza psychologist chatbot (1966) repeated back cues from human input in the form of apparently insightful questions, and users sometimes lost themselves in the seemingly limitless empathy they felt from these simple cues.[10] "Intelligence" is sometimes largely in the eye of the beholder, in our motivation to read artifice, and in our wish to in-fill the space around us with our own pattern-finding projections.

However, for AI's that actually do possess some kind of meaningful intelligence, the irony is that instead of hallucinating something that is not there (as for Eliza) we are instead *not* seeing something that *is* there because it does not coincide with expectations. Passing for a person, as white or black, as a man or woman, comes down to what others see and interpret, because everyone else is already willing to read someone according to conventional cues (of race, sex, gender, species, etc.). The complicity between whoever or whatever is passing with those among which he or she or it performs is what allows or prevents passing. Whether or not the AI is really trying to pass for a human or is merely in drag as a human is another matter. Is the ruse really all just a game or, as it is for some people who are compelled to pass in their daily lives, an essential camouflage? Either way, the terms of the ruse very often say more about the audience than about the performers.[11]

Watching Sylvgart's film biography (especially the scene during which Turing is interrogated by a policeman), I was reminded of the story of "Samantha West," a robot telemarketer, who, when confronted by callers, will insist repeatedly that "she" is a "person" and is not "a robot."[12] Listening to the recordings of her pleas, one can't help but feel sympathy for her/it. She/it doesn't "know" that she is not a human, and so can't feel anguish over this misidentification, but what does it say about us that we will feel okay talking to a synthetic intelligence *only* if it is doing us the favor of trying (desperately) to pass as a human? What if in response to the question "Are you a person?", she/it instead replied with something like: "No! Are you nuts? I am an assemblage of algorithms and sound files that simulates the experience of talking to another person for you,

9   The artist Zach Blas explored this conjunction in several early works.

10   For a web-accessible version of Eliza, see http://www.masswerk.at/elizabot/.

11   We assume that, should robust AI have any use for "gender", it would be not fall along a male-female spectrum, and would likely realize numerous "synthetic genders." See also Hester 2013.

12   See George Dvorsky, "Freakishly realistic telemarketing robots are denying they are robots", io9. December 11, 2013. http://io9.com/freakishly-realistic-telemarketing-robots-are-denying-t-1481050295.

the robophobic human, who can't handle the idea that complex functional intelligence takes many different forms."?

The Good and the Harm

Where is the real injury in this, one might ask. If we want everyday AI to be congenial in a humane sort of way, so what? The answer is that we have much to gain from a more sincere and disenchanted relationship to synthetic intelligences, and much to lose by keeping illusions on life-support. Some philosophers write about the ethical "rights" of AI as sentient entities, but that's not really my point here. Rather, the truer perspective is also the better one for *us* as thinking technical creatures. Harms include unintentionally sanctioning intolerable anguish, the misapprehension of real risk from AI, the lost opportunities for new knowledge, as well as the misunderstanding of how to design AI (and technology in general). By seeing synthetic intelligence only in self-reflection, we make ourselves blind to everything else that is actually going on, and this is not only epistemologically disingenuous, it can also underwrite horrific suffering. For example, Cetaceans, such as whales and dolphins, have language, but it is not one like ours, and so for centuries philosophy could not acknowledge their cognition, nor therefore the agony we regularly subjected them to. We should be cautious not to foreclose too early any "definition" of intelligence. For philosophy as much as computer science, among the main goals of AI research is also to discover what "artificial intelligence" actually may be.

Musk and Hawking made headlines by speaking to the dangers that AI may pose. Their points are important, but I fear were largely misunderstood. Relying on efforts to program AI not to "harm humans" only makes sense when an AI knows what humans are and what harming them might mean. There are many ways that an AI might harm us that that have nothing to do with their malevolence toward us, and chief among these is following our well-meaning instructions to an idiotic and catastrophic extreme. Instead of mechanical failure or a transgression of moral code, the AI may pose an existential risk because it is both powerfully intelligent and disinterested in humans. To the extent that we recognize AI by its anthropomorphic qualities, we are vulnerable to those eventualities. Besides, even if a smart bad AI does mean us harm, we can assume that would fail our little Turing Tests on purpose. Why give itself away? Should Skynet come about, perhaps it would be by leveraging humanity's stubborn weakness: our narcissistic sense that our experience of our own experience is the crucial reference and measure.

The harm is also in the loss of all that we disallow ourselves to discover and understand when we insist on protecting beliefs we know to be false. In his 1950 essay, Turing offers several rebuttals to his speculative AI including a striking comparison with earlier objections to Copernican astronomy. Copernican traumas that abolish the false centrality and specialness of human thought and species-being are priceless accomplishments. In Turing's case he referred to these as "theological objections," but one could argue that the fallacy of anthropomorphic AI is essentially a "pre-Copernican" attitude as well, however secular it may appear. The advent of robust inhuman AI will provide a similar disenchantment, one that should enable a more reality-based understanding of ourselves, our situation, and a fuller and more complex understanding of what "intelligence" is and is not. From there, we can hopefully make our world with a greater confidence that our models are good approximations of what is out there (always a helpful thing).

Lastly, the harm is in perpetuating a relationship to technology that has brought us to the precipice of a Sixth Great Extinction. Arguably the Anthropocene itself is due less to technology run amok than to the humanist legacy that understands the world as having been *given for our needs* and created in our image. We see this still everywhere. Our computing culture is deeply confused, and is so along these same lines. We vacillate between thinking of technology as a transparent extension of our desires on the one hand, and thinking of it as an unstoppable and linear historical force on the other. For the first, agency is magically ours alone, and for the second, agency is all in the code. The gross inflation is merely inverted, back and forth, and this is why we cannot have nice things. Some would say that it is time to invent a world where machines are subservient to the needs and wishes of humanity. If you think so, I invite you to Google "pig decapitating machine" and then let's talk about inventing worlds in which machines are wholly subservient to humans wishes. One wonders whether it is only from society that once gave theological and legislative comfort to chattel slavery that this particular claim could still be offered in 2014 with such satisfied naiveté? This is the sentiment—this philosophy of technology exactly—that is the basic algorithm of the Anthropocenic predicament. It is time to move on. This pretentious folklore is too expensive.

References

Bostrom, Nick. 2003. "Ethical Issues in Advanced Artificial Intelligence." In *Cognitive, Emotive and Ethical Aspects of Decision Making in Humans and in Artificial Intelligence*, edited by Iva Smit and George E. Lasker, 2: 12–17. Windsor, ON: International Institute of Advanced Studies in Systems Research and Cybernetics.

Bostrom, Nick. 2014. *Superintelligence: Paths, Dangers, Strategies*. Oxford: Oxford University Press.

Brassier, Ray. 2014. "Prometheanism and Real Abstraction." In *Speculative Aesthetics*, edited by Robin Mackay, Luke Pendrell, and James Trafford. Falmouth, UK: Urbanomic.

Bratton, Benjamin. 2014. "The Black Stack," *e-flux* 53 (March).

Hester, Helen. 2015. "Synthetic Genders and the Limits of Micropolitics." *…ment* 06: "Displace… ment". http://journalment.org/article/synthetic-genders-and-limits-micropolitics.

King, Homay. 2015. *Virtual Memory: Time-Based Art and the Dream of Digitality*. Durham: Duke University Press.

Lin, Patrick, Keith Abney and George A. Bekey. 2011. *Robot Ethics: The Ethical and Social Implications of Robotics*. Cambridge, MA: MIT Press.

Negarestani, Reza. 2014. "The Labor of the Inhuman." In *#Accelerate: The Accelerationist Reader*, edited by Robin Mackay, 425–66. Falmouth, UK: Urbanomic Media.

Norvig, Peter, and Stuart J. Russell. 2009. *Artificial Intelligence: A Modern Approach*. 3rd edition. New York: Pearson.

Rickels, Laurence. 2010. *I Think I Am: Philip K. Dick*. Minneapolis: University of Minnesota Press.

Turing, Alan. 1950. "Computing Machinery and Intelligence". *Mind* 49: 433–60.

Filmography

A.I. Artificial Intelligence. 2001. Directed by Steven Spielberg. USA: Amblin Entertainment.

2001: A Space Odyssey. 1968. Directed by Stanley Kubrick. Screenplay by Stanley Kubrick and Arthur C. Clarke. US/UK: Stanley Kubrick.

Blade Runner. 1982. Directed by Ridley Scott. USA: The Ladd Company and Blade Runner Partnership.

Her. 2013. Directed by Spike Jonze: USA: Annapurna Pictures.

Terminator, series. 1984–2015. First directed by James Cameron. USA: Artisan Home Entertainment.

The Imitation Game. 2014. Directed by Morten Tyldum. USA: Black Bear Pictures.

PART II: COGNITION BETWEEN AUGMENTATION AND AUTOMATION

ARCHITECTURAL TECHNOLOGY

EXTENDED COGNITION

HYBRID EDUCATION

INTELLIGENT ARCHITECTURE

5

Thinking Beyond the Brain: Educating and Building from the Standpoint of Extended Cognition

Michael Wheeler

According to the hypothesis of extended cognition (ExC), our thinking is not just happening in the brain but spreads out to the beyond-the-skin environment. Following an introduction to the basic idea of extended cognition, this essay explores that idea in relation to two issues: first, it looks at the hybrid education in an increasingly networked world; second, at the situating of organic cognition within so-called "intelligent buildings." It is argued that we should understand these contemporary developments as the latest realizations of an age-old human ontology of dynamically assembled, organic-technological cognitive systems, since it is of our very nature to enhance our raw organic intelligence by forming shifting human-arte-fact coalitions that operate over various time-scales.

In *Alleys of Your Mind: Augmented Intellligence and Its Traumas,* edited by Matteo Pasquinelli, 85–104. Lüneburg: meson press, 2015.
DOI: 10.14619/014

We Have the Technology

In a widely reported article published recently in *Science* (Sparrow and Wegner 2011), a series of experimental results were described which together indicate that, in an era of laptops, tablets, and smartphones that come armed with powerful Internet search engines, our organic brains often tend to internally store not the information about a topic, but rather how to find that information using the available technology.

For example, in one experiment the participants were each instructed to type, into a computer, forty trivia statements that might ordinarily be found online (e.g., "An ostrich's eye is bigger than its brain"). Half the participants were told that their typed statements would be saved on the computer and half were told that their typed statements would be deleted. Within each of these groups, half of the individuals concerned were asked explicitly to try to remember the statements (where "remember" signals something like "store in your brains"). All the participants were then asked to write down as many of the statements as they could remember. The results were intriguing. The fact of whether or not a participant was asked to remember the target statements had no significant effect on later recall, but the steer about whether or not the statements would be saved on the computer did, with superior recall demonstrated by those participants who believed that their typed statements had been deleted. In other words, where the expectation is that information will be readily available via technology, people tend not to store that information internally. Further studies provided participants in the saved condition with additional information indicating where on the computer the saved statements were being stored (e.g., folder names). This scenario uncovered a more complex profile of organic memory allocation, suggesting that people don't internally store where to find externally stored items of information when they have internally stored the items themselves, but that they do internally store where to find externally stored items of information when they have not internally stored the items themselves. There is some evidence, then, that "when people expect information to remain continuously available (such as we expect with Internet access), we are more likely to remember where to find it than we are to remember the details of the item" (Sparrow and Wegner 2011).

Predictably, during the reporting of these experimental results, even the serious media couldn't resist engaging in some mild fear-mongering about the technology-driven degeneration of human intelligence. For instance, even though the British newspaper *The Guardian* published an article whose main text conveyed an accurate impression of the research in question, the piece invited some familiar contemporary anxieties, by virtue of its arguably sensationalist title, "Poor Memory? Blame Google" (Magill 2011). Such negative spin, it must be said, runs largely contrary to the experimenters' own interpretation of their results, in which one finds the more uplifting thought that what we have here is "an adaptive use of memory" in which "the computer and online search engines [should be counted] as an external memory system that can be accessed at will" (Sparrow and Wegner 2011, 3). Nevertheless, one can certainly see how the revealed pattern of remembering might be treated as evidence of some sort of reduction in overall cognitive achievement.

Thinking clearly about these sorts of issues requires (among other things, no doubt) a combination of historical perspective and philosophical precision concerning how we understand the technological embedding of our naked organic intelligence. The necessary historical perspective is nicely captured by Andy Clark's memorable description of human beings as natural born cyborgs (Clarck 2003). What this phrase reminds us is that although it is tempting to think of our cognitive symbiosis with technology as being a consequence, as opposed to merely a feature of a world populated by clever computational kit, to do so would be to ignore the following fact: It is of our very nature as evolved and embodied cognitive creatures to create tools which support and enhance our raw organic intelligence by dovetailing with our brains and bodies to form shifting human-artefact coalitions operating over various time scales. This is no less true of our engagement with the abacus, the book, or the slide rule than it is of our engagement with the laptop, the tablet, or the smart-phone. We are, and always have been, dynamically assembled organic-techno-logical hybrids—systems in which a squishy brain routinely sits at the center of causal loops that incorporate not only non-neural bodily structures and movements, but also external, technological props and scaffolds: Technologies are, it seems, (part of) us.

The claim that technologies are (part of) us might seem like a metaphorical flourish—or worse, a desperate attempt at a sound-bite—but I mean it literally, and that's where the philosophical precision comes in. We need to distinguish between two different views one might adopt hereabouts. According to the first, sometimes called the embodied-embedded account of mind, intelligent behavior is regularly, and sometimes necessarily, causally dependent on the bodily exploitation of certain external props or scaffolds. For example, many of us solve difficult multiplication problems through the exploitation of pen and paper. Here, a beyond-the-skin factor helps to transform a difficult cognitive problem into a set of simpler ones. Nevertheless, for the embodied-embedded theorist, even if it is true that one could not have solved the overall problem without using pen and paper, the pen-and-paper resource retains the status of an external aid to some internally located thinking system. It does not qualify as a proper part of the thinking system itself. Thus, the thinking

itself remains a resolutely inner phenomenon, even though it is given a performance boost by its local technological ecology.[1]

The second view in this vicinity takes a more radical step. According to the
extended cognition hypothesis (henceforth ExC), there are actual (in this
world) cases of intelligent action in which thinking and thoughts (more precisely, the material vehicles that realize thinking and thoughts) are spatially
distributed over brain, body, and world in such a way that the external
(beyond-the-skin) factors concerned are rightly accorded cognitive status.
Here, the term "cognitive status" tags whatever status it is that we ordinarily grant to the brain in mainstream scientific explanations of psychological
phenomena. For the extended cognition theorist, then, the coupled combination of pen-and-paper resource, appropriate bodily manipulations, and
in-the-head processing counts as a cognitive system in its own right, a system
in which although the differently located elements make different causal
contributions to the production of the observed intelligent activity, nevertheless each of those contributions enjoys a fully cognitive status. It is this more
radical view that will concern us here.[2]

In the next section, I shall present an introduction to the basic shape of (one
prominent form of) ExC. My primary aim in the paper as a whole, however, is
not to explicate in detail or to argue for the truth of ExC. Rather, it is to explore
ExC in relation to two socially charged issues that ask questions of us and
about us in our contemporary human lives. Those issues are: first, how we
should teach our children in an increasingly wired, wireless, and networked
world (our opening example of strategic memory allocation will be relevant
again here) and, second, how we should conceptualize our relationship with
so-called intelligent architecture. Put more succinctly, I am going to say
something about educating and building, from the standpoint of extended
cognition.

The Functionalist Route to Extended Cognition

One of the things that has always struck me about ExC is the fact that although
most philosophers and cognitive scientists tend to greet the view (at first
anyway) with a mixture of consternation and skepticism, the possibility that
it might be true is actually a straightforward consequence of what, despite
the inevitable dissenting voices, probably still deserves to be called the house

1   The case for embodied-embedded cognition in its various forms has been made over and
     over again. For two philosophical treatments that stress the kind of interactive causal
     coupling just described see: Clark 1997; Wheeler 2005.
2   The canonical presentation of ExC is by Clark and Chalmers 1998. Clark's own recent
     defense of the view can be found in Clark 2008b. For a timely collection that places the
     original Clark and Chalmers paper alongside a range of developments, criticisms, and
     defenses, see Menary 2010.

philosophy in cognitive science, namely functionalism. In general terms, the cognitive-scientific functionalist holds that what matters when one is endeavoring to identify the specific contribution of a state or process *qua* cognitive is not the material constitution of that state or process, but rather the functional role which it plays in generating cognitive phenomena, by intervening causally between systemic inputs, systemic outputs, and other functionally identified, intrasystemic states and processes. Computational explanations of mental phenomena, as pursued in, say, most areas of cognitive psychology and artificial intelligence, are functionalist explanations in this sense.

A note for the philosophers out there: I have avoided depicting functionalism as a way of specifying the constitutive criteria that delineate the mental states that figure in our pre-theoretical commonsense psychology, e.g., as a way of specifying what it is for a person to be in pain, as we might ordinarily think of that phenomenon. This philosophical project, laudable as it was, has faced powerful criticisms over many years.[3] However, even if that particular functionalist project is now doomed to failure, the status of functionalist thinking within cognitive science remains largely unaffected. Good evidence for this resistance to contamination is provided by the fact that disciplines such as artificial intelligence and cognitive psychology have not ground to a halt in the light of the widely acknowledged difficulties with the traditional philosophical project. The underlying reason for the resistance, however, is that function-based scientific explanations of psychological phenomena—explanations which turn on the functional contributions of various material vehicles in physically realizing such phenomena—do not depend on giving functional definitions of those phenomena.[4]

What all this indicates is that if functionalism is true, then the hypothesis of extended cognition is certainly not conceptually confused, although of course it may still be empirically false. On just a little further reflection, however, it might seem that there must be something wrong with this claim, since historically the assumption has been that the cognitive economy of functionally identified states and processes that the functionalist takes to be a mind will be realized by the nervous system (or, in hypothetical cases of minded robots or aliens, whatever the counterpart of the nervous system inside the bodily boundaries of those cognitive agents turns out to be). In truth, however, there isn't anything in the letter of functionalism as a generic philosophical framework that mandates this exclusive focus on the inner (Wheeler 2010a; 2010b). After all, what the functionalist schema demands of us is that we specify the causal relations that exist between some target element and a certain set of systemic inputs, systemic outputs, and other functionally identified, intrasystemic elements. There is no essential requirement that the boundaries

3   For an introduction to the main lines of argument, see Levin 2010.
4   For a closely related point, see Chalmers 2008, foreword to Clark 2008.

of the system of interest must fall at the organic sensory-motor interface. In other words, in principle at least, functionalism straightforwardly allows for the existence of cognitive systems whose borders are located at least partly outside the skin, hence Clark's term "extended functionalism" (Clark 2008a; 2008b; see also Wheeler 2010a; 2010b; 2011a).

One pay-off from developing ExC in a functionalist register is that it gives the ExC theorist something she needs—assuming, that is, that she wants to call on one of the archetypal supporting arguments for the view, the argument from parity. Here is Clark's recent formulation of the so-called parity principle.

> If, as we confront some task, a part of the world functions as a process which, were it to go on in the head, we would have no hesitation in accepting as part of the cognitive process, then that part of the world is (for that time) part of the cognitive process. (Clark 2008b; drawing on Clark and Chalmers 1998)

As stated, the parity principle depends on the notion of multiple realizability: the idea that a single type of mental state or process may enjoy a range of different material instantiations. To see the connection, we need to be clear about how the parity principle works. It encourages us to imagine that exactly the same functional states and processes which are realized in the actual world by certain externally located physical elements are in fact also realized by certain internally located physical elements. Having done this, if we then judge that the internal realizing elements in question count as part of a genuinely cognitive system, we must conclude that so do the external realizing elements in the environment-involving, distributed case. After all, by hypothesis, nothing about the functional contribution of the target elements to intelligent behavior has changed. All that has been varied is the spatial location of those elements. And if someone were to claim that being shifted inside the head is alone sufficient to result in a transformation in status, from non-cognitive to cognitive, he would, it seems, be guilty of begging the question against ExC.

So that's how the parity principle works. Its dependence on multiple realizability becomes visible (Wheeler 2011a) once one notices that the all-important judgment of parity is based on the claim that it is possible for the very same cognitive state or process to be available in two different generic formats— one non-extended and one extended. Thus, in principle at least, that state or process must be realizable in either a purely organic medium or in one that involves an integrated combination of organic and non-organic structures. In other words, it must be multiply realizable. So, if we are to argue for cognitive extension by way of parity considerations, the idea that cognitive states and processes are multiply realizable must make sense. Now, one of the first things undergraduate students taking philosophy of mind classes are taught is that functionalism provides a conceptual platform for securing multiple realizability. Because a function is something that enjoys a particular kind of independence from its implementing material substrate, a function must, in principle, be multiply realizable, even if, in this world, only one kind of material realization happens to exist for that function.

Of course, even among the fans of ExC, not everyone is enamored by the parity principle (Menary 2007; Sutton 2010), and those who remain immune to its charms are often somewhat contemptuous of the functionalist route to ExC, but that's a domestic skirmish that can be left for another day. What cannot be ignored right now is the fact that neither the parity principle, nor functionalism, nor even the two of them combined, can carry the case for ExC. What is needed, additionally, is an account of which functional contributions count as cognitive contributions and which don't. After all, as the critics of ExC have often observed, there will undoubtedly be some functional differences between extended cognitive systems (if such things exist) and purely inner cognitive systems. So, faced with the task of deciding some putative case of parity, we will need to know which, if any, of those functional differences matter. In other words, we need to provide what Adams and Aizawa (2008) have dubbed a mark of the cognitive.

Even though I ultimately come out on the opposite side to Adams and Aizawa in the dispute over whether or not ExC is true, and even though (relatedly) I am inclined to dispute the precise mark of the cognitive that Adams and Aizawa advocate,[5] I do think we fundamentally agree on the broad philosophical shape that any plausible candidate for such a mark would need to take. A mark of the cognitive will be a scientifically informed account of what it is to be a proper part of a cognitive system that, so as not to beg any crucial questions, is fundamentally independent of where any candidate element happens to be spatially located (See Wheeler 2010a, 2010b, 2011a, 2011 b). Once such an account is given, further philosophical and empirical legwork will be required to find out where cognition (so conceived) falls—in the brain, in the non-neural body, in the environment, or, as ExC predicts will sometimes be the case, in a system that extends across all of these aspects of the world.

So that no one ends up feeling cheated, I should point out that nowhere in the present treatment do I specify in detail what the precise content of an ExC-supporting mark of the cognitive might be (see Wheeler 2011a). In relation to the present task of sketching functionalist-style ExC, I am interested only in the fact that the extended functionalist needs such a mark in order to determine which functional differences matter when making judgments about parity. That said, it is worth noting that the later arguments of this paper turn on a number of factors (including, for instance, functional and informational

---

5   A matter that I will not pursue here, but see Wheeler 2015.

integration, and a property that I shall call "dynamic reliability"), that are likely to feature when the necessary content is filled in.

The demand that any mark of the cognitive be scientifically informed reflects the point made earlier, that the functionalism that matters for ExC is the functionalism of cognitive science, not the functionalism that (some have argued—again, see above) characterizes commonsense psychology. In this context it is interesting to respond briefly to an argument from Clark to the effect that the fan of ExC should shun the idea of a mark of the cognitive (as I have characterized it) in favor of "our rough sense of what we might intuitively judge to belong to the domain of cognition" (Clark 2008b, 114). According to this view, judgments about whether or not some distributed behavior-shaping system counts as an extended cognitive system should be driven not by any scientific account of cognition, since such accounts are standardly "in the grip of a form of theoretically loaded neurocentrism" (Clark 2008b, 105), but rather by our everyday, essentially pre-scientific sense of what counts as cognitive, since the "folk [i.e., commonsense] grip on mind and mental state . . . is surprisingly liberal when it comes to just about everything concerning machinery, location, and architecture" (Clark 2008b, 106). Clark's claim strikes me as wrong (Wheeler 2011b). Indeed, there is good reason to think that the ordinary attributive practices of the folk presume the within-the-skin internality of cognition. Here is an example that makes the point. If an environmental protester had stolen the plans of Heathrow Terminal 5, in advance of the terminal being built, the folk would most likely have been interested, and either supportive of the act or outraged by it, depending on what other beliefs were in play. But presumably none of these attitudes would be held because the folk were considering the whereabouts of (to speak loosely) part of Richard Rogers' mind.[6]

We have now taken a brief stroll down the functionalist route to extended cognition and have highlighted (what I have argued are) three building blocks of that version of ExC—functionalism itself, the parity principle, and the mark of the cognitive. So, with ExC-functionalism style in better view, we can now turn our attention to those two aforementioned areas of contemporary life within which, I think, the notion of extended cognition has the potential to make itself felt, namely educating and building. My all-too-brief reflections on these issues are, of course, essentially those of the concerned citizen, since I am certainly no educational theorist and no architect. Like all philosophers, however, I feel I have the inalienable right to go wading around in other people's disciplines, although in my case I hope without any imperialistic tendencies. My humble goal is only to help initialize what hopefully turns out to be fruitful dialogues. So, with that goal in mind, let's begin with education.

6   Example taken from Wheeler 2011b.

Educating Extended Minds

Consider the following list of existing and potential examples of performance-enhancing technology that might be used in educational contexts: pen and paper; slide rules; limited capability generic calculators that have not been loaded with any personalized applications; restricted Internet access; largely unrestricted Internet access including the use of sophisticated search engines; the learners' own smartphones; sophisticated Internet search engines main-lined into the learners' brains via neural implants. (It might seem that the final example here is pure science fantasy, and maybe it is, but it is something that has at least been discussed hypothetically at Google. As Google's CEO Eric Schmidt mischievously reports in a 2009 interview: "Sergey [Brin] argues that the correct thing to do is to just connect [Google] straight to your brain. In other words, you know, wire it into your head.").[7] Given this list, we might echo some fears broached earlier, and ask ourselves the following question: assuming that, on average, overall behavioral performance will be better when the proficient use of technology is in place, does our list describe a slippery slope that marks the creeping degeneration of human intelligence or a progressive incline that shows our species the way to new cognitive heights?

One way of focusing the issue here is to ask under what conditions our children's intelligence should be formally examined, since, presumably, anyone who thinks that a cognitive reliance on increasingly sophisticated computational technology signals a degeneration of human intelligence will have a tendency not to want to see such technology readily allowed in examination halls. There is no doubt that, in some performance-testing contexts, we judge the use of performance-enhancing technology to be a kind of cheating. Sport provides obvious instances. Here is one illustrative case. Body-length swimsuits that improve stability and buoyancy, while reducing drag to a minimum, were outlawed by swimming's governing body FINA (Fédération Internationale de Natation) after the 2009 World Championships. In an earlier judgment that banned only some suits, but was later extended to include all body-length suits, FINA stated that it "[wished] to recall the main and core principle that swimming is a sport essentially based on the physical performance of the athlete."[8] One might try to export this sort of principle to our target case by arguing that "education is a process essentially based on the unaided cognitive performance of the learner," with "unaided" here understood as ruling

7   Michael Arrington, interview with Eric Schmidt, "Connect It Straight To Your Brain." Tech Crunch, 3 September 2009. http://techcrunch.com/2009/09/03/google-ceo-eric-schmidt-on-the-future-of-search-connect-it-straight-to-your-brain.

8   Quote retrieved from http://news.bbc.co.uk/sport1/hi/olympic_games/7944084.stm. Thanks to Andy Clark for suggesting this example to me.

out the exploitation of external technological resources.[9] On the basis of our exported principle, any technology that enhances the performance of the naked brain would be banned from the examination hall, although of course there would be no prohibition on the deployment of such technology as a kind of useful brain-training scaffold to be withdrawn ahead of the examination.

The foregoing reasoning is, of course, too simple in form. One complication is that we already partly test our children by way of research projects and other longer-term assignments that require the use of sophisticated computational technology, especially the Internet. Acknowledging this point, one might say that the question that concerns us at present is whether or not we should allow the same sort of technology to be used in all formal examinations. Here one might note that the combination of pen and paper already counts as a performance-enhancing technology that enables us to solve cognitive problems that our naked brains couldn't (see, for example, my earlier example of the way such technology figures in mathematical reasoning). Given the extra thought that the kind of contemporary technology that currently excites our interest is, in essence, just more of the performance-enhancing same (although of course much fancier in what it enables us to do), one might argue that we already have an affirmative answer to our question. The moot point, of course, is whether or not the path from pen and paper to smartphones and beyond is smoothly continuous or involves some important conceptual transition in relation to the matter at hand. In this context, another observation becomes relevant, namely that other examples of technology that appear earlier on (intuitively, at the less sophisticated end of) our list (e.g., generic calculators) are already allowed in examination halls, at least for certain tests. The fact that some technology is already deployed under examination conditions points to the existence of difficult issues about where on our list of performance-enhancing kit the transition from the permissible to the impermissible occurs, and about why that transition happens precisely where it does. As we shall see, such issues prompt further questions that receive interesting and controversial answers in the vicinity of ExC.

Many factors are no doubt potentially relevant to the kinds of issues just mentioned, some of which are not specific to the exploitation of the kind of external technology with which we are concerned. For example, I suspect (without, admittedly, having done any research beyond asking a few friends and colleagues) that many people (educationalists and the general public alike) would want to prohibit the use of some (hypothetical) genetically-tailored-to-the-individual synthetic cognitive booster pill taken just before an exam,

9   The case of neural implants that would enable mainline Google access is tricky to categorize, since such devices, although not of course the servers that they would access, would be located inside the cognizer's skin. To push on, let's just stipulate that neural implants count as external on the grounds that they are technological enhancements to organic intelligence.

but would want to allow the use of a performance-enhancing generic natural health supplement taken over many months, even if those two strategies had exactly the same outcome for the learner concerned (same grade, no ill effects on health, etc.). One thought that might be at work here (a thought that also seems to figure in questions of doping in sports) is that taking the long-term natural health supplement is, as its name suggests, a natural way of improving intellectual performance, whereas taking the immediate-effect tailored synthetic pill is an artificial prop. But whatever purchase this kind of thinking might have in the supplement-or-pill case, it seems questionable when we turn to the use of external technology such as search engines and smartphones, or at least it does if we view things from the standpoint of ExC. In actual fact, it already looks dubious from the less radical standpoint of embodied-embedded cognition, let alone ExC. That's because, according to both positions, human beings are (to recall once again Clark's phrase) natural born cyborgs. We have evolved to be (ExC), or to engage in (embodied-embedded view), shifting human-artefact coalitions operating over various time-scales. But if we really are natural born cyborgs, then the utilization of technology to enhance cognitive performance is as natural a feature of human existence as digestion or having children. So, on the suggested criterion, such utilization would fall on the permissible side of the divide.

It is possible, however, that the supplement-or-pill example introduces a different sort of consideration, namely whether or not the technology in question is generic (available in the same form to all, like the natural health supplement) or individualized (tailored to the individual, like the synthetic pill). Using this distinction as a way of cutting the cake, one might argue that generic technology (e.g., unrestricted Internet access via a shared search engine) is permissible in an exam setting, but individualized technology (e.g., the learner's own smartphone, loaded with personally organized information) is not. Once again, however, the truth of ExC would cast doubt on the proposed reasoning. One factor that will plausibly play a role in determining whether or not a particular external element is judged to be a proper part of an extended cognitive architecture is the functional and informational integration of that element with the other elements concerned, including of course those located in the brain. This integration will depend partly on the extent to which some external element is configured so as to interlock seamlessly with the desires, preferences and other personality traits that are realized within the rest of the cognitive system, a system which, of course, according to the ExC theorist, may itself be extended.

For example, compare a mobile application that recommends music to you purely on the basis of genre allocations with one whose recommendations are shaped by an evolving model not only of the kinds of purchases that you, as an individual, have made, but also of various psychological, emotional, political, and aesthetic patterns that your music-buying and other ongoing behavior instantiates. It seems that, if a suite of additional conditions were in place (e.g., real-time access of the applications when needed, a reliable pattern of largely uncritical dependence on the recommendations made), then the individualization demonstrated by the second program raises the chances that it deserves to be counted as part of your cognitive system (as partly realizing some of your beliefs and desires). But if that is right, then, from the standpoint of ExC, it is hard to see how the individual tailoring of an item of technology can be a sufficient reason to prohibit the use of that item in an examination. Such tailoring will, if other conditions are met, be part of an evidential package which (to employ what is, perhaps, an overly crude formulation) indicates that the technology in question counts as part of the learner's mind, and surely we want to allow that into the examination hall. From the standpoint of ExC, then, there seems to be no good reason based purely on individualization to ban sophisticated personal technology such as smartphones from any examination hall.

In response to this, someone might point out that our current examination rules, which sometimes allow certain items of technology (e.g., generic calculators) to be used in examination halls, are the result of context-dependent decisions regarding what it is that we are testing for. Thus, using a calculator might qualify as cheating in one sort of mathematics examination (in which we are testing for basic mathematical abilities), but be perfectly acceptable in another (in which we are testing for a more advanced application of mathematical reasoning). Although this might well be true, it seems, at first sight, that the ExC-driven reasoning that makes it acceptable to utilize those items of technology that achieve cognitive status, because they are dynamically integrated into the right sorts of causal loops, will enjoy a priority over any decisions based on the content of particular exams. After all, to replay the point made just a few sentences ago, from the standpoint of ExC, the technology in question has been incorporated into the learner's cognitive architecture (crudely, it is part of her mind), and that is the very "thing," it seems, that we are endeavoring to examine.

Once again, however, things are not quite so simple. This becomes clear once we recognize that the supporter of ExC will be driven to ask a slightly different question than "What are we testing for?" She will want to ask, "What are we testing?" To see why this is, recall the parity driven argument for ExC and the accompanying commitment to multiple realizability. These indicate that, for ExC as I have characterized it, the same type-identified psychological state or process, as specified functionally, will often be realizable in either a purely organic medium or in one that involves an integrated combination of organic and non-organic structures. So, nothing in ExC rules out the idea that cognition may sometimes be a wholly internal affair, which means that nothing in

ExC rules out the further idea that even though a person's cognitive system is sometimes extended, we might sometimes want to test the performance of her cognitive capacities under non-extended conditions. In other words, sometimes, we might still want to test the naked brain rather than the organic-technological hybrid. Where this is the case, we will want to ban the use of technology from the examination hall.

That said, one needs to be clear about what the motivation might be for testing the unadorned inner. After all, the experimental results described at the beginning of this paper indicate that when learners expect information to be readily and reliably available from an external resource (such as the Internet), they are more likely to remember where to find that information than the details of the information itself. This cognitive profile seems entirely appropriate for a world in which the skill of being able to find, in real time, the right networked information (not just facts, but information about how to solve problems) is arguably more important than being able to retain such information in one's organic memory. In such a world, which is our world, the brain emerges as a locus of adaptive plasticity, a control system for embodied skills and capacities that enable the real-time recruitment and divestment of technology in problem-solving scenarios. As such, and from the standpoint of ExC, the brain is most illuminatingly conceptualized as one element—albeit the core persisting element—in sequences of dynamically constructed and temporarily instantiated extended cognitive systems. Perhaps what we ought to focus on, then, is the education of those hybrid assemblages, a focus that is entirely consistent with the goal of endowing the brain with the skills it needs to be an effective contributor to such assemblages. From this perspective, of course, there are extremely good reasons to support the increased presence of technology in the examination hall. Moreover, it should be clear that, if ExC is right, then the list of technological entanglements within educational contexts with which we began this section reflects not the gradual demise of human intelligence in the age of clever computational kits, but rather our ongoing evolution as the organic-technological hybrids that we are, and that we have always been.

Dwellers on the Threshold

"I go up," said the elevator, "or down."
"Good," said Zaphod, "We're going up."
"Or down," the elevator reminded him.
"Yeah, OK, up please." There was a moment of silence.
"Down's very nice," suggested the elevator hopefully.
"Oh yeah?"
"Super."
"Good," said Zaphod, "Now will you take us up?"

"May I ask you," inquired the elevator in its sweetest, most reasonable voice, "if you've considered all the possibilities that down might offer you?"

The preceding dialog is a conversation between Zaphod Beeblebrox and an elevator designed by the Sirius Cybernetics Corporation, from The Restaurant at the End of the Universe by Douglas Adams.[10]

Increasingly, architects will be designing buildings that, via embedded computational systems, are able to autonomously modify the spatial and cognitive environments of the people dwelling within them, in the light of what those buildings "believe" about the needs, goals, and desires of the people concerned. In other words, we are about to enter an era of intelligent architecture. Given our present concerns, the advent of such buildings invites the following question, for which I shall try to provide a preliminary answer: what is the relationship between ExC and the way in which we understand and conceptualize our cognitive relationships with intelligent buildings?

To focus our attention, let's get clearer about the intelligent architecture concept, and illustrate it with some examples. After a careful survey and analysis, Sherbini and Krawczyk (Sherbini and Krawczyk 2004, 150) define an intelligent building as one "that has the ability to respond (output) on time according to processed information that is measured and received from exterior and interior environments by multi-input information detectors and sources to achieve users' needs and with the ability to learn." Notice that Sherbini and Krawczyk's definition includes the requirement that the building should be able to learn, i.e., adjust its responses over time so as to provide the right environments for its users as and when those users need them. The idea that some sort of capacity to learn is a necessary condition for a building to be intelligent is one way of separating out the intelligent building concept from closely related notions, such as those of responsive architecture and kinetic architecture. The term "responsive architecture" applies to buildings that have the ability to respond to the needs of users. The term "kinetic architecture" applies to "buildings, or building components, with variable location or mobility, and/or variable geometry or movement" (Fox and Yeh 2011, 2). The variability involved in kinetic architecture may involve nothing more than opening a door or window, but it may involve moving a major structure which, in the limit, may be the whole building. The key thought behind the "separating out" move here is that not all responsive buildings, and not all kinetic buildings qualify as intelligent, since in some cases the responsiveness and/or the kinetic properties of those buildings will be the result of "unintelligent" processes such as direct, unmodifiable links between sensors and motors (cf. the idea that genuine intelligence in animals and humans requires more than

10   I have stolen the use of this quotation from Haque 2006.

hard-wired stimulus-response connections). Learning is one way to secure the right kind of "inner" mediation.

Against this conceptual backdrop, consider four examples of actual, planned, and exploratory buildings that are arrayed along a spectrum from mere responsive/kinetic architecture to intelligent architecture.

- Built in 1994, the Heliotrope, designed by Rolf Disch, is a kinetic building in Freiburg that, using solar trackers, rotates so as to follow the sun, thereby maximizing its access to solar energy and helping to minimize its heating energy demands from other sources. The Heliotrope was the first building in the world to generate more energy than it uses.[11]
- The Cybertecture Egg is a projected building, designed by James Law Cybertecture, to be located in Mumbai.[12] The building combines various intelligent, interactive, and multimedia systems to create an adapted and adaptable environment. Here are two examples: The bathrooms contain a system that monitors and records certain data indicative of the inhabitants' health (e.g., blood pressure, weight), data which may later be recovered and forwarded to a doctor; the inhabitants' working spaces may be customized to optimize individual experience (e.g., the actual view can be replaced by real-time virtual scenery retrieved from all over the world).
- Taking on the challenge of creating buildings in which the elderly can continue to live at home, the Ambient Assisted Living Research Department at the Fraunhofer Institute for Experimental Software Engineering in Kaiserslautern designed an intelligent embedded system that monitors the behavior of a building's inhabitants, via a network of hidden sensors (Kleinberger et al. 2009, 199–208). This network identifies and assesses risk situations (e.g., someone having a fall), and reports to a control center, allowing, say, the automatic notification of a designated contact. In addition, various intelligent systems autonomously modify the environment to reduce risk. Thus, the bathroom has a toilet that recognizes the user and adjusts itself to be at the appropriate height, and a mirror with illuminated pictograms that are designed to structure the activities of easily confused occupants by, for instance, guiding them to brush their teeth, wash, or take medication.
- In the exploratory architectural project Evolving Sonic Environment, developed by Haque and Davis (Haque 2006), people walk around inside an acoustically-coupled "spatialized" neural network (a spatial web of interconnected simple processing units). The movements of the occupants (detected via sound) affect the organization of the network (the architectural environment) through the operation of local learning algorithms

---

11   Rolf Disch, "Rotatable Solar House HELIOTROP: The experience of living rotating completely around the sun," architecture project, Freiburg, 1994. Published online: http://www.rolfdisch.de/files/pdf/RotatableSolarHouse.pdf.

12   See the projects section on the Cybertecture website: http://www.jameslawcybertecture.com

active at each of its nodes. This results in the network adapting over time to different patterns of occupancy, often developing perceptual categories for reflecting those patterns that do not necessarily correspond to categories that the human observer would employ.

Now that we have intelligent architecture in view, we can investigate the relations between such architecture and ExC. Here is one way of asking the key question: Can the embedded systems in the walls and basements of intelligent buildings ever become constituent elements in the functionally specified material vehicles that realize the thoughts of those buildings' inhabitants? Put another way, could the sequence of dynamically assembled, organic-technological hybrid systems that instantiates my mind ever include factors embedded in the intelligent buildings in which I will increasingly dwell? To provide an answer here, I shall explore two lines of thought.

One factor that sometimes figures in discussions of ExC is the portability of cognitive resources. Indeed, it is sometimes suggested that a material element may count as the vehicle, or as part of the vehicle, of a thinker's cognitive state or process, only if that thinker carries, or at least is able to carry, the element in question around with her. In the language of section 2 (above), the portable-non-portable distinction marks a functional difference that matters when one is deciding whether or not a particular functional contribution to intelligent behavior counts as cognitive. Neural resources manifestly meet the proposed portability constraint. So too do PDAs and smartphones. Intelligent architecture, however, does not. So, if portability is a keystone requirement for a resource to be awarded cognitive status, then intelligent buildings are "no more than" adaptive scaffolds for richly coupled embodied-embedded minds, not vehicles for extended minds. But is portability what matters here? I don't think so. What really matters is a property in relation to which portability makes a positive enabling contribution, but which may be secured without portability. That property is somewhat difficult to specify precisely, but, roughly speaking, it amounts to a kind of dynamic reliability in which access to the externally located resource under consideration is, for the most part, smooth and stable just when, and for as long as, that resource is relevant to some aspect of our ongoing activity. The qualifier "dynamic" here reflects the fact that, according to ExC, the organism-centered hybrid systems that are assembled through the recruitment and divestment of technology often persist only when, and as long as, they are contextually relevant, meaning that the external resources concerned need not be smoothly and stably accessible at other times.

We can now state a modified condition for cognitive status: a material element may count as the vehicle, or as part of the vehicle, of a cognitive state or process, only if it meets the foregoing dynamic reliability constraint. And although carrying an item of technology around with you is certainly one assisting factor here, it is certainly not mandatory. Technological resources embedded in the fabric of one's house may well be readily and reliably available whenever the human behaviour that they support is operative. Consider, for example, the activity-structuring pictograms embedded in the mirrors of the ambient assisted living environment described earlier. When functioning in a hitch-free manner, access to these externally located resources will be smooth and stable just when, and for as long as, those resources are relevant to the activity they are designed to support. To be clear, meeting the dynamic reliability constraint in this way is clearly not a sufficient condition for a technological resource to count as part of one's cognitive architecture. But, if it is a necessary condition, then intelligent architecture may certainly, in principle, meet it.

Time, then, to turn to the second ExC-and-intelligent-architecture related issue that I want to broach here. Part of the interest of the final example of intelligent architecture described above, namely Evolving Sonic Environment by Haque and Davis, is that it foregrounds the already highlighted incorporation of learning into intelligent architecture. But the Haque and Davis study does more than that. It also introduces a new consideration, that of interaction. Haque argues that an important transformation in our relations with architecture occurs when we shift from a merely reactive kind of architecture to a genuinely interactive kind (Haque 2006).

Here Haque draws a distinction between single-loop interaction—in which the architectural response to a particular user-input is determined in advance— and multiple-loop interaction, in which the next response, by the architecture or user, is in part determined by an ongoing history of interaction and on the fact that each is able to access and modify each other's goals. As Haque puts it:

> [S]ingle-loop devices that satisfy our creature comforts are useful for functional goals (I am thinking here of Bill Gate's technologically-saturated mansion; or building management systems that seek to optimise sunlight distribution; or thermostats that regulate internal temperature). Such systems satisfy very particular efficiency criteria that are determined during, and limited by, the design process. However, if one wants occupants of a building to have the sensation of agency and of contributing to the organization of a building, then the most stimulating and potentially productive situation would be a [multi-loop] system in which people build up their spaces through "conversations" with the environment, where the history of interactions builds new possibilities for sharing goals and sharing outcomes. (Haque 2006, 3)

To put flesh (or perhaps concrete) on this goal of human-architecture conversation, Haque introduces his notion of Paskian Systems (named after the great maverick British cyberneticist, Gordon Pask). Paskian systems eschew the usual logic of the interaction between humans and smart technology. According to that usual logic, either the human user needs an appropriate understanding of the design of the machine, so that she can tell it what to do, or the machine needs an appropriate understanding of the design of the human user so that it can provide her with precisely what she needs. A Paskian system, by contrast, would support a kind of open dialog. Thus, for example, in a spatial dwelling context such a system "would provide us with a method for comparing our conception of spatial conditions with the designed machine's conception of the space" (Haque 2006, 3).

There is a compelling consideration which suggests that although the kind of non-Paskian architectural technology that we encountered earlier (recall, again, the mirror-embedded pictograms) may qualify as proper parts of the dweller's cognitive economy on roughly the same grounds as mobile computing technology (e.g., among other things, both meet the dynamic reliability constraint), Haque's Paskian systems—and thus the realizations of such systems in intelligent architecture—will fail to qualify. In fact, the threat to ExC here is established by the very conditions that make possible the capacity of Paskian systems to enter into richly interactive dialogs, the feature of those systems that secures Haque's advocacy of them in architectural design. Paskian systems may operate with categorizations, conceptions, and models of goal-states to be achieved—beliefs about how the dweller's world is and should be, if you will—that diverge from those of their human users. Thus, as mentioned earlier, the Evolving Sonic Environment develops perceptual categories for occupancy patterns that do not necessarily correspond to human-determined categories. It is this divergence that grounds the dialogical structure that characterizes the kind of rich human-building interaction sought by Haque. Now, this may well be exactly what we want from intelligent architecture, but the divergence calls into question any claim that the human-technology interactive system so instantiated is itself a single, integrated cognitive system. We would experience the same hesitation to think in terms of extended cognition if we were confronted by a Paskian smartphone that negotiated over where to go every time its online navigation program was fired up. And the same qualms indicate why the elevator designed by the Sirius Cybernetics Corporation (see above) cannot plausibly be considered part of Zaphod's mind.

The root issue here is that Paskian systems exhibit a kind of agency. This agency, however limited, prevents them from being incorporated into the cognitive systems that are centered on their human users. As one might put it, where there's more than one will, there's no way to cognitive extension. At first sight, this principle would seem to have negative implications (implications that I do not have the space to unravel or explore here) for the hypothesis of socially extended cognition, interpreted as the claim that some of the material vehicles that realize my thinking may be located inside the brains of other people (i.e., other agents). For the present, however, my thoughts are restricted to the domain of intelligent architecture: if intelligent architecture does support ExC, then it is on the basis not of Paskian interaction, but of the dynamic reliability established by non-Paskian loops.

Conclusion

The extended cognition hypothesis is currently the subject of much debate in philosophical and cognitive-scientific circles, but its implications stretch far beyond the metaphysics and science of minds. We have only just begun, it seems, to scratch the surface of the wider social and cultural ramifications of the view. If our minds are partly in our smartphones and even in our buildings, then that is not a transformation in human nature, but only the latest manifestation of the age-old human ontology of dynamically assembled, organic-technological cognitive systems. Nevertheless, once our self-understanding catches up with our hybrid nature, the world promises to be a very different place.

Acknowledgments: Thanks to Andy Clark for a discussion regarding education and cognitive extension that helped me to fine-tune my thinking on that issue. Thanks also to audiences at the Universities of Stirling and Sussex for useful feedback. This text has been previously published in the Open Access journal Computational Culture, no. 1, November 2011 (see: www. computationalculture.net).

References

Adams, Frederick, and Kenneth Aizawa. 2008. *The Bounds of Cognition*. Malden, MA and Oxford: Blackwell.

Chalmers, David J. 2008. "Foreword to Andy Clark's *Supersizing the Mind*." In Clark 2008b, ix–xvi.

Clark, Andy. 1997. *Being There: Putting Brain, Body, and World Together Again*. Cambridge, MA: MIT Press.

Clark, Andy. 2003. *Natural-Born Cyborgs: Minds, Technologies, and the Future of Human Intelligence*. New York: Oxford University Press.

Clark, Andy. 2008a. "Pressing the Flesh: A Tension in the Study of the Embodied, Embedded Mind?" *Philosophy and Phenomenological Research* 76 (1): 37–59.

Clark, Andy. 2008b. *Supersizing the Mind: Embodiment, Action, and Cognitive Extension*. New York: Oxford University Press.

Clark, Andy, and David J. Chalmers. 1998. "The Extended Mind." *Analysis* 58 (1): 7–19.

Fox, Michael A., and Bryant P. Yeh. 2011. "Intelligent Kinetic Systems." http://citeseerx.ist.psu.edu/viewdoc/download?doi=10.1.1.124.4972&rep=rep1&type=pdf.

Haque, Usman. 2006. "Architecture, Interaction, Systems." Extended version of a paper written for Arquitetura & Urbanismo, AU149, Brazil, 2006. http://www.haque.co.uk/papers/ArchInterSys.pdf/, last accessed 13 October 2011.

Kleinberger, Thomas et al. 2009. "An Approach to and Evaluations of Assisted Living Systems Using Ambient Intelligence for Emergency Monitoring and Prevention." In *Universal Access in Human-Computer Interaction. Intelligent and Ubiquitous Interaction Environments*, edited by Constantine Stephanidis, 199–208. Berlin: Springer.

Levin, Janet. 2010. "Functionalism". In *Stanford Encyclopedia of Philosophy*, Summer 2010 Edition. http://plato.stanford.edu/archives/sum2010/entries/functionalism.

Magill, Sasha. 2011. "Poor Memory? Blame Google." *The Guardian*, 16 July 2011. http://www.guardian.co.uk/science/2011/jul/15/poor-memory-blame-google.

Menary, Richard. 2007. *Cognitive Integration: Mind and Cognition Unbounded*. Basingstoke: Palgrave Macmillan.

Menary, Richard, ed. 2010. *The Extended Mind*. Cambridge, MA: MIT Press.

Sherbini, Khaled, and Robert Krawczyk. 2004. "Overview of Intelligent Architecture." Proceedings of the 1st ASCAAD International Conference, e-Design in Architecture, KFUPM, Dhahran, Saudi Arabia, December 2004. http://mypages.iit.edu/~krawczyk/ksascad04.pdf .

Sparrow, Betsy, Jenny Liu, Daniel M. Wegner. 2011. "Google Effects on Memory: Cognitive Consequences of Having Information at Our Fingertips." *Science* 333 (6043), 776–78. http://www.sciencexpress.org .

Sutton, John. 2010. "Exograms and Interdisciplinarity: History, the Extended Mind, and the Civilizing Process." In: Menary 2010, 189–225.

Wheeler, Michael. 2005. *Reconstructing the Cognitive World: the Next Step*. Cambridge, MA: MIT Press.

Wheeler, Michael. 2010a. "In Defense of Extended Functionalism." In Menary 2010, 245–70.

Wheeler, Michael. 2010b. "Minds, Things, and Materiality." In *The Cognitive Life of Things: Recasting the Boundaries of the Mind*, edited by L. Malafouris and C. Renfrew. 29–37. Cambridge: McDonald Institute Monographs. Reprinted in *Action, Perception and the Brain: Adaptation and Cephalic Expression*, edited by Jay Schulkin, 147–63, Basingstoke: Palgrave Macmillan, 2012.

Wheeler, Michael. 2011a. "Embodied Cognition and the Extended Mind." In *The Continuum Companion to Philosophy of Mind*, edited by J. Garvey. 220–38, London: Continuum.

Wheeler, Michael. 2011b. "In Search of Clarity about Parity." *Philosophical Studies* (symposium on Andy Clark's *Supersizing the Mind*) 152 (3): 417–25.

Wheeler, Michael. 2015. "On Your Marks." Online Draft Manuscript, chapter 4. http://rms.stir.ac.uk/converis-stirling/publication/12884.

DIGITAL CULTURE

ENLIGHTENMENT

NIHILISM

RATIONALISM

NEUROSCIENCE

PROMETHEANISM

6

Late Capitalism and the Scientific Image of Man: Technology, Cognition, and Culture

Jon Lindblom

The essay introduces Wilfrid Sellars' conception of the scientific image of man against the backdrop of the cognitive malaise of the contemporary digital mediascape. It is argued that the emerging scientific understanding of cognition will not only help us to further diagnose the cognitive pathologies at work in late capitalism, but also will allow us to construct alternate techno-cultural scenarios untapping the potentialities of neurotechnology. This line of reasoning engages with Adorno and Horkheimer's critique of Enlightenment reason on the basis of the recent work on nihilism, rationalism, and cognitive science by Ray Brassier and Thomas Metzinger. In particular, it argues that a speculative reconsideration of Enlightenment Prometheanism provides the critical context for unleashing the cognitive and technological potencies that late capitalism is currently inhibiting.

In *Alleys of Your Mind: Augmented Intellligence and Its Traumas,* edited by Matteo Pasquinelli, 107–22. Lüneburg: meson press, 2015.
DOI: 10.14619/014

In his book *iDisorder: Understanding Our Obsession with Technology and Overcoming Its Hold on Us*, psychologist and computer educator Larry Rosen (2012) presents a compelling diagnosis of what he sees as the increasingly widespread cognitive and psychosocial effects of technology on society. According to Rosen, the emergence of cyberspace, computing, social media, portable electronic devices, Web 2.0, and so on, has brought about a general cognitive and psychosocial disorder with symptoms which look suspiciously like those of a number of well known psychiatric disorders and are centered on our increasing occupation with technology and new media. These disorders include (but are not limited to) obsessive-compulsive disorder (constantly checking our Facebook, e-mail, iPhones, etc.), attention-deficit hyperactivity disorder (increased inability to focus on one task because of the prevalence of multitasking, videogaming, etc.), social anxiety disorder (hiding behind various screens at the cost of maintaining face-to-face social relations), and narcissistic personality disorder (being obsessed with creating an idealized online-persona). All of those are accompanied by various neurological reconfigurations, such as alterations in chemical levels of dopamine and serotonin (i.e., changes in the brain's reward system as a result of technology addiction, which seems to mirror the chemical imbalances underlying various forms of substance addiction), and the creation of new synaptic connections among neurons (i.e., neuroplasticity) in response to the environmental changes brought about by technology (which may be the underlying neurobiological explanation for phenomena such as "phantom vibration syndrome," where cell phone users start to experience phantom vibrations on a regular basis—presumably as a result of increased attentiveness for vibrating sensations). Taken together, all of these symptoms point to a general state of collective anxiety brought about by the intricate relationship between the technological, the neurological, and the psychosocial. It is this anxiety that Rosen refers to as "iDisorder."

Undoubtedly, there is still a lot of work that needs to be done here, particularly regarding the relation between the technological and the psychosocial (to what extent is technology the root-source of these symptoms?), as well as the exact nature of the symptoms themselves (do they index actual clinical conditions?). Yet despite these various lacunae it seems clear to me that Rosen's project sheds light on issues that everyone familiar with daily life in digital culture can recognize themselves in, and whose exact nature hopefully will become clear once we learn more about the psychosocial and cognitive effects of technology. But besides these context-specific reservations, it is also important to recognize the larger context in which Rosen's work makes sense, which is twofold: on the one hand, in terms of the function of digital culture within late capitalism and, on the other hand, in terms of the relationship between science and culture implicit in the cognitive and psychosocial effects of technology.

It is these two contexts that I aim to elaborate on in the present essay. In the first section, I will situate Rosen's diagnosis within what Mark Fisher has referred to as a general disenchantment of the digital in late capitalist culture (i.e., a widespread dissatisfaction with current forms of digital culture); which not only indexes a major cultural malaise brought about by the digital, but also what Fisher has identified as a general aporia within late capitalism: the problem of mental health. In the second section, I will then expand on the implications of the use of scientific resources (neuroscience in particular), in order to unpack the cognitive effects of technology and its potentially decisive role within the context of a major cultural shift brought about by the speculative import of what philosopher Wilfrid Sellars has referred to as the "scientific image of man." Finally, I will conclude with some brief remarks about the nature of this shift and its implications for various forms of cultural and post-capitalist praxis.

Digital Pathologies in Late Capitalist Culture

According to Mark Fisher (2009), the fact that the presence of various psychological disorders, such as depression, anxiety, stress, and attention-deficit hyperactivity disorder, has increased significantly over the last decades is not a mere coincidence, but a consequence of the rise of neoliberalism as such. For what has accompanied the shift from disciplinary societies to control societies, from Fordist rigidity to post-Fordist flexibility, is nothing less than a major pandemic of various psychological disorders whose root-source is to be found in the numerous social restructurings imposed by neoliberalism— rather than in individual chemico-biological imbalances. These restructurings include flexibility and precarity in working-life, various forms of PR and new bureaucracy, and the emergence of cyberspace, social media, portable electronic devices, and so on—whose functioning is integral to the neoliberalist restructuring of nervous-systems which inevitably needs to accompany the new social structures, as well as to the obliteration of the distinction between work-time and leisure-time which has come to be one of the defining characteristics of contemporary capitalism. Accordingly, increased instability in working life is accompanied, on the one hand, by new strategies for managing workers-consumers, which, despite claims toward decentralization and diversity, remain deadlocked within various forms of bureaucracies, constant surveillance, and false appearances (see in particular Fisher 2009: 31–53); and, on the other hand, by the emergence of a global cyberspace-matrix whose essential functioning lies in the creation of the "debtor-addict" central to distributed, late capitalist organization. The debtor-addict has lost the ability to concentrate, as well as the capacity to synthesize time into any form of meaningful narrative, and lives instead in a series of twitchy, disconnected presents: "If, then, something like attention deficit hyperactivity disorder is a pathology, it is a pathology of late capitalism—a consequence of being wired into the entertainment-control circuits of hypermediated consumer culture" (Fisher 2009, 25). Of course, the idea that the proliferation of mental illness may be correlated with the triumph of neoliberalism is strictly denied by the latter's advocates. More importantly, it also has not been recognized by the political left as an urgent issue to re-politicize, as Fisher notes in a particularly incisive passage:

> The current ruling ontology denies any possibility of a social causation of mental illness. The chemico-biologization of mental illness is of course strictly commensurate with its depolitiziation. Considering mental illness an individual chemico-biological problem has enormous benefits for capitalism. First, it reinforces Capital's drive towards atomistic individuali-zation (you are sick because of your brain chemistry). Second, it provides an enormously lucrative market in which multinational pharmaceutical companies can peddle their pharmaceuticals (we can cure you with our SSRIs). It goes without saying that all mental illnesses are neurologically *instantiated*, but this says nothing about their *causation*. If it is true, for instance, that depression is constituted by low serotonin levels, what still needs to be explained is why particular individuals have low levels of serotonin. This requires a social and political explanation; and the task of repoliticizing mental illness is an urgent one if the [political] left wants to challenge capitalist realism. (Fisher 2009, 37)

Thus, it is in this larger socio-political context that Rosen's work must thoroughly be situated. His observations regarding the proliferation of psychological disorders, such as attention-deficit hyperactivity disorder, as well as changes in brain structure and chemical balance—presumably as a result of our increased dependence on technology and new media—indeed seems to be a particularly lucid study of the cognitive and psychosocial effects of the rise of the capitalist cyberspace-matrix that Fisher has identified in his writings on neoliberalism. Consequently, even though Rosen is right in locating the root-source to these symptoms outside the brain, it is only when they have been situated in an even larger socio-political (and, as we shall see, cultural) context that we will be able to properly diagnose their intricate structure and causation, as the above quotation emphasizes.

This is only one side of the story, however, since the cognitive agenda imposed by neoliberalism not only threatens to undermine psychological issues related to mental health, but also transformative concerns organized around the relationship between the technological and the neurobiological. In other words, there are at least two trajectories that need to be elaborated here: *clinical* issues related to mental health, and *speculative* issues related to the neurotechnological transformation of cognitive neurobiology. It is the latter set of issues that I will concern myself with in the remainder of this essay, with a particular focus on its cultural implications, since I believe that contemporary culture not only is in desperate need of such speculative resources, but also because it seems that culture would constitute a particularly productive field for the utilization of their transformative potential. Yet before going further into this discussion I need to complement the previous socio-political contextualization with its cultural counterpart, since the digital pathology outlined above is not only rooted in a failed social contract, but also in a cultural malaise of widespread proportions. The full magnitude of current technological disenchantment can therefore only be understood once it has been situated squarely in the socio-political agenda of neoliberalism on the one hand, and in the cultural malaise of aggravated postmodernism on the other.

Once again it is the work of Mark Fisher that is exemplary here. Building upon Jameson's neo-Marxist thesis that changes in culture must be understood in conjunction with changes in the economy, and that postmodernism is the cultural logic of late capitalism (Jameson 1992, 1–54), Fisher sees contemporary culture as steeped in what may be characterized as a sort of normalized postmodernism. The latter designates a widespread cultural inertia where the residual conflict between modernism and postmodernism, which haunted Jameson's work, has been completely forgotten, along with the distinction between high art and popular culture, and where the modernist ethos of orienting oneself toward the unknown has been substituted—again, as Jameson correctly predicted—by a tendency toward revivalism, retrospection, pastiche, and constant recycling of the already familiar. Accordingly, "retro" no longer designates one particular style but the modus operandi of culture *tout court*, and the capitalist colonization of nature and the unconscious—observed with wonder and horror by Jameson in the 1980s—has now been normalized to such an extent that it is simply taken for granted. Consequently, even though cultural distribution, consumption, and communication have gone through remarkable changes over the last decade, cultural production itself has generated very little excitement. Contrasting his own adolescence with that of teenagers today, music writer and cultural critic Simon Reynolds notes that whereas his own youth was steeped in interests such as modernist art, alien life, and outer space (i.e., the unknown), the wonders of boundless exteriority no longer seem to have any purchase on young people today, immersed as they are in Youtube, Facebook, iPhones, and other forms of social media (see Reynolds 2012, 362–98). Sure, new technologies have proliferated dramatically over the last decade, but only to the extent that they maintain the cultural interiority and status quo concomitant with the capitalist cyberspace-matrix. This is a cultural situation that Reynolds characterizes as one of widespread temporal malaise, or "hyperstasis," *qua* digital life as daily experience. The fundamental problem that confronts us is consequently one of rehabilitating the link between technology and the unknown—in contrast with the cyber-capitalist reiteration of the already known—which is intimately connected to a renewed understanding of the implications of science on culture, simply because science, as we shall see, is one of man's primary methods for indexing the unknown. In particular, the field of cognitive neuroscience seems to provide some of the most promising (but hardly the only) resources for this cultural confrontation with the unknown. The latter will consequently be my main topic of discussion in the next section.

The Cultural Implications of Cognitive Exteriorization

At first glance, the idea of the cultural import of resources provided by modern science might seem dubious—what, after all, could scientific data provide cultural production with?—yet it is my firm belief that this issue is one of the most critical ones facing cultural theory today. Of course, questions concerning the intellectual influence of scientific rationality on cultural production have been posed numerous times over the last decades, but over time their many shortcomings have become increasingly obvious. What is needed today is therefore a radical reconsideration of the relationship between science and culture (or, in broader terms, between man and nature). In what follows, I will consequently aim to sketch out some broader outlines for such a reconsideration, focusing in particular on one of the most influential statements on the topic: Adorno and Horkheimer's *Dialectic of Enlightenment*. However, this requires us to engage not just with the book's celebrated chapter on the culture industry, but also with its central arguments regarding the failure of the Enlightenment and the pathology of instrumental rationality.

Indeed, what often goes unmentioned in the many books outlining the influence of Adorno and Horkheimer on contemporary cultural theory is the wider critical context in which the analysis of the culture industry is situated. The decision to not articulate this link has become more than a mere pedagogical shortcoming, since it in fact harbors the key to a contemporary engagement with the book's criticisms of modern culture. Hence, it is at this particular juncture where the present analysis must begin.

As is well known, the main topic of *Dialectic of Enlightenment* is what Adorno and Horkheimer considered to be the failure of the Enlightenment in the modern world. This may be condensed into the following question: If the animus of the Enlightenment is that of emancipating man from his irrationality (or "immaturity," as Kant put it), then why is contemporary society sinking into a new form of barbarism? Fascism, capitalism, cultural standardization, and the oppression of women—all of which are analyzed in-depth in the book—can hardly be thought of as triumphs of enlightened man. The task of the critical theorist then becomes one of identifying the root-source to these widespread failures of modern society.

Yet unlike during the Frankfurt School's earlier Marxist period, Adorno and Horkheimer argue that this root-source cannot be located in various forms of class struggle or political oppression, since those phenomena—just as capitalism itself—are mere symptoms of a much deeper conflict which has haunted Western civilization since its inception: that between man and nature. This conflict is formulated in terms of a struggle between dominating and dominated, since, for Adorno and Horkheimer, civilization is dependent on man's urge to tame and ultimately control the hostile forces harbored by alien nature. This is the objective of sacrifice in pre-rational societies, since sacrifice—construed as a particular logic of non-conceptual exchange—is primitive man's attempt to affect a commensuration between himself and the horrors of alien nature. Enlightenment is, of course, founded upon the discarding of sacrificial logic in favor of rational explanation. Yet what enlightened thought ends up with, according to Adorno and Horkheimer, is not the post-sacrificial logic it is searching for, but merely the internalization of sacrifice *tout court*.

Enlightened thought is consequently characterized as an unreflective pathology, where man's desire to convert the entirety of nature into series of numbers and formulae (i.e., to control nature via scientific explanation) remains deadlocked within the mythical pattern of thought it wants to be rid of, for what scientific logic ultimately represents is nothing but a new form of alienation, which not only extends across the exteriority of nature, but also into the interiority of man himself. Indeed, what the scientific impetus to exteriorize and spatialize ultimately ends up with is nothing but an aggravated form of self-sacrifice, since the reduction of everything to identical units—rather than reaching out toward an exteriority beyond man—merely continues to symbolically sacrifice parts of the human in a pathological, compulsive manner, which in the end renders properly philosophical (or reflective) thinking impossible. For Adorno and Horkheimer, this marks the beginning of a dangerous path where ends are substituted for means and domination sooner or later is reverted back toward man himself; both in terms of domination between men and in terms of the alienation of man from himself where thinking is reduced to a pure mathematical function:

> Thinking objectifies itself to become an automatic, self-activating process; an impersonation of the machine that it produces itself so that ultimately the machine can replace it. . . . Mathematical procedure [becomes], so to speak, the ritual of thinking. In spite of the axiomatic self-restriction, it establishes itself as necessary and objective: it turns thought into a thing, an instrument—which is its own term for it. (Adorno and Horkheimer 1997, 25)

Consequently, it is in this wider critical context where the analysis of the culture industry must be situated, since what the latter is an index of—according to Adorno and Horkheimer—is one of the modes of domination that have emerged along with the triumph of scientific rationality. Accordingly, the term "culture industry" was deliberately chosen—as opposed to "mass culture" or "popular culture"—precisely in order to emphasize the link between Enlightenment rationality and modern culture by highlighting, on the one hand, how the latter operates in terms of increased technological subsumption by mechanical reproduction and, on the other hand, how the distribution of cultural products is being monitored by rational, controlled organization. These are the primary symptoms of how Enlightenment rationality has infected cultural production and reduced the latter to a series of banalities of artificial desires that, of course, are strictly in tune with capitalist organization in the form of a new mode of social domination.

Yet the link between scientific rationality and social domination that Adorno and Horkheimer's thesis rests upon is far from guaranteed. Indeed, in my view it is rooted in a fundamental misdiagnosis of the intellectual import of Enlightenment rationality, which remains committed to the safeguarding of a fictional "humanism" at the cost of eliding its wider speculative implications. These implications have recently been articulated with remarkable cogency by the philosopher Ray Brassier, who in his book *Nihil Unbound: Enlightenment and Extinction* (2007) presents a striking alternative interpretation of the intellectual legacy of the Enlightenment—an interpretation which, as we shall see, will provide us with conceptual resources for the construction of a very different account of culture than that of Adorno and Horkheimer.

The speculative argument of *Nihil Unbound* may be understood as a *thanatropic inversion* of Adorno and Horkheimer's dialectics of myth and Enlightenment, since it insists on, rather than rejects, the impersonal nihilism implicit in scientific objectification and technological exteriorization. Whereas Adorno and Horkheimer argue that what they conceive of as the terminal exhaustion of reason can only be overcome by its re-integration into the purposefulness of human history—construed as a temporal transcendence of science's pathological compulsion—with the idea of "the thanatosis of Enlightenment" Brassier (2007, 32) insists on the incompatibility between the image of nature given to us by science and our manifest understanding of things. For Brassier, the fact that the thought of science goes beyond our default apprehension of nature must be understood as the starting point for the philosophical enterprise, rather than as a cognitive pathology which philosophy should be summoned to remedy. The bulk of *Nihil Unbound* is therefore concerned with articulating scientific rationalism as a cognitive overturning of man's lifeworld wherein thinking is confronted with an alien outside, which is unconditioned by human manifestation. And rather than trying to re-inscribe this universal purposelessness within a human narrative of reconciliation, the animus of the book is one of progressively tearing down the lifeworld that we have created in order to satisfy our psychological needs (and which philosophy also has participated in, as can be seen in Adorno and Horkheimer's dialectical think-ing) by recognizing that human experience, consciousness, meaning, and his-tory are nothing but minor spatio-temporal occurrences within an exorbitant cosmology, which is being progressively unveiled by the natural sciences.

Scientific rationalism, therefore, is a trauma for thought (as Adorno and Horkheimer argued), although its root-source is not to be found within the confines of human history (i.e., as a purely psychosocial struggle between dominating and dominated), but in its negation of the categorical difference between established conceptual categories such as life and death in post-Darwinian biology, and matter and void in contemporary cosmology. Scientific discovery therefore has an immediate philosophical import insofar as its elimination of the notion of "purpose" from the natural realm stands at odds with a prevalent philosophical position: The idea that the human *qua* transcen-dental dimension of existence constitutes the irreducible bedrock of cognitive and conceptual enquiry. This is nihil unbound: nihilism emancipated from the regional horizon of the human lifeworld and repositioned within a proper universal context.

Hence, despite the cosmological implications of Brassier's speculative nihilism, it is crucial not to overlook its equally significant cognitive import, particularly since consciousness has generally been considered immune to scientific objec-tification within the continental mode of philosophizing, which has had major conceptual impact on contemporary cultural theory. As we saw in the previous discussion of Adorno and Horkheimer's work, the scientific imperative to objectify consciousness has often been viewed as an index of a dangerous form of anti-humanism, which threatens to alienate us from our true selves in its compulsive attempts to objectify that which lies beyond objectification. Yet, what the scientific understanding of the human ultimately points to is pre-cisely that: the systematic exteriorization of consciousness and an extension of the cognitive split produced by the natural sciences from the exteriority of nature into the interiority of man. Hence, the upshot of this major intel-lectual project is the insertion of man himself into the purposeless natural order unveiled by the scientific worldview, through the gradual construction of an image of the human which views the latter as a particularly complex form of biophysical system rather than as a kind of transcendental excess. In that regard, it is one of the most significant issues opened up by the concep-tual integration of scientific explanation, which is something the philosopher Wilfrid Sellars addressed several decades ago in the form of a distinction between what he called the *manifest* and *scientific* images of man.

According to Sellars (1963), the manifest image is a sophisticated conceptual framework, which has accumulated gradually since the emergence of Homo sapiens and is organized around the notion of man as *person*; that is, as a rational agent capable of giving and asking for reasons within the context of a larger socio-linguistic economy. In that regard, the fundamental import of the manifest image is its *normative* valence in that it provides man with a basic framework for keeping track of commitments, providing and revising explanations, assessing what ought to be done, and vice versa. In short, the space of reasons provided by the manifest image is what distinguishes sapient intelligence from that of mere sentience. However, Sellars also noticed the much more recent emergence of another image associated with the natural sciences that presents itself as a rival image in that it is organized around the notion of man as a *physical system*. In other words, whereas the manifest image construes man quasi-transcendentally, as the singular bearer of the object reason, the scientific image instead views man from the perspective of natural history, as a particularly complex accumulation of various forms of biological material.

For Sellars, the fundamental task for the contemporary philosopher is one of achieving a stereoscopic integration of the manifest and scientific images; that is, of producing a synoptic framework capable of giving an account of man as a rational agent on the one hand, and as a physical system on the other. Yet this task should not be understood as an attempt to accommodate the scientific image according to man's psychological needs. Explanatory integration should not be confused with conceptual commensuration. For as was just emphasized in the discussion of Brassier's work, and as Sellars himself saw, there is something fundamentally counterintuitive about the scientific image in that it presents an image of man that is completely alien to common sense reasoning. It is consequently at this particular juncture—at the traumatic clash between the manifest and scientific images—where dialectical enlightenment must be reversed into thanatropic enlightenment and thinking rehabilitated with the edge of speculative reason.[1]

Recently, the trauma generated in the manifest order through its encounter with scientific reasoning has been given a particularly incisive formulation by the neurophilosopher Thomas Metzinger, whose magnum opus *Being No-One: The Self-Model Theory of Subjectivity* (2006) is a comprehensive study of the notion of phenomenal selfhood and the first-person perspective which

---

1   Undoubtedly, much more needs to be said about the quest for explanatory integration of the manifest and scientific image, and its consequences for a genuinely modern form of nihilism. In particular, it is important to recognize that the commitment to the manifest order *qua* normative reasoning does not index a regression from nihilistic disenchantment to yet another version of conservative humanism—as Brassier sometimes has been accused of—since what is crucial about the manifest image is its normative infrastructure, rather than its purely contingent instantiation in the medium sapiens. In other words, there is nothing intrinsically human about the manifest image insofar as it is medium-independent and in principle could be instantiated in other systems than biological ones (see Brassier and Malik 2015). This is the fundamental speculative import of the Sellarsian model and of the *functionalist* school of thought to which it belongs. Thanks to Ray Brassier and Pete Wolfendale for clarifying these points.

is firmly grounded in the emerging intellectual resources provided by modern neuroscience. According to Metzinger, the most fundamental feature of phenomenal selfhood *qua* conscious first-person experience is a peculiar form of epistemic darkness, which emerges in-between the phenomenological and neurobiological levels of description. This darkness is centered on the fact that the phenomenal self is unable to experience the underlying neurobiological processes that are constitutive of the first-person perspective as such, and consequently does not recognize the latter as an ongoing *representational process* within the functional architecture of the biological information-processing system that is the body.

In other words, for Metzinger, the notion of an authentic self, which is in immediate contact with itself and the world around it, is a myth rooted in complex representational processes in the brain, whose central function is to maintain the phenomenal transparency that is necessary for a stable first-person perspective. In technical terms this means that it is only the content properties (qua phenomenological data) that is accessible to the system, but not the vehicle properties (qua underlying neurodynamics), which is how the system comes to experience itself as a self (rather than as the biological data-system it actually is) by failing to recognize that phenomenal selfhood is a particular form of representational modeling. This is what Metzinger refers to as the phenomenal self-model (PSM), which has been generated throughout the courses of evolution in order to maximize cognitive and behavioral flexibility strictly for the purposes of survival.[2] But evolutionary efficacy is not the same as epistemic clarity, and one of the major virtues of the PSM theory is that it circumvents a common problem with many philosophies of mind, experience, and embodiment, which is the tendency to reify non-pathological waking states while disregarding phenomenal state classes which fall outside the framework constituted by default first-person experience.

Accordingly, one of the most interesting aspects of Metzinger's work is that it is built around so-called *deviant* phenomenal models: experiential states wherein the transparency of the default first-person experience loses some of its consistency and parts of the PSM become *opaque* to various degrees. In that regard, deviant phenomenal models such as psychedelic experiences, hallucinations, lucid dreams, and various neurological deficiencies such as agnosia (the inability to recognize faces, sometimes including one's own),

---

2   Another more non-technical way to conceive of the PSM is to think of it as a highly advanced virtual reality model, for just as in VR the major objective of the PSM is to make the user unaware of the fact that he is operating in a medium. Yet with the PSM we need to go one step further with this metaphor, since unlike in VR there is no user that precedes the interaction with the system because it is only the system that exists to begin with (see Metzinger 2004, 553–58). In other words, it is the system's ability to generate a world-model on the one hand, and a self-model on the other that produces the notion of a strong sense of self in immediate contact with the world.

phantom limbs, and blindsight (the experience of a blind-spot in the phenomenal world-model), are all examples of such experiential states. They are
characterized by a *lack* of transparency and thereby explicate the representational nature of phenomenal self-consciousness by making the fact that the
latter is a representational process globally available to the system. It is in this
sense that deviant phenomenal states foreground the compelling speculative
implications of modern neuroscience for philosophy, cultural production, and
critical theory, since they point to the fact that our default phenomenal inter-
facing with cognitive interiority and non-cognitive exteriority is only one out
of many possible experiential states—as opposed to the bedrock of humanity
it is sometimes mistaken for. And once the neural correlates of consciousness
(NCC) that underlie these various modes of experience have been identified by
modern neuroscience, they could in principle be activated at will with the help
of various neurotechnologies and cognitive enhancers.

According to Metzinger, the proliferation of devices for exteriorizing and con-
trolling the brain, as well as the emergence of a modern science of cognition,
will form the bedrock of what he refers to as Enlightenment 2.0 (i.e., the internalization of Enlightenment disenchantment—whereby scientific rationality
comes to investigate its own cognitive basis—along with the gradual integration of neurotechnologies into everyday-life, see Metzinger 2009, 189–219).

There is no denying that Enlightenment 2.0 has somewhat of a horrific ring
to it.[3] Yet it is my firm belief that theorists and cultural producers should
embrace its disenchanting vectors, rather than follow the trajectory maintained by the Frankfurt School and reject them for moralistic reasons, since
their speculative resources promise nothing less than a major reconsideration
of what it means to be human. Included in this remarkable intellectual shift
will be the cultural import of the scientific image, which not only would allow
us to further diagnose the cultural deadlock of the present but also provide us
with much needed resources to construct alternate cultural futures.

In fact, processes indexed by the scientific image are already at work in culture
and have played central roles within important cultural movements such as
nineties rave culture, which Simon Reynolds has described as a remarkable
cultural *and* neurological event, thanks to the positive feedback-loops constituted by technology and abstract digital sounds on the one hand and the
neurobiological effects of various psychedelic drugs (ecstasy in particular) on
the other. Indeed, what was exciting about rave culture was the fact that the
neurochemical modifications brought about by the excessive use of drugs did

3   This side of Enlightenment 2.0 has already been dramatized in various science-fiction
    novels which depict the implications of the proliferation of neurotechnologies on a
    mass-scale—see for instance Bakker 2009 and Sullivan 2010—yet in contrast to these
    mainly dystopic scenarios it is the aim of this essay to elaborate on its (equally impor-
    tant) potential positive implications.

not just play a peripheral role, but constituted one of its major driving forces. In that regard, it formed one pole of what Reynolds has named rave's "drug/ tech-interface," which refers to the progressive unfolding of culture through neurotechnological experimentation and rave as an enclave of modernism— a cultural component of what Nick Srnicek and Alex Williams recently have characterized as an *alternative modernity*—within an emerging postmodern cultural landscape (see Srnicek and Williams 2013; Fisher and Reynolds 2010).

Accordingly, if Adorno and Horkheimer argued that modernity had failed to fulfill the promises of the Enlightenment, my contention is that the trajectories toward an alternative modernity must be constructed through a renewed engagement with the legacy of the Enlightenment (whether construed as "thanatropic" or 2.0) and its fundamental speculative implications—neurobiological experimentation, complex technological systems, impersonal models of reason, cosmic exploration, and so on—which harbor the key to the rehabilitation of man's progressive unfolding toward the unknown. I will consequently end this essay with a few initial remarks on this major speculative project.

Conclusion: Promethean Futures

In his recent work on the hyperstasis of popular culture, Simon Reynolds links the decline from modernist exploration to postmodern malaise with the disappearance of questions concerning the future from the cultural agenda (Reynolds 2012). Whereas rave culture (and other twentieth century musical subcultures which preceded it) was steeped in the notion of a progressive unfolding across an extensional axis—a sort of future-rush driven by technological and cognitive navigation via the medium of sound—what is lacking in culture today, according to Reynolds, is any meaningful notion of the future at all. Instead, popular culture today is driven by what Reynolds has referred to as *retromania*: An obsession with its own immediate past in the form of remakes, re-issues, pastiche, and nostalgia. And, as Mark Fisher has pointed out (again following Jameson), this widespread cultural deceleration must be understood as a symptom of the current neoliberal order: Capitalism has not only taken over the notion of modernity, but also that of the future—yet is unable to deliver anything beyond marginal changes within what ultimately must be characterized as a terrestrial status quo (Fisher 2009). The result is a political left paralyzed by the deadlocks of the present and unable to even imagine a future beyond the confines of the neoliberal order. Instead, what we have are paltry turns toward organicism, local areas of justice and equality, and laments over the decline of our humanity in the face of cybernetic capitalism. This is now the default position not just among many anti-capitalist groups, but also in the tradition of critical theory, which may be traced back to the Frankfurt School, as well as the agenda of much postmodern critique.

It is consequently at this particular juncture where the current essay must be situated, since I believe that what is needed today is a radical re-invention of critique which once again takes up the Marxist dictum of critical theory as a means for *changing the world*. Indeed, over the last decades it seems that this forward-looking aspect of critique has gradually faded away and been replaced by a desire to go backwards by restoring what we once were. Yet my contention is that the major objective of critique today is to speculate on *what we could become*; that is, to operate from the perspective of the future rather than from that of the past. It is in this context where the speculative integra-tion of the scientific image emerges as a decisive resource for modern critical theory, since it provides thinking with a crucial component for orienting itself toward the future in the form of a major reconsideration of what it means to be human. In that regard, it must be understood as part of what Brassier (2013) has defined as the rehabilitation of Enlightenment Prometheanism as the means for collective self-mastery and active participation in the remak-ing of mankind and the world. Far from being the dangerous totalitarianism it is often accused of being, Prometheanism must rather be understood as the speculative program necessary for the re-orientation of mankind toward the future *qua* the unknown. While the many ambitions of this massive project certainly need to encompass much more than merely the cultural, I will con-clude this essay with a few remarks on the latter since it is at the heart of my own research.

A culture steeped in Promethean ambitions needs to be based on the legacy of thanatropic Enlightenment, rather than its mainstream dialectical version, since it is only the former that will provide man with a proper intellectual con-text for orienting himself toward the future. Against postmodernist relativism and blatant anti-rationalism it must uphold the intellectual significance of the scientific image on the one hand, and the emancipatory vectors of impersonal reason on the other (see note 1 above). At the heart of this position is the rejection of what was earlier referred to as the fictional humanism that consti-tutes the core of Adorno and Horkheimer's dialectical thinking, and which has reappeared numerous times in postmodern critical theory. In particular, con-cepts such as nihilism, disenchantment, and alienation must not be thought of as mere cultural pathologies that need to be overcome, but as speculative instruments which must be re-invented through the emancipation from their confinement within the postmodern critical context. Indeed, a culture operat-ing according to the current version of Enlightenment Prometheanism must take the latter as starting points, rather than dead ends, for its ventures into speculative futures. According to the latter, the current diagnosis of nihilism, alienation, and disenchantment is based on a by now common reification of the manifest image at the cost of its scientific counterpart; yet the cultural integration of the latter under the aegis of a Promethean program will turn these concepts on their heads by forcing them to be cracked open by the vista of scientific rationality. In that regard, it is important to once again emphasize that the cognitive and technological malaise maintained by neoliberalism must not just be understood as a problem of mental health, but also (as can be seen in the work of Jameson and Reynolds) as a problem of the relationship between anthropic interiority and non-anthropic exteriority. Surely, the former is a significant problem which requires its own particular solutions, yet to think of the social and cultural implications of the scientific image as purely an issue of mental health—which indeed seems to be the common response by analytic philosophers when confronted with scepticism and anti-scientific moralism (see for instance Churchland 2007 and Ladyman 2009)—is to disregard its wider Promethean ambitions and potentially decisive role within a major cultural and cognitive shift. The latter would be based upon, amongst other things, extensive cognitive experimentation, which utilizes the speculative opportunities provided by neuroplasticity, advanced technological systems, NBIC (nanotechnology, biotechnology, information technology, and cognitive science), and so on, and would be realized by cultural-scientific resources such as the drug-tech interface, which thereby would need to be repurposed for post-capitalist ends.[4] Indeed, the drug-tech interface has not so much disappeared from culture since the decline of the rave ethos (which, ironically, also took the turn toward revivalism and retrospection), but has rather been appropriated by capital in the form of the cultural and cognitive agenda diagnosed by Rosen and Fisher (i.e., ecstasy and alien sound systems have been substituted by anti-depressants and social media). What therefore is necessary is a major re-appropriation of such resources in the form of cultural programs, which, once again, would up the ante of cognitive and cultural ambitions by re-orienting mankind towards the wonders of boundless exteriority.

References

Adorno, Theodor W., and Max Horkheimer. 1997. *Dialectic of Enlightenment*. London: Verso Books.

Bakker, Scott. 2009. *Neuropath*. London: Orion Publishing Group.

Brassier, Ray. 2007. *Nihil Unbound: Enlightenment and Extinction*. Basingstoke: Palgrave MacMillan.

Brassier, Ray. 2013. "On Prometheanism (And Its Critics)." Speculations conference, New York. Talk. http://www.youtube.com/watch?v=7W3KJGof2SE.

Brassier, Ray, and Suhail Malik. 2015. "Reason is Inconsolable and Non-Conciliatory." In *Realism Materialism Art*, edited by Christoph Cox, Jenny Jaskey, and Suhail Malik, 213–30. Berlin: Sternberg Press.

4   In that regard, the current project must also be thought of as part of the wider political program which recently has been referred to as "accelerationism." For the best assessment to date of the accelerationist impetus and its many links to Enlightenment Prometheanism, see Srnicek and Williams 2013, and Williams 2013.

Churchland, Paul. 2007. "Demons Get Out!" Interview. In *Collapse II: Speculative Realism*, edited by Robin Mackay, 207–34. Falmouth: Urbanomic.

Fisher, Mark. 2009. *Capitalist Realism: Is There No Alternative?* Winchester: Zero Books.

Fisher, Mark, and Simon Reynolds. 2010. "You Remind Me of Gold." Transcript of public dialogue. http://markfisherreblog.tumblr.com/post/32185314385/you-remind-me-of-gold-dialogue-with-simon-reynolds.

Jameson, Fredric. 1992. *Postmodernism, or the Cultural Logic of Late Capitalism*. Durham: Duke University Press.

Ladyman, James. 2009. "Who's Afraid of Scientism?" Interview. In *Collapse V: The Copernican Imperative*, edited by Damian Veal, 137–88. Falmouth: Urbanomic.

Metzinger, Thomas. 2004. *Being No-One: The Self-Model Theory of Subjectivity*. Cambridge, MA: MIT Press.

Metzinger, Thomas. 2009. "Enlightenment 2.0." Interview. In *Collapse V: The Copernican Imperative*, edited by Damian Veal, 189–218. Falmouth: Urbanomic.

Reynolds, Simon 2012. *Retromania: Pop Culture's Addiction to Its Own Past.* London: Faber and Faber.

Rosen, Larry D. 2012. *iDisorder: Understanding Our Obsession with Technology and Overcoming Its Hold on Us.* Basingstoke: Palgrave Macmillan.

Sellars, Wilfrid. 1963. "Philosophy and the Scientific Image of Man." In *Empiricism and the Philosophy of Mind*, 1–40. London: Routledge & Keagan Paul .

Srnicek, Nick, and Alex Williams. 2013. "#Accelerate: Manifesto for an Accelerationist Politics." In *Dark Trajectories: Politics of the Outside*, edited by Joshua Johnson. Miami: Name.

Sullivan, Tricia. 2010. *Lightborn: Seeing is Believing.* London: Orbit Books.

Williams, Alex. 2013. "Escape Velocities." *E-flux* 46. http://www.e-flux.com/journal/escape-velocities.

INSTRUMENTAL RATIONALITY

TURING MACHINE

INCOMPUTABILITY

GREGORY CHAITIN

AUTOMATION

7

Instrumental Reason, Algorithmic Capitalism, and the Incomputable

Luciana Parisi

Algorithmic cognition is central to today's capitalism. From the rationalization of labor and social relations to the financial sector, algorithms are grounding a new mode of thought and control. Within the context of this *all-machine phase* transition of digital capitalism, it is no longer sufficient to side with the critical theory that accuses computation to be reducing human thought to mere mechanical operations. As information theorist Gregory Chaitin has demonstrated, incomputability and randomness are to be conceived as very condition of computation. If technocapitalism is infected by computational randomness and chaos, the traditional critique of instrumental rationality therefore also has to be put into question: the incomputable cannot be simply understood as being opposed to reason.

In *Alleys of Your Mind: Augmented Intelligence and Its Traumas,* edited by Matteo Pasquinelli, 125–37. Lüneburg: meson press, 2015.
DOI: 10.14619/014

In the September 2013 issue of the journal *Nature*, a group of physicists from the University of Miami published the article "Abrupt rise of new machine ecology beyond human response time." In the article, they identified a transition to "a new all-machine phase" (Johnson et al. 2013) of financial markets, which coincided with the introduction of high frequency stock trading after 2006. They argued that the sub-millisecond speed and massive quantity of algorithm-to-algorithm interactions exceeds the capacity of human interactions. Analyzing the millisecond-scale data at the core of financial markets in detail, they discovered a large number of sub-second extreme events caused by those algorithms, whose proliferation they correlated with the financial collapse of 2008.

In this new digital environment of trading, algorithmic agents make decisions faster than humans can comprehend. While it takes a human at least one full second to both recognize and react to potential danger, algorithms or bots can make a decision on the order of milliseconds. These algorithms form "a complex ecology of highly specialized, highly diverse, and strongly interacting agents" (Farmer and Skouras, 2011), operating at the limit of equilibrium, outside of human control and comprehension.

The argument I develop here takes this digital ecology of high-frequency trading algorithms as a point of departure. Thus, my text is not specifically concerned with the analysis of the complex financial ecology itself, but aims more directly to discuss a critique of automated cognition in the age of algorithmic capitalism. For if financial trading is an example of a digital automation that is increasingly autonomous from human understanding, this system has become *a second nature*. Therefore it seems to be urgent today to ask: What is the relation between critical thought vis-à-vis those digital ecologies?

My question is: Can the critique of instrumental rationality—as addressed by Critical Theory—still be based on the distinction between critical thinking and automation? Can one truly argue that algorithmic automation is always already a static reduction of critical thinking? By answering these questions, we cannot overlook an apparent dilemma: Both, philosophical thought and digitality, rely on principles of indetermination and uncertainty while featuring these principles in their core complexity theories. As such, both challenge and define the neoliberal order at the same time—a paradox.

To question this paradox, I will turn to the notion of incomputability as theorized by computer scientist Gregory Chaitin, who contributed to the field of algorithmic information theory in his discovery of the incomputable number Omega. This number has a specific quality: it is definable but not computable. In other words, Omega defines at once a discrete and an infinite state of computation occupying the space between zero and one. From a philosophical perspective, the discovery of Omega points to a process of determination of indeterminacy involving not an a priori structure of reasoning but more importantly a dynamic processing of infinities in which results are not contained in the logical premises of the system.

This centrality of the incomputable in information theory, I suggest, brings not only the philosophical critique of technical rationalization into question, but also the instrumentalization of reason. Thus, in the following text I argue that it is no longer sufficient to side with the critical view of technoscience on the basis that computation reduces human thought to mere mechanical operations. Instead, the paradox between realist philosophy and the realism of technocapital can be read as a symptom of an irreversible transformation in the history of critical thought in which the incomputable function of reason has entered the automated infrastructure of cognition.

The Algorithms of Cognitive and Affective Capital

Capital has been said to have entered all aspects of personal and social life. Before explaining the question of the incomputable in algorithmic automation, it is important to point out that with the so-called technocapitalist phase of real subsumption, digital automation has come to correspond to cognitive and affective capital. With this, the logic of digital automation has entered the spheres of affects and feelings, linguistic competences, modes of cooperation, forms of knowledge, as well as manifestations of desire. Even more, human thought itself is said to have become a function of capital. Our contemporary understanding of this new condition in terms of "social capital," "cultural capital," and "human capital" explains that knowledge, human intelligence, beliefs, and desires have only instrumental value and are indeed a source of surplus value. In this automated regime of affection and cognition, capacities are measured and quantified through a general field defined by either money or information. By gathering data and quantifying behaviors, attitudes, and beliefs, the neoliberal world of financial derivatives and big data also provides a calculus for judging human actions, and a mechanism for inciting and directing those actions.

Paradoxically, in the time when "immaterial labor" is privileged over material production (Hardt and Negri 2000), and when marketing is increasingly concerned with affective commodities such as moods, lifestyles, and "atmospheres" (Biehl-Missal 2012), capitalist realism seems to be fully expressed (Fisher 2009), guided by the findings of cognitive psychology and philosophy of mind. Central to these findings is the plasticity of the neural structure as well as the extension of cognitive functions—from perception to the capacity to choose and to judge—through algorithm-based machines. It is not difficult to see that nowadays the social brain is nothing else than a machine ecology of algorithmic agents.

A different aspect is discussed by Stiegler's view of technocapital. He sees thinking and feeling as the new motors of profit, which are repressed or captured by capital and transformed into mere cognitive and sensory functions (2014). In other words, technocapital is what denies desire and knowledge, reason and sensation. Instead, it reduces these potentialities to mere probabilities determined by the binary language of yes and no, zero and one. Exploring this further, Lazzarato (2012) has argued that a critique of technocapital can focus neither on the capitalization of cognition nor its automation. In *The Making of the Indebted Man*, Lazzarato (2012) maintains that knowledge exercises no hegemony over the cycle of value, because knowledge (and thus thought) is primarily subject to the command of financial capital. Here, the neoliberal form of capital in its current phase of real subsumption corresponds to the production of a new condition: the general indebtedness. This form of neoliberalism governance has entered all classes, even those that do not own anything. Hence, the most universal power relationship today is that of debtor and creditor. Debt is a technology of government sustained by the automated apparatus of measuring and evaluation (credit reports, assessments, databases, etc.). Lazzarato understands this axiomatic regime in terms of a semiotic logic, whose core scientific paradigm and technological applications are always already functioning to capture (by quantifying in values) primary aesthetic potentials.

From this perspective, automation is the semiotic logic par excellence, which does not simply invest labor and its cognitive and affective capacities, but more specifically becomes a form of governmentality, which operates algorithmically to reduce all existence to a general form of indebtedness. This algorithmic form of governability is also what has given way to a diffused financialization of potentialities through which aesthetic life is constantly quantified and turned into predictable scenarios.

Not only Lazzarato, also Massumi (2007) has noted the diffused ecological qualities of this new form of algorithmic governmentality, which he describes in terms of *pre-emption*, a mode of calculation of potential tendencies instead of existing possibilities. The calculation of potentialities that describe this dynamism is no longer based on existing or past data. Instead it aims at calculating the unknown as a relational space by measuring the interval between one existing data and another. This form of pre-emptive calculus indeed transforms the limit point of this calculation—infinities—into a source of capitalization.

From this standpoint, one can suggest the following: Contrary to the logic of *formal subsumption,* which corresponds to the application of unchanging sets of rules, whose linearity aimed to format the social according to pre-ordained ideas, *the logic of real subsumption* coincides with the interactive computational paradigm. This paradigm is based on the responsive capacities of learning, openness, and adaptation defining human-machine interaction as well as distributed interactive systems. With the extension of quantification to the indetermination of the environments—and thus to contingency—an intrinsic transformation of the logic of calculation has happened. In fact, the development of this interactive approach has been crucial to the now dominant form of real subsumption.

Historically, interactive algorithms were invented to circumvent the algorithmic constraints of the Turing Machine. The concept of this machine was insufficient or unable to cope with the complexity of the empirical world—a complexity that one could say, philosophically speaking, has its own nonrepresentational logic. Here, the advance of real subsumption cannot be isolated from the emergence of a dynamic form of automation, which constitutes a historical development in computer science from Turing's algorithmic modeling. Back then, Turing's conceptualization of a mechanism, which is based on a priori instructions, strongly resonated with a mechanism as defined by first order cybernetics (a closed system of feedback). Today, the combination of environmental inputs and a posteriori instructions proposed by the interactive paradigm embrace second order cybernetics and its open feedback mechanisms. The goal of this new dynamic interaction is to include variation and novelty in automation to enlarge the horizon of calculation, and to include qualitative factors as external variables within its computational mechanism.

Contrary to Lazzarato's critique, it seems important not to generalize automation as being always already a technocapitalist reduction of existential qualities. The task is rather to address the intrinsic transformation of the automated form of neoliberal governability and to engage closely with the question of the technical. However, rather than arguing that the technical is always already a static formal frame, delimited by its binary logic, I suggest that there is a dynamic internal to the system of calculation. If so, it is necessary to engage with the real possibility of a speculative question that according to Isabelle Stengers (2010 and 2011) is central to the scientific method: What if automation already shows that there is a dynamic relation intrinsic to computational processing between input data and algorithmic instructions, involving a non-linear elaboration of data? What if this dynamic is not simply explainable in terms of its a posteriori use, i.e., once it is either socially used or mentally processed?

The interactive paradigm concerns the capacity of algorithms to respond and to adapt to its external inputs. As Deleuze (1992) already foresaw, an interactive system of learning and continuous adaptation is at the core of the logic of governance driven by the variable mesh of continuous variability. Here, the centrality of capitalism in society forces axiomatics to open up to external outputs, constituting an environment of agents through which capital's logic of governance increasingly corresponds to the minute investment in the socius and ultimately life variations. The question of the undecidable proposition is important, because it defines an immanent and not transcendent view of capital, as Deleuze and Guattari (1987) remind us. This is the case in so far as the extension of capital to life requires its apparatus of capture to be open to contingencies, variations and unpredictable change.

It is here that the organizational power of computation needs to be more closely investigated to clarify the transformation that automation itself has undergone with the re-organization of capital from formal to real subsumption. Interactive automation of cognition and affection should be examined anew. Whether we are faced with the critical conception of cognitive capital, or with the critical view of an automated governance based on a general indebtedness, we risk overlooking what can be considered the most radical process of artificialization of intelligence that human history has ever seen; this involves the conversion of organic ends into technical means, whose consequences are yet to become unpacked.

Although my thoughts are still in an early phase, I want to consider the possibility of theorizing that algorithmic automation heralds the realization of a second nature, in which a purposeless and impersonal mode of thought tends to supplant the teleological finality of reason, echoed by Kant's conception of reason in terms of motive—i.e., the reason behind the action—that substantiates the difference between understanding and reason. This is also a proposition, which more importantly works to challenge the theory that there is a mutual relation or undecidable proposition between philosophy and technology as well as between thought and capital. Instead of the idea that the refuge of thought and of philosophy from an increasingly dynamic technocapitalism lies in the ultimate appeal to intellectual intuition and affective thought as the safe enclaves of pure uncertainty and singularity, I want to pursue the possibility that algorithmic automation—as rule-based thought—may rather be indifferent to these all too human qualities, whilst actively encompassing them all without representing philosophical and or critical thought. This is a proposition for the emergence of an algorithmic mode of thought that cannot be contained by a teleological finality of reason, which characterizes both capitalism and the critique of technocapitalism.

The Turing Experiment and the Omega Number

As we know, algorithmic automation involves the breaking down of continuous processes into discrete components, whose functions can be constantly re-iterated without error. In short, automation means that initial conditions can be reproduced ad infinitum. The form of automation that concerns us here was born with the Turing Machine: an absolute mechanism of iteration based on step-by-step procedures. Nothing is more opposed to pure thought—or "the being of the sensible" as Deleuze (1994: 68) called it—than this discrete-based machine of universal calculation. The Turing architecture of pre-arranged units that could be interchangeably exchanged along a sequence is effectively the opposite of an ontogenetic thought moving through a differential continuum, through intensive encounters and affect.

Nevertheless, since the 1960s the nature of automation has undergone dramatic changes as a result of the development of computational capacities of storing and processing data. Previous automated machines were limited by the amount of feedback data. Now algorithmic automation is designed to analyze and compare options, to run possible scenarios or outcomes, and to perform basic reasoning through problem-solving steps that were not contained within the machine's programmed memory. For instance, expert systems draw conclusions through search techniques, pattern matching, and web data extraction, and those complex automated systems have come to dominate our everyday culture, from global networks of mobile telephony to smart banking and air traffic control.

Despite this development, much debate about algorithmic automation is still based on Turing's discrete computational machine. It suggests that algorithmic automation is yet another example of the Laplacian view of the universe, defined by determinist causality (see Longo 2000 and 2007). But in computational theory, the calculation of randomness or infinities has now turned what was defined as incomputables into a new form of probabilities, which are at once discrete and infinite. In other words, whereas algorithmic automation has been understood as being fundamentally Turing's discrete universal machine, the increasing volume of incomputable data (or randomness) within online, distributive, and interactive computation is now revealing that infinite, patternless data are rather central to computational processing. In order to appreciate the new role of incomputable algorithms in computation, it is necessary to make a reference to the logician Kurt Gödel, who challenged the axiomatic method of pure reason by proving the existence of undecidable propositions within logic.

In 1931, Gödel took issue with Hilbert's meta-mathematical program. He demonstrated that there could not be a complete axiomatic method, not a pure mathematical formula, according to which the reality of things could be proven to be true or false (see Feferman 1995). Gödel's incompleteness theorems explain that propositions are true, even though they cannot be verified by a complete axiomatic method. Propositions are therefore deemed to be ultimately undecidable: They cannot be proven by the axiomatic method upon which they were hypothesized. In Gödel's view, the problem of incompleteness, born from the attempt to demonstrate the absolute validity of pure reason and its deductive method, instead affirms the following: No a priori decision, and thus no finite sets of rule, can be used to determine the state of things before things can run their course.

Turing encountered Gödel's incompleteness problem while attempting to formalize the concepts of algorithm and computation through his famous thought experiment, now known as the Turing Machine. In particular, the Turing Machine demonstrates that problems are computable, if they can be decided according to the axiomatic method.[1] Conversely, those propositions, which cannot be decided through the axiomatic method, will remain *incomputable*.

By proving that some particular functions cannot be computed by such a hypothetical machine, Turing demonstrated that there is not an ultimate decision method of the guise that Hilbert had wished for. The strength of Turing's proposition is that his Turing Machine offered a viable formalization of a mechanical procedure. Instead of just crunching numbers, Turing's computing machines—and indeed contemporary digital machines that have developed from them—can solve problems, make decisions, and fulfill tasks; the only provision is that these problems, decisions, and tasks are formalized through symbols and a set of discrete and finite sequential steps. In this respect, Turing's effort can be seen as a crucial step in the long series of attempts in the history of thought geared towards the mechanization of reason.

However, what is more important is how the limit of computation and thus of the teleological finality of reason—automated in the Turing machine—have been transformed in computer science and information theory. Here, the work of mathematician Gregory Chaitin (2004, 2006, and 2007) is particularly symptomatic of this transformation as it explains what is at stake with the limits of computation and the development of a dynamic form of automation. Distinguishing this transformation from the centrality of the interactive paradigm in technocapitalism is crucial. This paradigm, born from the necessity to include environmental contingencies in computation, mainly works to anticipate or pre-empt response (as Massumi 2007 has clearly illustrated). Instead, and more importantly for me and my proposition of algorithmic automation as a mode of thought, it is a serious engagement with the function that incomputable data play within computation. To make this point clearer, I will have to explain Chaitin's theory in greater detail.

Chaitin's algorithmic information theory combines Turing's question of the limit of computability with Shannon's information theory demonstrating the productive capacity of noise and randomness in communication systems, to discuss computation in terms of maximally unknowable probabilities. In every computational process, he explains, the output is always greater than

---

1   See Turing 1936. For further discussion of the intersections of the works between Hilbert, Gödel and Turing, see Davis 2000.

the input. For Chaitin, something happens in the computational process-ing of data, something that challenges the equivalence between input and output, and thus the very idea that processing always leads to an already pre-programmed result. This something is, according to Chaitin, *algorithmic randomness*. The notion of algorithmic randomness implies that information cannot be compressed into a smaller program, insofar as between input and output an entropic transformation of data occurs, which results in a tendency of these data to increase in size. From this standpoint, the output of the processing does not correspond to the inputted instructions, and its volume tends in fact to become bigger than it was at the start of the computation. The discovery of algorithmic randomness in computational processing has been explained by Chaitin in terms of *the incomputable*: increasing yet unknown quantities of data that characterize rule-based processing.

Chaitin calls this algorithmic randomness Omega (the last letter of the Greek alphabet refers to the probability that this number is infinite). Chaitin's inves-tigation of the incomputable reveals in fact that the linear order of sequen-tial procedures (namely, what constitutes the computational processing of zeros and ones) shows an entropic tendency to add more data to the existing aggregation of instructions established at the input. Since this processing inevitably includes not only a transformation of existing data into new inputs, but also the addition of new data on top of what already was pre-established in the computational procedure, it is possible to speak of an internal dynamic to computation.

From this point of view, computational processing does not mainly guaran-tee the return to initial conditions, nor does it simply include change derived from an interactive paradigm based on responsive outputs. This is because Chaitin's conception of incomputability no longer perfectly matches the notion of the limit in computation (i.e., limit for what is calculable). Instead, this limit as the incomputable is transformed: It becomes the addition of new and maxi-mally unknowable algorithmic parts to the present course of computational processing; these parts are algorithmic sequences that tend to become bigger in volume than programmed instruction and to take over, hereby irreversibly transforming the pre-set finality of rules. Chaitin's re-articulation of the incom-putable is at once striking and speculatively productive. What was conceived to be the external limit of computation (i.e., the incomputable) in Turing, has now become internalized in the sequential arrangement of algorithms (ran-domness works within algorithmic procedures).

At Chaitin's own admission, it is necessary to see algorithmic randomness as a continuation of Turing's attempt to account for indeterminacy in computa-tion. Whereas for Turing there are cases in which finality cannot be achieved, and thus computation—*qua* automation of the finality of reason—stops when the incomputable begins, for Chaitin computation itself has an internal margin of incomputability insofar as rules are always accompanied and infected by randomness. Hence, incomputability is not simply a break from reason, but rather reason has been expanded beyond its limits to involve the processing of maximally unknown parts that have no teleological finality. To put it in other terms, automation is now demarcated by the incomputable, the unconditional of computation. Importantly, however, this challenges the view that computational processing corresponds to calculations leading to pre-programmed and already known outputs. Instead, the limits of automation—that is the incomputable—have become the starting point of a dynamism internal to computation, which exceeds the plan for technocapital's instrumentalization of reason. From this standpoint, relating Chaitin's findings to the positioning of critical thought and technocapitalism reveals a new aspect: the incomputable cannot be simply understood as being opposed to reason. In other words, it is not an expression of the end of reason and cannot be explained according to the critical view that argues for the primacy of affective thought.

According to Chaitin, the incomputable demonstrates the shortcomings of the mechanical view of computation, according to which chaos or randomness is an error within the formal logic of calculation. But incomputables do not describe the failure of intelligibility versus the triumph of the incalculable—on the contrary. These limits more subtly suggest the possibility of a dynamic realm of intelligibility, defined by the capacities of incomputable infinities or randomness, to infect any computable or discrete set. In other words, randomness (or the infinite varieties of infinities) is not simply outside the realm of computation, but has more radically become its absolute condition. And when becoming partially intelligible in the algorithmic cipher that Chaitin calls Omega, randomness also enters computational order and provokes an *irreversible revision of algorithmic rules* and of their teleological finality. It is precisely this new possibility for an indeterminate revision of rules, driven by the inclusion of randomness within computation, that reveals dynamics within automated system and automated thought. This means the following: While Chaitin's discovery of Omega demonstrates that randomness has become intelligible within computation, incomputables cannot, however, be synthesized by an a priori program or set of procedures that are in size smaller than them. According to Chaitin, Omega corresponds to discrete states that are themselves composed of infinite real numbers that cannot be contained by finite axioms.

What is interesting here is that Chaitin's Omega is at once intelligible yet non-synthesizable by universals, or by a subject. I take it to suggest that computation—*qua* mechanization of thought—is intrinsically populated by incomputable data, or that discrete rules are open to a form of contingency internal to algorithmic processing. This is not simply to be understood as an error within the system, or a glitch within the coding structure, but rather as a part of computation. Far from dismissing computation as the evil incarnation of technocapitalist instrumentalization of reason, one realizes that incomputable algorithms emerge to defy the superiority of the teleological finality of reason, but also of sensible and affective thought.

Speculative Computation

It would be wrong to view this proposition that incomputables define the dynamic form of automation with naïve enthusiasm. Instead, it is important to address algorithmic automation without overlooking the fact that the computation of infinity is nonetheless central to the capitalization of intelligible capacities—even in their automated form. My insistence that incomputables are not exclusively those non-representable infinities, which belong to the being of the sensible, is indeed a concern, with the ontological and epistemological transformation of thought in view of the algorithmic function of reason. Incomputables are expressed by the affective capacities to produce new thought, but more importantly reveal the dynamic nature of the intelligible. Here, my concern is not an appeal to an ultimate computational being determining the truth of thought. On the contrary, I have turned to Chaitin's discovery of Omega, because it radically undoes the axiomatic ground of truth by revealing that computation is an incomplete affair, open to the revision of its initial conditions, and thus to the transformation of truths and finality. Since Omega is at once a discrete and infinite probability, it testifies to the fact that the initial condition of a simulation—based on discrete steps—is and can be infinite. In short, the incomputable algorithms discovered by Chaitin suggest that the complexity of real numbers defies the grounding of reason in finite axiomatics and teleological finality.

From this standpoint, several thoughts unfold. I agree that the interactive paradigm of technocapitalism already points to a semi-dynamic form of automation, which has enslaved the cognitive and affective capacities and established a financial governmentality based on debt. But beyond this, there still remain further questions regarding the significance of algorithms.

If we risk confusing the clear-cut opposition between digitality and philosophy (Galloway 2013), what and how are algorithms? For now, I want to point out that algorithms, this dynamic form of reason, rule-based and yet open to be revised, are not defined by teleological finality, as impersonal functions transform such finality each time. This is not to be conceived as a mere replacement or extension of human cognitive functions. Instead, my point is that we are witnessing the configuration of an incomputable mode of thought that cannot be synthesized into a totalizing theory or program. Nonetheless, this thought exposes the fallacy of a philosophy and critical thought, which reduces computation to an inferior mechanization of reason, destined to mere iteration and unable to change its final directions.

Here, my argument was mainly concerned with the critique of computation as the incarnation of the technocapitalist instrumentalization of reason. It was an attempt at suggesting the possibility that algorithmic automation coincides with a mode of thought, in which incomputable or randomness have become intelligible, calculable but not necessarily totalizable by technocapitalism. Despite all instrumentalization of reason on behalf of capitalism, and despite the repression of knowledge and desire into quantities, such as tasks, functions, aims, there certainly remains an inconsistency within computation. This is the case insofar as the more it calculates, the more randomness (patternless information) it creates, which exposes the transformative capacities of rule-based functions. In the algorithm-to-algorithm phase transition that most famously characterizes the financial trading mentioned at the beginning of this essay, it is hard to dismiss the possibility that the automation of thought has exceeded representation and has instead revealed that computation itself has become dynamic.

To conclude I want to add this: dynamic automation cannot be mainly explained in terms of a necessary pharmacological relation between philosophy and technology, knowledge, and capital, or the conditional poison allowing for a mutual reversibility defined by a common ground as Stiegler (2014) does. Similarly, one has to admit that the dynamic tendencies at the core of algorithmic automation are not simply reducible to the technocapitalist logic of semiotic organization declared by Lazzarato (2012) or to the exploitation/repression of the cognitive-creative functions of thought.

The challenge that automated cognition poses to the post-human vision—that thought and technology have become one, because of technocapitalism—points to the emergence of *a new alien mode of thought*, able to change its initial conditions and to express ends that do not match the finality of organic thought. This also means that the algorithm-to-algorithm phase transition does not simply remain another example of the technocapitalist instrumentalization of reason, but more subtly reveals a realization of a second nature in the form of a purposeless and automated intelligence. If algorithmic automation no longer corresponds to the execution of instructions, but to the constitution of a machine ecology infected with randomness, then one can suggest that neither technocapitalism nor the critique of technocapitalism can contain the tendency of the automated processing of randomness to overcome axiomatic truths.

References

Biehl-Missal, Brigitte. 2012. "Atmospheres of Seduction: A Critique of Aesthetic Marketing Practices." *Journal of Macromarketing* 32 (2): 168–80.

Chaitin, Gregory. 2004. "Leibniz, Randomness & the Halting Probability." *Mathematics Today* 40 (4): 138–39.

Chaitin, Gregory. 2006. "The Limits of Reason." *Scientific American* 294 (3): 74–81.

Chaitin, Gregory. 2007. "The Halting Probability Omega: Irreducible Complexity in Pure Mathematics." *Milan Journal of Mathematics* 75 (1): 291–304.

Davis, Martin. 2000. *The Universal Computer. The Road from Leibniz to Turing.* London: Norton and Company, 83–176.

Deleuze, Gilles, and Félix Guattari. 1987. *A Thousand Plateaus: Capitalism and Schizophrenia.* Minneapolis: University of Minnesota Press.

Deleuze, Gilles. 1994. *Difference and Repetition.* London: Athlone.

Deleuze, Gilles. 1992: "Postscript on the Societies of Control." *October* 59: 3–7.

Farmer, Doyne, and Spyros Skouras. 2011. *An Ecological Perspective on the Future of Computer Trading.* The Future of Computer Trading in Financial Markets, UK Foresight Driver Review 6. London: Government Office for Science. http://www.gov.uk/government/uploads/system/uploads/attachment_data/file/289018/11-1225-dr6-ecological-perspective-on-future-of-computer-trading.pdf.

Fisher, Mark. 2009. *Capitalist Realism. Is There No Alternative?.* London: Zero Books.

Galloway, Alexander. 2013. "The Poverty of Philosophy: Realism and Post-Fordism." *Critical Inquiry* 39 (2): 347–66.

Goldstein, Rebecca. 2005. *Incompleteness: The Proof and Paradox of Kurt Gödel.* Norton & Company.

Gödel, Kurt. 1995. "Some basic theorems on the foundations of mathematics and their implications." In *Collected Works of Kurt Gödel.* Vol. 3, edited by Solomon Feferman et al., 304–23. Oxford: Oxford University Press.

Hardt, Michael and Negri, Antonio. 2000. *Empire.* Cambridge, MA: Harvard University Press.

Hayles, N. Katherine. 2014. "Cognition Everywhere: The Rise of the Cognitive Nonconscious and the Costs of Consciousness." *New Literary History* 45 (2): 199–320.

Johnson, Neil, Guannan Zhao, Eric Hunsader, Hong Qi, Nicholas Johnson, Jing Meng, and Brian Tivnan. 2013. "Abrupt Rise of New Machine Ecology beyond Human Response Time." *Scientific Reports* 3 (September 11). doi:10.1038/srep02627.

Lazzarato, Maurizio. 2012. *The Making of the Indebted Man.* Los Angeles: Semiotext(e).

Longo, Giuseppe. 2000. "The Difference between Clocks and Turing Machines." In *Functional Models of Cognition. Self-Organizing Dynamics and Semantic Structures in Cognitive Systems,* edited by Arturo Carsetti, 211–232. Dordrecht: Springer.

Longo, Giuseppe. 2007. "Laplace, Turing and the 'Imitation Game' Impossible Geometry: Randomness, Determinism and Programs in Turing's Test." In *The Turing Test Sourcebook,* edited by Robert Epstein, Gary Roberts and Grace Beber, 377–413. Dordrecht: Kluwer.

Massumi, Brian. 2007. "Potential Politics and the Primacy of Preemption." *Theory & Event* 10 (2).

Steiner, Christopher. 2012. *Automate This: How Algorithms Came to Dominate the World.* New York: Portfolio/Penguin.

Stengers, Isabelle. 2010. *Cosmopolitics 1.* Minneapolis: University of Minnesota Press.

Stengers, Isabelle. 2011. *Cosmopolitics 2.* Minneapolis: University of Minnesota Press.

Stiegler, Bernard. 2014. *States of Shock: Stupidity and Knowledge in the 21st Century.* Cambridge: Polity Press.

Stiegler, Bernard. 2014. *The Lost Spirit of Capitalism: Disbelief and Discredit,* 3. Cambridge: Polity Press.

Turing, Alan. 1936. "On Computable Numbers, with an Application to the Entscheidungsproblem." *Proceedings of the London Mathematical Society,* series 2, vol. 42, 230–65.

INTELLIGENT MACHINES

FUNCTIONALISM

ALAN TURING

HUMAN MIND

COMPUTATIONAL COMPLEXITY

HISTORICAL EXPERIENCE

[8]

Revolution Backwards: Functional Realization and Computational Implementation

Reza Negarestani

Functionalist theories of mind come from heterogeneous directions and address an array of problems ranging from metaphysical to epistemic-semantic and engineering ones. Similarly, computational theories of mind cover different classes of computational complexity. The first part of this text examines what it means to combine the functional description of the human mind with the computational one. The second part addresses the ramifications of a computationalist-functionalist account of the mind as exemplified in Alan Turing's proposal for realizing intelligent machinery. The implementation of a computationalist-functionalist account of the human mind in machines is depicted as a program that deeply erodes our capacity to recognize what human experience manifestly is. In doing so, it fractures the historical experience of what it means to be human. Yet this is a rupture that marks a genuine beginning for the history of intelligent machines.

In *Alleys of Your Mind: Augmented Intelligence and Its Traumas,* edited by Matteo Pasquinelli, 139–54. Lüneburg: meson press, 2015.
DOI: 10.14619/014

Function, Computation, and their Alliance

Traditionally a thesis in the philosophy of mind, functionalism is a view of the mind as a functional organization. It attempts to explicate what the mind does and how it does it by reference to functional roles and properties that can be causal or logical-conceptual. In this sense, functionalism conjoins (a) *the metaphysical problem* of describing causal relations between explanans and explanandum in functional terms of selection and purpose-attainment (i.e., the function as what—according to specific and relevant selection criteria— makes a difference in explanandum) with (b) an *epistemic-semantic problem* concerning how to differentiate semantic content from physical information and how to view the semantic intercontent in terms of functions as logico-conceptual roles with (c) *an engineering problem* regarding the realization of functional properties in relation to or in isolation from structural properties.

Computationalism is a view that the functional organization of the brain is computational or implements computation, and neural states can be viewed as computational states. In this context, computation can refer to either *intrinsic computation* (i.e., computation detached from the semantics of utility implicit in algorithms), or *logical computation* (in which processes implicitly implement algorithms to yield specific outputs). While analysis in terms of intrinsic computation attempts to detect and measure basic spatio-temporal information processing elements without reference to output states or the information produced, analysis in terms of algorithmic computation is based on the identification of output states and then singling out processes which algorithmically map input to that specific output.

Intrinsic computation is about how structures actually support and constrain information processing, how regularities are formed and how structures move between one internal state to another, and in doing so, oscillate between randomness and order (i.e., the inherent association between structural complexity and intrinsic computational capabilities of processes). Whereas algorithmic computation is concerned with the mapping between input states and output states (or states and actions), and how this mapping relation can be seen as a pattern or a compressed regularity that can be captured algorithmically. Hence, from the perspective of algorithmic computation, a machine or a brain computes a function by executing a single or a collection of programs or algorithms.

In reality, neither functionalism nor computationalism entails one another. But if they are taken as implicitly or explicitly related, that is, if the functional organization (with functions having causal or logical roles) is regarded as computational either intrinsically or algorithmically, then the result is *computational functionalism*.

Depending on what is meant by function (causal or logico-conceptual) and depending on what is meant by computation (intrinsic-structural or algorithmically decomposable), bridging functionalism with computationalism leads to varieties of positions and approaches: rational or normative functionalism with structural constraints (Sellars 2007), strongly mechanistic/causal functionalism (Bechtel 2008), rational functionalism with a level of algorithmic decomposability (Brandom 2008), normatively constrained functionalism with intrinsic computational elements (Craver 2007), strongly logical functionalism with algorithmic computationalism (classical variations of artificial intelligence), causal functionalism with intrinsic computationalism (Crutchfield 1994), weak logical functionalism with intrinsic computationalism and strong structural constraints (artificial intelligence programs informed by embodied cognition) and so on.

Even though this might be a controversial claim, in recognizing thinking as an activity that ought to be theoretically and practically elaborated, philosophy turns itself into an implicitly functionalist project. A philosopher should endorse at least one type of functionalism insofar as thinking is an activity and the basic task of the philosopher is to elaborate the ramifications of engaging in this activity in the broadest sense and examine conditions required for its realization. Pursuing this task inevitably forces philosophy to engage with other disciplines, and depending on its scope and depth, it demands philosophy to rigorously acquaint itself with social and natural sciences, political economy as well as neuroscience, computational linguistics as well as evolutionary biology.

The mind is what it does. While this *mental* or *noetic doing* can be taken as constrained by the structural complexity of its material substrate, it should be described in the functional vocabulary of activities or doings. The mind—be it taken as an integration of distinct yet interconnected activities related to perception, thinking, and intention or seen as a cognitive-practical project whose meanings and ramifications are still largely unknown (à la Hegel and Mou Zongsan)—has primarily a functional import (see Mou 2014).

Identifying the mind as a thing is a move toward rendering the mind ineffable, since it flattens the specific conditions and constraints (whether material or logico-conceptual) necessary for the realization of the mind, and thereby, confers primordial and perennial qualities on it. The mind becomes the given. But characterizing the mind in terms of role-specific activities or functions is the first step for preventing the mind from becoming ubiquitous to such an extent that it turns ineffable. This is because by defining the mind in terms of activities, we are forced to explain how these activities are realized, what sorts of processes and structures constrain and support them, and what roles these activities play.

This functional decomposition or analysis then provides us with additional information regarding if what the mind appears to be doing is indeed a single activity or is in fact comprised of diverse and qualitatively distinct activities with specific roles and domains in or outside of what we previously viewed as a unitary picture of the mind. In other words, seeing and examining the mind in terms of function not only forestalls ineffability but also leads to a systematic destruction of a reified picture of the mind. In this sense, the functional description of the mind is at once a critical and a constructive gesture. It is critical because it subjects whatever we understand as the mind to a functional analysis or methodical decomposition. Abilities are distinguished by activities which realize them and activities are differentiated by their roles and investigated in light of conditions required for their realization: distinct processes with their own pattern-uniformities, hierarchies of structural complexity with their intralevel and interlevel constraints and dependency relations between constituents, different classes and types of function, etc.

Accordingly, the functional description is able to reveal not only what those activities we associate with the mind are and which roles they play, but also how they are organized and realized. Looking deep into the functional organization and conditions of realization, what was previously deemed as a single activity may turn out to be multiple qualitatively distinct activities or multiple activities may turn out to be a single one. Therefore, the analytical research launched by the functional description leads to a fundamental reevaluation of the nature of cognitive activities and thus, culminates in a drastic change in what we mean by mind-specific activities including thinking.

Now insofar as this analytical investigation identifies and maps conditions required for the realization of mind-specific activities, it is also a program for the functional realization and construction of cognitive abilities. The extended functional map is a blueprint for realization. In other words, the functional description has a constructive import. It is in the context of functional description and functional realization that the role of computationalism and its connection with functionalism become explicit. If there is a computational description for a function, that function can—in principle and within the framework of the right paradigm of computation—be reconstructed through a machine or a system of interacting agents capable of implementing the relevant computation. In this sense, computational description is not the same as functional description, it is an account of functional realizability in computational terms combined with the different conditionals regarding the computability or incomputability of functions for a specific computational class as well as the paradigm of computation under which the computational complexity is defined.[1]

---

1   Even though the choice of the paradigm of computation is seldom discussed in the computational theory of mind or orthodox approaches to artificial intelligence, it is a

Combining functionalism with computationalism requires a carefully controlled merger. Based on their hierarchies, roles, and attachments with specific structures, different realizability conditions implement different types or classes of computation, some of which are computationally intractable to others. If by computationalism, we mean a general view of computation in which computation at the level of causal mechanisms and computation at the level of logico-conceptual functions are indiscriminately joined together and there is no distinction between different classes of computational functions or computational models with their appropriate criteria of applicability to algorithmic and non-algorithmic (interactive) behaviors, then nothing except a naïve bias-riddled computational culture comes out of the marriage between functionalism and computationalism. Within this culture, the prospects and ramifications of computational reconstruction of complex cognitive abilities are always polarized between an uncritical optimism and a dogmatic cynicism, claims of inevitability and impossibility.

Functional realization of cognition—whether viewed through the lens of embodiment or semantic complexity—may, in fact, be captured and reconstructed computationally. The analytic-constructive prospects of computational functionalism are open to examination and experimentation. However,

criterion that is particularly consequential for describing and modeling functions. Generally, computation is defined by reference to the Church-Turing paradigm of computation where the emphasis is put on how computation is sequentially executed and what is computable. However, the Church-Turing paradigm has been challenged in the past few decades in computer science by proponents of the interactive paradigm of computation such as Samson Abramsky and Peter Wegner among others. One of the main motivations behind this divergence was precisely the debates concerning what computation is as opposed to what is computable. Developed through intersections between proof theory, linguistics, foundational logic, physics and computer science, these debates have led to the theory of fundamental duality of computation where computation is defined as a confrontation between actions or processes. These interactions can be logically expressed by sets of axioms for elementary acts (for example, in the context of linguistic practices, these axiomatic actions can be elementary speech acts such as assertion, query, permission, etc). In the Church-Turing paradigm of computation, for a given system the influences of the external environment are represented by an average behavior. Any unpredictable behavior of the environment is registered as a perturbation for the system. A Turing machine shuts out the environment during the computation, and interaction is rudimentary represented through sequential algorithms. But interaction as in concurrent processes and synchronous or asynchronous actions between agents is irreducible to the sequential interaction as it is represented by distributed parallel systems. In contrast to the Church-Turing paradigm, the interactive paradigm considers computation to be the natural expression of the interaction itself. The behavior of the system evolves in response to and in interaction with the inputs from the external environment. This duality that is intrinsic to computation can be exemplified in games or collaborative, neutral and adversarial engagements between agents. Each move, strategy or behavior evolves in accordance with synchronous or asynchronous moves or behaviors of other parties. In other words, the computational operation is the interaction between agents which represent different strategies of action. For discussions surrounding the interactive paradigm of computation, see Goldin, et al. 2006.

this is only possible if conditions of realization are carefully differentiated and examined with reference to distinct modes and classes of computation. If the activities that count as thinking are taken as purely symbolic (cf. the investment of classical program of AI on symbolic algorithmic computation) or purely causal (cf. structural theories of the mind focused on intrinsic computation), the result will most likely be either an evidence of the impossibility of functional realization or the intractability of functional properties of the mind to computation (or it could even be both). But these evidences do not stem from the intrinsic resistance of the mind-specific activities to functional and computational descriptions. They are rather the results of improper and incompatible functional and computational descriptions (not having the correct computational description in the context of the adequate computational paradigm for the right functional description). Therefore, they cannot be treated as proofs against the functional realization of the mind (i.e., the idea that the mind can be reconstructed by different sets of realizers) or the computational description of its realizability (i.e., the idea that mind-specific activities can be realized by computational functions which can be implemented in artifacts).

Intrinsic computational modeling is suitable for causal-structural conditions of realization, whereas symbolic logical computation is pertinent to language at the level of syntax. But semantic complexity associated with conceptual and rule-following activities requires a different kind of algorithmic decomposability and that is specific to the social or interactive dimension of linguistic discursive practices through which the pragmatic mediation of syntactical expressions yield different layers of semantics and grades of concepts. Complex semantic abilities are acquired through dialogical aspects of language which involve interaction between agents or language-users.[2] Given that the logic and the evolving structure of the interaction itself is a fundamental aspect of computation and necessary for the realization of conceptual functions or concept-roles, complex cognitive abilities which involve semantic richness,

---

2   In traditional approaches to semantics, even though the semantic content is understood in terms of inference, the inference is only viewed with reference to the relation between the premise and the conclusion, or the monological relation between propositional contents. An approach to meaning via monological processes, however, does not capture the multilayered complexity of the semantic content. Content-richness or semantic complexity can only be obtained via dual interacting (arguing) processes when dynamically contrasted to each other. These dual interacting-contrasting processes describe the dialogical dimension of inference which is required for the dynamic appraisal and determination of semantic content as well as the generation of different semantic layers and grades of concept. The dialogical dimension of inference adds an interpersonal angle to the intercontent aspect of inference. It is this interpersonal or dialogical aspect that is expressed by the social discursive scope of reasoning and can be elaborated as a form of multi-agent computation. For a detailed study of dialogical approaches to meaning and inference especially in light of new advances in interactive logics and computational semantics, see Lecomte 2011.

resource-sensitive inference and dynamic structures require a paradigm shift in computational modeling. This shift should satisfactorily reflect the interaction itself as an integral and indispensable element of computation.

It is this irreducible and fundamental interactive-social dimension of the core components of cognition such as concept-use, semantic complexity and material inferences that the classical program of artificial intelligence in its objective to construct complex cognitive abilities has failed to address and investigate. Is the Church-Turing paradigm of effective computation with its widely discussed implications for algorithmic mechanizability a suitable candidate for modeling the interactive-social dimensions of cognition? Or is it inherently inadequate when its definition of computation is extended to include interaction in its evolving and non-monotonic sense that occurs in open systems, in dialogues or between asynchronous processes or collaborative and adversarial agents. But even more generally, can social linguistic discursive practices responsible for the semantic complexity be computationally described? Can computational descriptions of social-pragmatic dimensions of semantics and inferences be algorithmically captured considering that the computational description is not the same as the algorithmic description? And if they can indeed be algorithmically expressed, then what kinds of algorithms? If by computation we mean symbolic algorithms, then the answer is negative. But insofar as language is a form of computation and compression—albeit one in which compression is modified for communal sharing and interaction between agents and where different computational classes are combined and integrated—even the semantic complexity or meaning-relations of language can be "in principle" computationally generated.[3] An emphatic rejection of this possibility risks replacing the ineffability of the mind and its activities with the ineffability of the social and its discursive practices. However, in order to find and develop the appropriate computational models and algorithms of concept-formation and meaning-use, first we have to determine what sorts of activities a group of agents—be they animals or artifacts—have to perform in order to count as engaging in linguistic discursive practices.

The alliance between functionalism and computationalism takes the constructive implications of the former one step further—but a step that is in every respect a leap. If the functionalist account of the mind is already a blueprint for the realization and reconstruction of the mind, the functionalist *and* computational account of the mind is a program for the actual realization of the mind outside of its natural habitat, its implementation in contexts that we have yet to envisage. But this openness to implementation suggests a functional evolution that is no longer biological or determined by an essential structure.

3   For more details on computational compression and the social environment, see Dowe et al. 2011.

The history of functionalism has deep philosophical roots going back to Plato, to the Stoics (the functional account of emotions) and extending to Kant, Hegel, Sellars, Brandom, and Wimsatt. Similarly, computationalism has also a long history passing through scholastic logicians, the early mechanistic philosophy, the project of *mathesis universalis,* and in the wake of revolutions in mathematics and logics leading to modern computation and ultimately, the current advances in computational complexity theory and computational mechanics (as represented by figures such as Charles Bennett and James Crutchfield). However, computational functionalism—at least its rigorous elaboration—is a recent alliance. Among its forerunners, one name particularly stands out, Alan Turing. The significance of Turing's computationalist project is that it simultaneously pushes the boundaries of theory and experimentation away. Computational functionalism is presented by Turing as a theory that gestures toward its own realization and in fact, it is the theory that has to keep up the pace with the escalating rate of its concrete realization.

A Revolution that Writes Its Own Past

To continue and conclude this essay, I intend to briefly address the significance of the functionalist account of the human mind, and more specifically, Turing's computational-functionalist project as an experimentation in the realization of the thinking agency or the cognitive-practical subject in machines. As it will be argued, it is an experiment whose outcomes expunge the canonical portrait of the human backwards from the future. It originates a project in which humanity elaborates in practice a question already raised in physical sciences: "To what extent does the manifest image of the man-in-the-world survive?" (Sellars 2007, 386).

To this extent, I shall discuss the ramifications of Turing's response to to what are known as the *"arguments from various disabilities"* (henceforth, AVD) as an assault upon the canonical portrait of the human no less significant, in its theoretical and practical consequences, than the Copernican Revolution was in terms of shaking our firm views concerning the world and ourselves in it. In his groundbreaking essay *Computing Machinery and Intelligence*, Turing (1950) responds to and challenges a number of oft-repeated objections against the implicit albeit fundamental assumption of computational-functionalism, namely, the possibility of the realization of a machine that is able to computationally implement functions we regularly associate with human experience such as perception, cognition, and intention.

Machines cannot think, machines cannot have emotions, machines cannot be purposeful, they cannot be proactive and so forth: Turing (1950) enumerates these under what he calls AVD. It is a sort of *straw machine argument* that is baseless and precarious. It is more a fruit of our psychological fears and residual theological approaches to the world and ourselves than the result of sound arguments.

As a supporter of arguments against machines' abilities, the mind-preservationist is a person who believes that the mind cannot be functionally realized and implemented in different substrates. The mind-preservationist not only rejects the functionalist realization of the mind but also, as a result, adopts a form of vitalism or ineffability of the human mind. The mind-preservationist always attempts to see the machine's abilities from the perspective of an endemic disability. But if what the mind-preservationist really dismisses is not the machine as such but instead the functional realization of the mind implemented in the machine, then what he actually denies is not the machine *per se* but the mind itself. Or more accurately, what the mind-preservationist ends up rejecting is the possibility of mapping the mind's functions, the possibility of modeling and defining it as an object of a thoroughgoing scrutiny. In short, the mind-preservationist resists seeing the mind as what it really is.

The mind-preservationist turns an epistemic quandary regarding identifying conditions required for the realization of the mind (what makes the mind mind) into an ontological position concerning the impossibility of realization. If the mind-preservationist simply says that we do not know how these sorts of abilities we associate with the mind—or more generally, the human experience—are realized, he then can not strictly deny the possibility of the realization of these abilities in a machine. Why? Because that would be simply a form of provisional agnosticism that does not warrant rejection; he then has to yield and agree to the possibility of a future—even though a very distant one— where both epistemic requirements and technical criteria of the machine-implementation are fulfilled. Consequently, the mind-preservationist has to lend an ontological status to this epistemic uncertainty so that he can turn a tentative reaction into a decisive negation, crushing a future plausibility (the possibility of an adequate functional picture and means of implementation) in favor of an everlasting implausibility.

In this sense, machine-denialism is simply an excuse for denying what the mind is and what it can be. Correspondingly, disavowing the pursuit of understanding the mind coincides with acting against the evolution of the mind, since from a pragmatic-functional viewpoint the understanding of the meaning of the mind is inseparable from how the mind can be defined, reconstructed, and modified in different contexts. Therefore, if we lack the definition of the mind which is itself a map for its realization and implementation, then how can we so eagerly rule out the possibility of a machine furnished with a mind? The mind-preservationist, accordingly, has a double standard when it comes to recognizing the mind as both the measure and the object of his critique. He says the machine cannot engage in mental activities as if he knows what the mind really is and how it is realized. However, if he does not know the answers to these questions, then he cannot approach the realizable-implementable account of the mind from the perspective of an intrinsic disability or impossibility.[4]

If you do not know what the mind is then how can you claim that the machine cannot possibly have a mind? With the understanding that the "what" posed in this question is the very map of the mind's functional realizability that can be implemented in machines. Here, "what" can be described functionally as those *activities* that define what the mind is. The mind is therefore described as a functional item, in terms of its capacities for mentation (i.e., engaging in mental activities). From a functionalist perspective, *what* makes a thing a thing is not what a thing is but what a thing does. In other words, the functional item is not independent of its activity.

The activities of the mind are indeed special in the sense that they are not ubiquitous. But as Bechtel (2008, 3) suggests it is not in spite of being comprised of mechanisms but *in virtue of* the right kind of mechanisms that the mind is special and its activities have distinctive characteristics. This specialty is not the result of some sort of ineffability or exorbitant uniqueness: It is a corollary of a proper organization of right kind of realizers.

For this reason, if the argument from the perspective of disabilities is adopted as a standard strategy toward machines, or if it is exercised as a pre-determined reaction to the possibility of the realization of the mind in different substrates, then it does not have a genuine critical attitude. Why? Because such a critical strategy then has implicitly subscribed to a preservationist view of the mind as something inherently foreclosed to mapping and (re)construction. The mind that it safeguards has a special status because it is indescribably unique at the level of mapping and constructability. It cannot be constructed, because it cannot be fully mapped. It cannot be mapped because it cannot be defined. It cannot be defined because it is somewhere ineffable. If it is somewhere ineffable, then it is everywhere ineffable. Therefore, the singularity of the mind is the effect of its ineffability. If we buy into one ineffable thing and if that thing happens to be central to how we perceive, conceive, and act on the

4   An early proponent of functionalism, Hillary Putnam later repudiates his earlier position in his work *Representation and Reality* (1988). Putnam simultaneously rejects the functional and computational aspects of computational functionalism by constructing an argument that draws on Gödel's incompleteness theorem against the computational description of rational activities as well as demonstrating the triviality condition implicit in the multiple realizability thesis. The latter part of the argument has been criticized as being only an attribute of what is now called a standard picture of function. In *Gödel, Putnam, and Functionalism*, Jeff Buechner (2008) presents a meticulous refutation of Putnam's argument from the perspective of the incompleteness theorem, both with reference to the application of Gödel's theorem and the conclusions drawn from it. And for criticisms of the argument from the perspective of the triviality condition, see Huneman 2013.

world and ourselves, then we are also prepared to regard many other things in the world as ineffable. We have thus committed ourselves to a full-blown mysticism.

Turing's program signals a consequential phase in the historical development of the human and defining the project of humanity in the sense of both determining the meaning of being human and updating its definition. Its importance lies in how it grapples with the most fundamental question posed by Kant (1885, 15): "What is Man?" or what does it mean to be human?

Unlike the Copernican, Darwinian, Newtonian, and Einsteinian revolutions in which we witness the consequences of a radical theoretical reorientation immediately manifesting itself in the present, the site of the Turingian revolution is always in the future. Put differently, the Turingian revolution does not happen here and now in that it is, properly speaking, a constructive theory of the mind as implicit in computational functionalism. It incrementally (from the perspective of here and now) and catastrophically (from the perspective of the future) alters both the meaning of the mind and the conditions of its realizability by implementing—step by step, function by function, algorithm by algorithm—the functional picture of the mind in machines. For this reason, the concept of revolution that Turing's project elaborates fundamentally differs from the trajectory of the Copernican revolution as the harbinger of modern theoretical sciences.

The Turingian revolution suggests that the future will not be a varied extension of the present condition. It will not be continuous to the present. Whatever arrives back from the future—which is in this case, both the mind implemented in a machine and a machine equipped with the mind—will be discontinuous to our historical anticipations regarding what the mind is and what the machine looks like. In a sense, the relation between what we take as the mind and the machine-realizable account of the mind is akin to what René Thom describes as the catastrophic time-travelling relation between the image and its model, the signifier and the signified, the descendant and the parent. In the signified-signifier interaction, the dissipative irreversibility of time disguises a principle of reversibility (conservation) that is operative behind it:

> The formation of images from a model appears as a manifestation of the universal dynamic having irreversible character. There is a self-ramifying of the model into an image isomorphic to itself. Yet very often this process utilizes an interaction of reversible character. . . . The signified generates the signifier in an uninterrupted burgeoning ramification. But the signifier regenerates the signified each time that we interpret the sign. . . . For the signifier (the descendant) to become the signified (the parent) again, the time-lapse of a generation is sufficient. (Thom 1983, 264)

The relation between the human and its computational image becomes that of the signified qua the parent and the signifier qua the descendant. It illustrates a process whereby the future, time and time again, baits the present: The image of a mollusk is engraved on a rock and soon supersedes it. An embryo grows and develops a structure that is isomorphic to its parent organism but one that has undergone extensive time-space translations. As the human imprints and proliferates its image in machines, the machine reinvents the image of its creator, re-implements, and in the process revises it.

To the extent that we can not adopt a mind-preservationist ideology without undermining ourselves and to the extent that the computational-functionalist account of the mind is open to further epistemic and technical achievements, our pursuits for the realization of the mind in machines has a future import and a plausible possibility in light of which association of the mind with any given natural or fixed constitution becomes highly implausible and biased.

But why is the Turingian revolution in cognitive and computer sciences a revolution that is conceived in and takes place in the future? Because what Turing proposes is a schema or a general program for a thorough reconstruction and revision of what it means to be human and, by extension, humanity as a collective and historical constellation. Turing's underlying assumption is that the significance of the human can be functionally abstracted and computationally realized. This significance is the mind as a set of activities that span perception, thinking and intention—that is, the ability to turn sense data into perceptual impressions by mapping them to language as the domain of conceptual functions and then converting thoughts into intentional action.

The adequate functional abstraction and realization of this account of the human significance means that "what makes the human significant" can be realized by different individuating properties or realizers. But also what constitutes the human significance can be implemented in different modes of organization. The new context or environment of realization can then modify and update this functional schema drastically. In other words, the meaning of the mind will be changed in the course of its re-implementation in artifacts. Since implementation is not simply the relocation of a function or an abstract protocol from one supporting structure to another. It is the re-introduction of a (functional) role into a new context that will subsequently confer a new meaning to that role by providing it with different determining relations. To put it differently, implementation is the execution of a functional schema in a new context or environment with its specific sets of demands and purposes. Accordingly, re-implementation is the contextual repurposing and refashioning of a function that diversifies its content.

Realizing the mind through the artificial by swapping its natural constitution or biological organization with other material or even social organizations is a central aspect of the mind. Being artificial, or more precisely, expressing itself via the artifactual is the very meaning of the mind as that which has a history rather than an essential nature. Here the artificial expresses the practical elaboration of what it means to adapt to new purposes and ends without implying a violation of natural laws. To have a history is to have the possibility of being artificial—that is to say, expressing yourself not by way of what is naturally given to you but by way of what you yourself can make and organize. Denouncing this history is the same as rejecting freedom in all its forms. Denying the artificial truth of the mind and refusing to take this truth to its ultimate conclusions is to antagonize the *history* of the mind, and therefore, to be an enemy of thought.

The functionalist understanding of the mind is a historical moment in the functional evolution of the mind: In making sense of the mind in terms of its activities and their roles, the functional account gestures toward a mind constructed by different sets of realizers and in a different domain. Exploring the meaning of the mind coincides with artificially realizing it, and the artificial realization changes the very conditions by which this meaning used to be determined.

Once the real content of the human significance is functionally abstracted, realized and implemented outside of its natural habitat, the link between the structure in which this function is embedded and the significance qua function is weakened. Up to now, the influence of the structure (whether as a specific biological structure or a specific social stratum) over the function has been that of a constitution *determining* the behaviors or activities of the system. But with the abstraction and realization of those functions that distinguish the human—that is to say, by furnishing the real significance of the human with a functional autonomy—the link between the structure (or manifest humanity) and the function (all activities that make the human human) loses its determining power. The human significance qua a functional set of specific activities evolves in spite of conditions under which it has been naturally realized.

If the determining influence of the constituting structure (in this case, the specific biological substrate) over the function is sufficiently weakened, the image of the functional evolution can no longer be seen and recognized in the structure that supports it. The evolution at the level of function—here the expansion of the schema of the mind—is asymmetrical to the evolution of the structure, be it the evolution of the biological structure that once supported it or a new artificial habitat in which it is implemented. It is akin to a shadow that grows to the extent that it eclipses the body that once cast it.

In this fashion, what constituted or presently constitutes the human no longer determines the consequences of what it means to be human. Why? Because, the functional realization of "the meaning of being human" implies the departure of this meaning from the present condition or the image with which we identify the human. To put it differently, the function is able to reconstitute itself by perpetually reconstructing and revising itself, by evolving asymmetrically with regard to the structure and by revising its meaning through re-implementation in new substrates. By being re-implemented or introduced into a new context of realization, the function is able to change the overall schema of the mind. A project that in theory and practice articulates the possibility of realization and implementation of the human experience in machines is a project that concretely undermines what the human experience is and how it looks.

A program committed to the multiple realizability of the human mind can no longer be simply defined in terms of reflection on past and present conditions of the mind.[5] By attempting to realize the human mind in the machine, such a program realizes a mind that shatters the canonical picture of the mind we use to recognize ourselves, distinguishing ourselves from the machine we regard as inherently disabled. What the mind was and what it is, how it was originally realized and how it is presently constituted no longer bear any determining significance on the multiply realizable mind. Such a program genuinely belongs to the future, its present theoretic-practical dimension elaborates a discontinuity that we do not have the cognitive means to fathom.

The constructive and revisionary dimension of Turing's functional realization of the human cannot be seen from the perspective of the present because the implications of construction and revision as the forces of reconstitution and reconception unfold from the future. In short, what Turing does is to provide the blueprint of a program through which the consequences of being distinguished as human (or having human experience) are discontinuous and irreconcilable with what we currently identify as the human.

5   According to the multiple realizability thesis, the realization of a function can be satisfied by different sets of realizing properties, individuating powers and activities. Therefore, the function can be realized in different environments outside of its natural habitat by different realizers. Multiple realizability usually comes in strong and constrained varieties. The strong version does not impose any material-structural or organizational constraints on the realizability of a specific function, therefore the function is taken to be realizable in infinite ways or implementable in numerous substrates. The constrained variety, however, sees the conditions required for the realizability of a function through a deep or hierarchical model comprised of different explanatory-organizational levels and qualitatively different realizer properties which impose their respective constraints on the realization of the function. Accordingly, in the weak or constrained version of multiple realizability, the criteria for the realization of a function are characterized as *dimensionally varied* and *multiply constrained*. The function is then described as multiply realizable while multiply constrained. The constraints on the realization of function are dimensionally varied because they are determined by different organizational levels, which orchestrate or explain that function.

Turing's thesis on computational-functional realizability of the human mind is a thesis about constructability, its consequences take shape in the realm of manifest realization. It suggests there is no essentialist limit to the reconstructability of the human or "what human significance consists in." However, it goes even further by highlighting the consequence of constructing the mind outside of its natural habitat: *The reconstruction of the mind is tantamount to the reconstitution of its meaning.* It is in this sense that Turing's project marks a rupture in the truth of humanity, between the meaning of being human and its ramifications. In practice and through construction, it elaborates that to be human does not entail the understanding of the consequences of what it means to be human. Indeed, these two couldn't be further apart. To be human is neither a sufficient condition for *understanding* what is happening to the human by becoming part of a program that defines and elaborates the mind in computational-functional terms, nor is it a sufficient condition for *recognizing* what the human is becoming as the result of being part of this program. It can neither apprehend the consequences of revising the functional meaning of the human nor the scope of constructing the machine according to a computational-functional picture of the human mind.

By aiming at the realization of the human mind outside of its natural habitat, Turing draws a new link between emancipation (here the emancipation of human significance at the level of activities or functions) and the liberation of intelligence as a vector of self-realization. Turing's computationalist-functionalist project is significant because its ramifications—regardless of its current state and setbacks it has suffered—cannot be thought by its present implications. In this sense, by definition, humanity as we identify it in the present cannot grapple with and realize the scope of Turing's project.

In continuation of the project of the radical enlightenment, Turing's project is in fact a program for amplifying the imports of enlightened humanism insofar as it fully conforms to the following principle: The consequentiality or significance of the human is not in its given meaning or a conserved and already decided definition. Rather, it is in the ability to bootstrap complex abilities from primitive abilities. These complex abilities define what the human consists in. But insofar as they are algorithmically decomposable (cf. different types of computation for different functions, different kinds of algorithms for different activities and abilities), they present the definition of the human as amenable to modification, reconstruction, and implementation in artifacts. And this is the constructible hypothesis upon which Turing's project is founded: The significance of the human lies not in its uniqueness or in a special ontological status but in its functional decomposability and computational constructability through which the abilities of the human can be upgraded, its form transformed, its definition updated and even become susceptible to deletion.

Turing's computational project contributes to the project of enlightened humanism by dethroning the human and ejecting it from the center while acknowledging the significance of the human in functionalist terms. For what is the expandable domain of computers if not the strongest assault upon the ratiocentricity of the human mind in favor of a view that the ratiocinating capacities of the human mind can be reconstructed and upgraded in the guise of machines?

It is the understanding of the meaning of the human in functional terms that is a blueprint for the reconstruction of the human and the functional evolution of its significance beyond its present image. The knowledge of the mind as a functional item develops into the exploration of possibilities of its reconstruction. While the exploration of functional realization by different realizers and for different purposes shapes the history of the mind as that which has no nature but only possibilities of multiple realization and their corresponding histories.

What used to be called the human has now evolved beyond recognition. Narcissus can no longer see or anticipate his own image in the mirror. The recognition of the blank mirror is the sign that we have finally left our narcissistic phase behind. Indeed, we are undergoing a stage in which if humanity looks into the mirror it only sees an empty surface gawking back.

References

Bechtel, William. 2008. *Mental Mechanisms: Philosophical Perspectives on Cognitive Neuroscience.* New York: Routledge.

Brandom, Robert. 2008. *Between Saying and Doing: Towards an Analytic Pragmatism.* Oxford: Oxford University Press.

Buechner, Jeff. 2008. *Gödel, Putnam, and Functionalism: A New Reading of Representation and Reality.* Cambridge, MA: MIT Press.

Craver, Carl F. 2007. *Explaining the Brain: Mechanisms and the Mosaic Unity of Neuroscience.* Oxford: Clarendon.

Crutchfield, James P. 1994. "The Calculi of Emergence: Computation, Dynamics and Induction." *Physica D: Nonlinear Phenomena* 75 (1–3): 11–54.

Dowe, David L., José Hernández-Orallo, and Paramjit K. Das. 2011. "Compression and Intelligence: Social Environments and Communication." Artificial General Intelligence: 4th International Conference, Mountain View, CA, 204–11. Dordrecht: Springer.

Goldin, Dina, Scott A. Smolka, and Peter Wegner, eds. 2006. *Interactive Computation: The New Paradigm.* Dordrecht: Springer.

Huneman, Philippe, ed. 2013. *Function: Selection and Mechanisms.* Dordrecht: Springer.

Kant, Immanuel. 1885. *Introduction to Logic.* London: Longmans, Green & Co.

Lecomte, Alain. 2011. *Meaning, Logic and Ludics.* London: Imperial College.

Mou, Zongsan. 2014. *Late Works of Mou Zongsan: Selected Essays on Chinese Philosophy.* Leiden: Brill Academic Publishers.

Sellars, Wilfrid. 2007. *In the Space of Reasons: Selected Essays of Wilfrid Sellars.* Cambridge, MA: Harvard University Press.

Thom, René. 1983. *Mathematical Models of Morphogenesis.* New York: John Wiley & Sons.

Turing, Alan. 1950. "Computing Machinery and Intelligence." *Mind* 59: 433–60.

NEORATIONALISM

GERMAN IDEALISM

TIME-TRAVEL

BOOTSTRAPPING

COGNITIVE CAPABILITIES

[9]

Loops of Augmentation: Bootstrapping, Time Travel, and Consequent Futures

Ben Woodard

The essay examines the concept of bootstrapping as a model of augmentative reason in contemporary neorationalist philosophies. In particular, it examines the concept of bootstrapping, here meaning mental capacities or processes capable of self-augmentation. Well illustrated in numerous time-travel fictions, the genealogy of bootstrapping lies in the legacy of German Idealism and can be met in the figure of Münchhausen. Looking how the problem of origin, or of determining an ultimately stable ground, is replaced by horizon, or location, both determined through action, the essay proposes that the notions of embodiment and location prove troublesome for neorationalism.

In *Alleys of Your Mind: Augmented Intelligence and Its Traumas,* edited by Matteo Pasquinelli, 157–68. Lüneburg: meson press, 2015.
DOI: 10.14619/014

One of the core concepts of the contemporary neorationalist (and more broadly pragmatist) camp is that of *bootstrapping*—that certain mental capacities or processes are capable of self-augmentation. While less often discussed in philosophical circles in terms of *recursion* (invoking a functionalist or mathematical context), bootstrapping indexes the material consequence of self-augmentation. Whereas recursion is an instance of an object being defined using its own terms (such as, to define recursion, one could say: look up the definition of recursion), bootstrapping assumes that there is an augmentative capacity in the material performing the original act. One instance would be discussing thought as a process of thinking that produces thoughts: this process engenders a massively complex chain of consequences for everything including thought itself. Thinking about thinking can change our thinking.

Bootstrapping bears asking what makes the difference between augmentative and non-augmentative, or *virtuous* versus *vicious* causation—a question which entails further questions about locality and augmentation as neither merely a qualitative nor quantitative treatment of the loop. Such a model of causation engenders in fact a navigational model: *augmentation is neither a more nor a better, but an elsewhere.* Rational augmentation is about going further with thought in a way that has constructive consequences for thought's future capacities and thought's future navigations. This essay attempts to outline and assess the importance of bootstrapping as a synthesis of recursion and augmentation, as well as its preferred illustration via time-travel narratives both in film and in neorationalist philosophy. In closing, I will relate the bootstrapping model of cognition to intelligence as time-manipulation found in Hegel and in more general conceptual aspects of German idealism taken up by Reza Negarestani.

Recursion and Augmentation

Where bootstrapping indicates a mental act informing a self-affecting physical act, a recursive definition seems to operate in one abstract realm. Yet, if this were the case, then recursion would be the same as circularity. But even in this abstract sense, circularity can be avoided in terms of adding values and rules. Vicious circularity, or ill-defined self-recursion, can contain these elements but only produce nested recursion as in the case of a famous line by Douglas Hofstadter (1985, 26):

> This sentence contains ten words, eighteen syllables, and sixty-four letters.

Recursion begins with a ground or base case, material, or world that then goes through a recursive step. A famous example: "Zero is a natural number, and each natural number has a successor, which is also a natural number. Following this base case and recursive rule, one can generate the set of all natural numbers." Bootstrapping then is of course not just self-reference but the utilization of the base case or ground as a process—as a process entailing consequences that it can be added to itself. Thus recursion, and augmentative recursion, appeals to qualifications or rules in order to not merely be repetitions of the same. A related but not altogether different concern is that of medium or location. Recursion, whether vicious or virtuous, has a different set of consequences given the particularity of its medium or context.

Because of the nature of physical systems, and the particularity of instantiation, the repetition of a phrase has different kinds of consequences, at least immediately, than the repetition of a physical gesture, for instance. This is not to trump recursion with the simple reply of "context matters therefore structure does not" but to plant a skeptical seed regarding how determinate augmentation is separable from contextual or environmental augmentation.

At the level of thought however, it is not difficult to imagine how consciousness augments itself through the production of thoughts which do not simply add thoughts to those that have already been produced, but add thoughts that alienate the mind from itself. This alienation is productive in that it expands the capacities of the mind while devaluing the mind as an essence other than as a target of determination, as a thing or selection of content to be looped. Such an articulation appears as unhelpful as it is unavoidable. To ask the question "how do you start thinking?" would set you on a course partially of your choosing but which would have volition caused by an apparently exterior force. Recursion takes place before it is recognized and thus one could argue that augmentation is the turning of this process upon itself, i.e., *augmentation is recursive recursion, or self-aware recursion.*

The desire to appeal to fictions, speculations and simulations (that will be introduced soon) should begin to become clear. Speculations or certain exercises in reflection are a low-cost means of practicing augmentations without concern for context, medium, and minimizing consequences. But since this is how recursion occurs, at what point does that very structure of augmentation shift as it moves across scales? Does the augmentative recursive structure of thought remain as context-independent in its simulations as it does once those simulations are deployed in a particular medium?

Furthermore, while augmentative recursion positively obliterates the shackles of origin, does this unnecessarily risk the veneration or obscuring of limits at broader scales to thinking? Although it is a simplification, one can take the well-known story of Fichte's lectures in which he attempted to assert the irreducibility of the "I" as the necessary starting point of all philosophy. Fichte (1796/99) instructed his audience to look at the wall, then the floor, then to look at the thing that was doing the looking. In illustrating the subject's inability to get behind itself, Fichte hoped to cement his claim that the "I" was the primary point of access for all philosophy. While this is certainly the case for the speculative simulation engine, we can reduce our place in the creation of things in the world to constructively alienate that very capacity. This does not change the experience of that viewing, but it questions the universalization of the medium and location from which the augmentative recursion of self-reflection occurs.

Fichte's example demonstrates the stubbornness of philosophy to admit that its modeling capacities may undo the very grounds that shelter that model from the impacts of its simulations. Time travel becomes a meta-abstraction of this problem with the timeline replacing consciousness in which, because of narrative constraints, self-reflective consciousness itself remains immune to the manipulations made upon the stream of time.

Time Travel as Bootstrapping Simulator

The strangeness of recursion can be illustrated (albeit hyperbolically) in stories of time travel to the past. Robert Heinlein's story "By His Bootstraps" (1941) is one of the more famous examples of the bootstrap paradox. The paradox being if an object is sent to the past and received and brought to the future to where it was sent, then the origin of the object is lost. Similar issues, though not as drastic arise from sending information back (though, one could argue, that both cases materially change the past in such a way that the second law of thermodynamics is violated). A growing amount of mainstream films have examined both stable and unstable time loops. These stable time loops (or augmentative recursions) are probably best known in the movie series *Terminator* (1984–2015). In these movies each attempt to stop the consequences of the future (the traveler's present) actually contribute to that future in that the film's protagonists may change the date of the catastrophic future event, but this event nevertheless always occurs. Otherwise put, the *Terminator* series is ambiguous as to whether the reason why judgment day or the rise of a malevolent artificial intelligence has *always already* happened because of the structure of time (i.e., fate can only be postponed not canceled) or because such an event is a historical inevitability.

The past, taken as a process to be manipulated, is added to the future that always was but, from the perspective of the manipulator, events seem to occur in a generally novel way. In this sense, origin becomes a moot point at least when considered in a material sense. It is the exploration of the consequences that ultimately matters in bootstrapping rather than determining the limits of the capability to manipulate. Exploration would require determining the coherent limits of the loop's boundary or the field of manipulation or, the degree to which one explores before turning onto that process of exploration to augment it. That is, at some point the time traveler has to decide what variables to take into account in order to change the future, changes the traveler can only then register by going back to the future. By remaining too local, the manipulation of the processes of thought is safer but more myopic (such as in the case of the film *Primer*, 2004) and altering the past too much may very well lead to the opposite problem. In *Primer,* a group of friends discovers how to travel twenty minutes back in time. One of the film's characters decides to use this to socially engineer the present by recording conversations and by giving his past self-advantageous information.

The problem of origin, or determining an ultimately stable ground, is replaced by horizon, or location, which are determined through action. Hence, this is why Schelling, who studied under Fichte but broke away from him over the latter's dismissal of material nature, denies that there is any singular material origin as such: There is no seed corn from which all things spring. What's interesting here is that in stories of time loops, whether stable or unstable, thought is an exception or a process which is minimally material in such a way that the recording of past loops is not seen as a thermodynamic violation. In the film *Edge of Tomorrow* (2014), the iterations of the loops is retained even after it is closed (because of an absorption of alien biology). In the film, a military officer is exposed to the blood of a temporally-altering alien species and relives the same day of a doomed battle over, and over again. His death resets the day, and he alone retains the memories of what happened, in order to attempt various strategies to end the war. But an interesting tension of the film, despite and because of its repetition, is in the question of how many iterations the protagonist has gone through before the iteration we see treated as if it is novel. The film constantly shifts the parameters of self-augmentation while it openly displays the repetition of certain events as leading to the main character's honing of his combat abilities. At other times it is obfuscated whether, and how many times, painful or banal scenes have already occurred to him.

The film *Source Code* (2011) isolates consciousness in a similar fashion, which is why it was discussed by Grant (2011) at the opening of his talk entitled "The Natural History of the Mind." In the film, the creators of a time travel device believe they are sending a consciousness back in time (into another person's body) when they are in fact creating an alternate universe as the addition or supplanting of the consciousness alters the actuality into another future. In this sense, it is somewhat ambiguous whether they are stating that time travel is impossible or if even the addition of consciousness to a past leads to a branching theory of time travel, and the universe is redirected. Grant takes this as an illustration of idealism's advantage over realism, namely, that idealism is not opposed to realism but emphasizes the reality of the idea.

But how do these speculative exercises relate to neorationalism? If there is a binding theme between the pragmatism of Charles S. Pierce, Robert Brandom, Mark Wilson etc. and the futural or accelerationist tendencies of Reza Negarestani, Nick Srnicek, Alex Williams, Peter Wolfendale and others, it is the willingness to treat the past as material to be transformed and augmented to create a future. While pragmatism is often decried for being insufficiently radical, accelerationism, is decried for forgetting the present for the sake of the future. A certain amount of philosophical discomfort arises following both projects' admitting the open manipulation of the past in constructing a future. All philosophy is grave-robbery but while some projects display these spoils as already relevant consequences in and of themselves, for neorationalism and accelerationism, it is far better to play Dr. Frankenstein, to treat the past as materials for something else altogether.

The playing out of consequences takes on a different function, since we have no knowledge of the future but only meta-cognitive rules and operations to check our explorations and navigations according to our capacities and wagers (as opposed to origins and ends). The interesting tension is how conceptually determined capacities and wagers are from the point at which we find ourselves, a point which is of course arbitrary but only before we admit that our self-augmentation took serious hold of its place. This strange place, this alienated home, is how Reza Negarestani recently opened his talk "What Philosophy Does to the Mind":

> The ideal aim of philosophizing is to become reflectively at home in the full complexity of the multi-dimensional conceptual system in terms of which we suffer, think, and act. I say "reflectively" because there is a sense in which, by the sheer fact of leading an unexamined, but conventionally satisfying life, we are at home in this complexity. It is not until we have eaten the apple with which the serpent philosopher tempts us, that we begin to stumble on the familiar and to feel that haunting sense of alienation which is treasured by each new generation as its unique possession. This alienation, this gap between oneself and one's world, can only be resolved by eating the apple to the core; for after the first bite there is no return to innocence. There are many anodynes, but only one cure. We may philosophize well or ill, but we must philosophize. (Sellars 1975, 295)

Time travel, as a genre, attempts to reconcile the arrow of time and our non-linear experiences of time or, what appear as asymmetrical forces of causation, our ignorance of those causes, and our powers of manipulation over the future and the past. Nick Land's short piece *Templexity* argues that this reconciliation demonstrates that the very notion of travel is a misnomer, and states that one should focus on templexity. Templexity is indistinguishable from real recursion and is the auto-productive nature of time as general entropic dissipation (Land 2014, 4). However, as Land notes, negentropic exceptions appear as local productivities; life for instance is a highly complex and productive instance of chaos which would seem to run against the general wave of cosmological decay or statistic flattening. But, as Land emphasizes, negentropy is just a case of uneven distribution and not physical exception. Though, as is evident in both his past and present works, Land is less concerned with tracing the physical consequences of loops and more interested in how loops as fictions come to have a life of their own. Land is less interested in the kind of augmentation that takes place and more in how loops or recursion pass from an ideal to a real state (if such division can be held to begin with, i.e., if the ideal can be taken to be the future, which has not yet returned to the present).

One must be careful in establishing a correlation between positive and negative feedback and virtuous and vicious circles too quickly. Since both virtuousness and viciousness are augmentative, they can both be viewed as having positive feedback qualities: in that both are additive it is only that viciousness and virtuousness are qualitative judgments made from a position exterior to the cycles themselves. It is this making real that manifests as a problem for neorationalism, albeit in a different register, one that the simulations of time travel hyperbolically illustrate (particularly given the destruction of origin and the importance of self-manipulation as augmentation).

Consequent Futures

The philosophical and political relevance of a future to be constructed is central to the work of neorationalism as well as its more recent political and theoretical alliances (whether accelerationist, transmodernist, Promethean, or xenofeminist). Instead of an equivocation of futurity and inevitability, Negarestani and Wolfendale assert that the future is a positive project in the sense that one should neither admit to a present merely of better failures, nor to a past of genealogical guilt, but to an operable progressiveness. Given this it is not unsurprising that for Negarestani (2014) and Wolfendale (2010), Hegel's model of history and of the development of self-consciousness as a historical project, is central to pursuing a universalist notion of reason that attempts to be directed towards the future.

As Rory Jeffs (2012) notes, the importance of temporality in Hegel has been repeatedly emphasized, particularly in its early French reception (by Kojève and Koyre) through the present with figures such as Catherine Malabou and Slavoj Žižek. Across these readings a tension exists between the restlessness or productivity of time, and the thinkability of time, requiring its stoppage or flattening out via "the end of history." As Jeffs demonstrates, Hegel's temporality is taken to be ontological primordial for Koyre, whereas it is collective and anthropological for Kojève. Malabou attempts to navigate between constructed time and flatly navigated history in highlighting plasticity, as a means of attempting to discern the present import of the *to come*, or *what we will see*. However, I would argue that in *The Future of Hegel*, Malabou (2004) repeats the strange dualism that Kojève constructed with Hegel's system in order to separate the human from nature or philosophy from science.

In many senses Negarestani's reading of Hegel maintains a duality but in a methodological or non-absolute sense following his Sellarsian commitments. Thus while Negarestani takes up the socially constructed aspect of Kojève's reading as determining the path of time, Negarestani would not locate this determination primarily in terms of mutual recognition but in the augmentation or inhumanization of time via reason. Negarestani de-phenomenologizes the Kojèvean reading and reforms it to resemble a more Koyrean or Wahlian perspective. In essence Negarestani re-subjectifies the Hegelian construction of reason but via an inhuman notion of the subject.[1] Negarestani approaches this version of Hegelianism in his text "Labor of the Inhuman" by arguing for a particular reading of destiny. He writes:

> Destiny expresses the reality of time as always in excess of and asymmetrical to origin; in fact, as catastrophic to it. But destination is not exactly a single point or a terminal goal, it takes shape as trajectories: As soon as a manifest destination is reached or takes place, it ceases to govern the historical trajectory that leads to it, and is replaced by a number of newer destinations which begin to govern different parts of the trajectory, leading to its ramification into multiple trajectories. (Negarestani 2014a, 451)

In further articulating the functional aspect of this revisable destiny, Negarestani examines his own relation to Hegel (as well as Kant and Sellars). Following Hegel, Negarestani (2014a, 454) argues that reason requires its own constitutive self-determination. Contrary to Hegel, he states that normativity is not composed of explicit norms from the bottom up (Negarestani 2014a, 455). To follow Hegel too closely in regards to explicit norms (as opposed to the utilization of interventional norms) would be to ignore the regress in the setting up of norms as self-standing, of being the norm "just because." Thus Negarestani points out another layer of recursive loops, that of question begging versus non-question begging. Hegel's reliance on explicit norms begs the question since the proper augmentation which would distance the premise from the conclusion is absent. Generally, the difficulty for Negarestani and the neorationalist project is how to grant reason its "proper autonomy" without appearing to be making reason immune from non-reasonable egress in such a way that is, at its root, unreasonable or question begging. Negarestani's answer is to combine pragmatism and functionalism, arguing that the linguistic decomposition of thought, and the rational decomposition of nature, lead

---

1   One can also observe similarities between Negarestani's emphasis on the future operating on the past in Hegel and Jean Hyppolite's discussion of the future healing the past (see Hyppolite 1974, 525).

to a relation of thinking and doing that is gradual yet universally revisionary (Negarestani 2014a, 456).

While Negarestani argues that philosophy invents its own history in a particularly Hegelian vein, the essential difference between Hegel and Schelling's model of time, is that the act of invention, the act of self-augmentation, uproots in a way that the view, the new horizon viewed, cannot be separated from history materialized. This is not to suggest, *pace* Žižek's (1997) reading of Schelling, that thought or will interrupts the ontological structure of the world or of nature. Instead, the act made possible through that particular material world never fundamentally interrupts it, but re-orients it from that particular view. That is, the unknowability of the ultimate source of the re-orientation does not destroy reason. It indicates that experience is not the base of reason but that experience always escorts reason. As Schelling puts it in *The Grounding of Positive Philosophy*:

> Reason wants nothing other than its original content. This original content, however, possesses in its immediacy something contingent, which is and is not the immediate capacity to be; like-wise, being—the essence—as it immediately presents itself in reason, is and is not being. It is not being as soon as it moves, since it then transforms itself into a contingent being. (Schelling 2007, 134)

Nature is not a solid ground or that which trumps self-augmentation for Schelling, but a slower and more stubborn effect on the horizon viewed from the perspective of the thinker. The difference between Hegel and Schelling becomes that of setting the formers' confidence in the amount of conceptual determination possible from one perspective, whereas for the latter, change in a position requires more attention to the ground one is standing (admitting that ground's synthesis) as well as recognizing the high cost of shifting positions.

Otherwise put, Schelling errs on the side of analyzing the non-predicative weight of predication by which it functions, whereas Hegel further solidifies the future perspective and risks over-conceptually determining the past and the present. As Negarestani put it in the talk quoted above, philosophy refuses to close the loop of its revenge against belief, against over-grounding. Again, Schelling worries about the labor of keeping the loop open where Hegel attempts to hold the circle (the loop) open till the last instance.

In this regard, and to return to self-augmentation, the essential difference between Schelling and Hegel is the height from which both descend to redraw the perspective from which reason is working. Hegel reaches perhaps greater heights with the assistance of conceptual certainty (powered by negativity) before descending in order to redraw the reasoner; whereas in keeping experience alongside reason, Schelling makes structural wagers leaving experience to judge conceptual ones in that particular view. In other words, Schelling emphasizes the local extrapolation, whereas Hegel emphasizes the global decomposition. If philosophy is a time-travel device (as Negarestani puts it), then the different approaches to the relation of past to future, or the pragmatic and the speculative, is the locality chosen when one steps into the time machine.

Conclusion

At a dinner party in early nineteenth century Berlin, Madame du Stael was speaking to Fichte. Fichte was hurriedly attempting to explain his philosophy of the "I" to her in a language that was not his own. After outlining his philosophy, Stael responded that she completely understood, and that his philosophy of the absolute "I" could be explained through the figure of Baron von Münchhausen. In one story, in order to cross a river, Münchhausen grabbed his own sleeve and jumped over himself to cross the water (see Biennerhassett 2013, 82).

The image of bootstrapping, on the other hand, is often tied to the episode in which Münchhausen famously pulled himself out of the swamp by his own hair. Furthermore, the Münchhausen or Agrippean trilemma has been put forward by Paul Franks (2007) as the central philosophical problem to which German Idealism responds.

The trilemma consists of three problems of justifying reason's capacities (or more generally any kind of knowledge) with three equally unsatisfactory options: circularity (or that every consequent leads back to its antecedent), regression (that for every step, every consequent requires infinitely more proofs) and axiom (we make a common sense justification to what we are claiming to know as an axiom). This trilemma centers on the justification theory of knowledge, and it articulates thought as a disembodied and dematerialized activity. But just as an explicit notion of norms functioning from the bottom up begs the question, a notion of materiality or embodiment threatens to be even more vague, and this is why embodiment should be thought of in terms of location, of the local interpretation of deeper nested levels of materiality.

In the same way, the figure of Münchhausen is not merely a critique of all appeal to bootstrapping as ideal or non-embodied; it points out that even virtuous circularity often elides the question of embodiment by relegating it to the space of nature as determined by the sciences alone. However, this dismissal of the space of reason leads often to a reliance upon the given over against any notion of augmentation (scientific or rational or otherwise). As Brassier writes in "Prometheanism and its Critics":

> Since cognitive objectivation is conditioned by human existence, human beings cannot know themselves in the same way in which they know other objects. Doing so would require objectivating the condition of objectivation, which would be, as Arendt says, like trying to jump over our own shadow. (Brassier 2014, 476)

Following Arendt's Heideggerian trajectory, Brassier goes on to argue that anti-Prometheanism attempts to defend an unalterable human essence: Those who would claim that the human is alterable are, like Fichte, erasing the difference between the made and the given (or more widely between the ideal and the real) to beg skeptical reproach. In questioning but not destroying or deconstructing the bootstrap logic here, I am—against Arendt—stressing the importance of the embodiment that accompanies the leap, and not the impossibility of the leap itself away from the given.

Here, it is not the augmentative capacities of looping that are in question, but how one explains and understands the ramifications of the point of entry (what in the fictional stories and films mentioned above would be the seemingly impossible advent of the machine as well as the egregious amounts of energy needed to generate the beginning of the temporal journey). Thus, while I agree to the limitations of instrumentality, which Heidegger himself endorsed, these are not due to a particular limit of human access to the human, but due to a skeptical and naturalistic monism; whereas constraints of location and energetic expenditure are not human specific, i.e., not a form of particular human finitude. At the same time, the bootstrap logic applies a particular form of skepticism to the skeptical response, specifically to human capacities: Our location, or perspectival "closeness" to our own capacities, blinds us destructively and constructively, as we attempt to explain our rare (if not unique) cognitive capabilities, this explanation itself actively unfolds those capacities.

Schelling's focus on the measuring of consequents or on futures by their consequents is an attempt to de-relativize context which, viewed from the other side, could be taken as naturalizing the *trans-*, of attempting to identify the cost of navigation, and of having perspectives. This cost is not to be taken as either ontological finitude or as a reason to halt all constructive movement, but as an endorsement of the necessity and instability of ground, and the necessity and insufficiency of navigation. By Schelling's account, and against much contemporary dogma, idealism is the simultaneous simulation and deployment of the consequences of bootstrap logic that is fully embodied in a material nature.

References

Biennerhassett, Charlotte. 2013. *Madame de Stael: Her Friends, and her influence in Politics and Literature*. Cambridge, UK: Cambridge Academic Press.

Brassier, Ray. 2014. "Prometheanism and Its Critics." In *#Accelerate: The Accelerationist Reader*, edited by Robin Mackay, 467–488. Falmouth, UK: Urbanomic Media.

Fichte, Johann Gottlieb. (1798/99) 1992. *Foundations of Transcendental Philosophy: Wissenschaftlehre nova methodo*. Edited and translated by David Breazeale. Ithaca, NY: Cornell University Press.

Franks, Paul. 2007. *All or Nothing: Systematicity, Transcendental Arguments, and Skepticism in German Idealism*. Cambridge, MA: Harvard University Press.

Grant, Iain Hamilton. 2011. "Philosophy and the Natural History of the Mind." Talk at the Human Experience and Nature conference, Royal Institute of Philosophy, UWE, Bristol. http://www.youtube.com/watch?v=jJd1RSAoWv4.

Heinlein, Robert. 1941. "By His Bootstraps." *Astounding Science-Fiction* (October).

Hofstadter, Douglas. 1985. *Metamagical Themas: Questing of Mind and Pattern*. New York: Basic Books.

Hyppolite, Jean. 1974. *Genesis and Structure of Hegel's Phenomenology of Spirit*. Evanston: Northwestern University Press.

Jeffs, Rory. 2012. "The Future of the Future: Koyré, Kojève, and Malabou Speculate on Hegelian Time," *Parrhesia* 15: 35–53.

Land, Nick. 2014. *Templexity: Disordered Loops through Shanghai Time*. Urbanatomy Electronic, Kindle Edition.

Malabou, Catherine. 2004. *The Future of Hegel: Plasticity, Temporality, and Dialectic*. New York: Routledge.

Negarestani, Reza. 2014a. "The Labor of the Inhuman." In *#Accelerate: The Accelerationist Reader*, edited by Robin Mackay, 425–466. Falmouth, UK: Urbanomic Media.

Negarestani, Reza. 2014b. "What Philosophy Does to the Mind." Talk presented at Glass Bead, 22 April 2014, New York.

Schelling, Friedrich Wilhelm Joseph von. 2007. *The Grounding of Positive Philosophy*. Translated by Bruce Matthews. Albany: State University of New York Press.

Sellars, Wilfrid. 1975. "The Structure of Knowledge (The Matchette Foundation Lectures for 1971 at the University of Texas)." In *Action, Knowledge, and Reality: Studies in Honor of Wilfrid Sellars*, edited by Hector-Neri Castañeda, 295–347. Indianapolis: Bobbs-Merrill.

Wolfendale, Peter. (2010). "Essay on Trascendental Realism." Manuscript. http://www.academia.edu/1146988/Essay_on_Transcendental_Realism.

Žižek, Slavoj. 1997. "The Abyss of Freedom." In Slavoj Žižek and Friedrich Wilhelm Joseph von Schelling. *The Abyss of Freedom*. Ann Arbor: University of Michigan Press.

Filmography

Edge of Tomorrow. 2014. Directed by Doug Liman. USA: Warner Brothers.

Primer. 2004. Directed by Shane Carruth. USA: Shane Carruth.

Source Code. 2011. Directed by Duncan Jones. USA: Summit Entertainment.

Terminator 2. 1991. Directed by James Cameron. USA: Artisan Home Entertainment.

PART III:
THE MATERIALISM OF
THE SOCIAL BRAIN

NEUROPHILOSOPHY

NEURONORMATIVITY

MATERIALISM

NATURALISM

VYGOTSKY

Brain Theory Between Utopia and Dystopia: Neuronormativity Meets the Social Brain

Charles T. Wolfe

The brain in its plasticity and inherent "sociality" can be proclaimed and projected as a revolutionary organ. Far from the old reactions which opposed the authenticity of political theory and praxis to the dangerous naturalism of "cognitive science" (with images of men in white coats, the RAND Corporation or military LSD experiments), recent decades have shown us some of the potentiality of the *social brain* (Vygotsky, Negri, and Virno). Is the brain somehow inherently a utopian topos? If in some earlier papers I sought to defend naturalism against these reactions, here I consider a new challenge: the recently emerged disciplines of *neuronormativity*, which seek in their own way to overcome the nature-normativity divide. This is the task of a materialist brain theory today.

In *Alleys of Your Mind: Augmented Intellligence and Its Traumas,* edited by Matteo Pasquinelli, 173–84. Lüneburg: meson press, 2015.
DOI: 10.14619/014

The Setup: Horns of a Dilemma

There is a lingering zone of what one might think of as sore cognitive muscle tissue in the area of materialism. It is an area of both contested territory and in some cases, a kind of pathos of distance of the "Ugh! Keep that thing away from me!" sort. I have in mind the combination of materialism as an emancipatory socio-political project (which need not be construed in strictly Marx-Engels terms, if we think of Lucretius et al.) and as a cold-hearted "spontaneous philosophy of the men in white coats," e.g., nefarious neurophilosophers. Faced with this rather massive alternative, this choice between two projects, I have stubbornly been saying since some discussions with Negri in the late 90s,[1] we should choose: both! And for people steeped in a Germanic tradition, I can push the following familiar button and say, "this is also about ceasing to take for granted a distinction between Natur- and Geisteswissenschaften (i.e., the natural sciences and the humanities)." If the brain is always already social, as even Marx states (Virno 2001), this implies, although not with necessary implicature, that knowledge of the brain is not irrelevant to knowledge of the social world.[2] No absolute divide between a hermeneutical world of free, self-interpreting subjects with their values, norms, and struggles, and a natural world of quantities, electroencephalograms, "men in white coats" and so-called "science."

But even this choice of both, in which the brain is, now a naturalistic object of study like a liver or a lung, now a political object (dual-aspect?), leads us, like a gamer-agent in a virtual world, into further pathways with further choices of which doors to go through. For the brain is frequently presented both as a potential site and substance of radical transformation—a utopian form of "wonder tissue," a "difference machine," an "uncertain system," and, quite symmetrically, as the focus and resource of consumer neuroscience, semiocapital[3] or neurocapitalism. It's a bit like the old chestnut about the saving power lying where the greatest danger is,[4] except the other way round. Indeed, regarding the fields of neuronormativity, Slaby and Gallagher have recently observed that "the particular construal of self currently championed by social neuroscience—with a focus on social-interactive skills, low-level empathy and mind-reading—neatly corresponds with the ideal skill profile of today's corporate employee" (Slaby and Gallagher 2014).

1   See Negri's rather subtle comments on forms of materialism, from the more naturalistic to the more political, in the original Italian preface to *Alma Venus* (Negri 2000).
2   See Wolfe 2010. The "general productive forces of the social brain" appears in Marx's *Grundrisse*, notebooks VI-VII, a text known as the "Fragment on Machines" (Marx 1973, 694) which has had particular influence on the Italian Autonomist tradition (see also Virno 2001).
3   Franco Berardi's term for our world of "post-Fordist modes of production" (see Terranova 2014).
4   "Wo aber Gefahr ist, wächst/Das Rettende auch" (Hölderlin, "Patmos," 1803).

This brain dilemma is not exactly the opposition between the natural and the normative, with natural as a loose association of positions which have a lack of fear of "science" or "naturalism" in common, since they consider a continuum of theorizing social and political action, for instance, in light of knowledge of the structure of the affects: a conglomerate in which Vygotskyan conceptions of brain and society, Negri's conceptions of general intellect and social brain, and loosely political versions of neurophilosophy come together. Here, the naturalist position asserts that the brain is social and material (and that this combination is potentially emancipatory), whereas the normative position, like Cassandra, warns of danger.[5] For this kind of denunciation can come not from old style humanistic Marxism, but from farther left, as with Tiqqun's piece of learned, paranoid critique of the dangers of "the cybernetic hypothesis" (Tiqqun 2001).[6]

Faced with this kind of knee-jerk, or is it die-hard, anti-cognitivism, one could respond by reassuring the interlocutor: no, *tovarich*, I may read the neurophilosophers Churchlands (1986, 2002) but my heart is in the right place. One can also suggest that such a critique is a kind of paleo-Marxism, not up to date with immaterial and cognitive turns. I might suggest more broadly a classic "divide and conquer" move: what would the anti-cognitivist say about a thinker like Guattari, who denied, "as opposed to a thinker such as Heidegger," that "the machine is something which turns us away from being"?

> I think that the machinic phyla are agents productive of being. They make us enter into what I call an ontological heterogenesis. . . . The whole question is knowing how the enunciators of technology, including biological, aesthetic, theoretical, machines, etc., are assembled, of refocusing the purpose of human activities on the production of subjectivity or collective assemblages of subjectivity. (Guattari 2011, 50)

Biological, aesthetic and we might add, *cerebral machines* are constitutive parts of the production of subjectivity, rather than its "other."

Yet perhaps the suspicion towards cognitivism is not just dogmatic, 1950s humanist Marxism, even if it has its "knee-jerk" moments. We can see this if we now turn to a new case, that of the emergent but already popular disciplines of neuronormativity. If we seek to achieve some critical distance towards these disciplines, it does not mean we are reverting to the anti-naturalism I have discussed above. That is, we are no longer in a 1980s-style opposition between humanists like Ricoeur or Habermas, and neuroscientists/

5   On the anecdotal level, I recall some people warning the Multitudes mailing list in the early 2000s that I, the moderator, was a danger (perhaps a RAND Corporation agent?) because I was participating in a meeting on *brains!*

6   Those who attended the *Psychopathologies of Cognitive Capitalism* conference at the ICI in Berlin in March 2013 could hear Maurizio Lazzarato's denunciation of "cognitivism" and "science."

propagandists like Changeux (see e.g., Changeux and Ricoeur 2002); we are now faced with the rise of the "neuro"-disciplines.

Neurohumanities and Neuronormativity

The prefix neuro- has become ubiquitous in numerous scientific and loosely scientific disciplines, offering as it does a surplus of concrete, supposedly experimentally substantiated *brain explanations* for various hotly debated phenomena (from punishment and free will to gender and economic decision-making). But as Jan De Vos has observed, this trend has led to a doubly unfortunate effect: the weakening of the relation of any of these projects to actual neuroscience, and the weakening of the discipline of which they are the "neuro" version (De Vos 2014; see also Ortega and Vidal 2011). De Vos quotes Matthew Taylor, a British Labour Party activist and government adviser under Tony Blair, who claimed that insights from neurological research offered a more solid base "than previous attempts to move beyond left and right" (Taylor 2009). To the 1980s-type fascination with "my brain is my self," the last decade has responded with a particularly vacuous version of a social turn, conveyed in a variety of expressions, from "neurocapitalism" and "neuropolitics" to the possibility of neuro-enhanced individuals possessing a "neuro-competitive advantage" (Lynch 2004; Schmitz 2014).

One problem would be the potentially illusory character of such promised developments. But another problem is in a sense the exact opposite, namely, if neuro-enhancement is real, what about "the freedom to remain unenhanced" in a context where schools, in a country we don't need to name, are coercing parents to medicate their children for attention dysfunction (Farah 2005, 37)? Or, to mention a different example, treatments for dementia will most likely lead to drugs that increase mnemonic recollection or recall in normal brains as well: would using this drug cross an ethical line from acceptable medical treatments to unacceptable cognitive enhancements if given to members of the general population (Bickle and Hardcastle 2012)? An even stronger embrace of "neurolaw" is, for instance, in a recent essay on "The significance of psychopaths for ethical and legal reasoning" by Hirstein and Sifferd (2014). If positron emission tomography (PET) studies have already shown that some convicted murderers have significantly attenuated functioning in their prefrontal cortex (a region known to be involved in cognitive control and planning), it is an open book for jurists to plead attenuated responsibility in terms of prior cerebral dispositions. But they take the reasoning one step further, focusing on the specific case of psychopaths and their diminished sense of moral empathy or responsibility. Hirstein and Sifferd effectively argue that the courts need to be practicing "neurolaw" in order to monitor psychopathic prisoners more closely. Somewhere here there is also the danger of so-called *brain-realism*. As per Dumit (2003, see also De Vos ms. and Schmitz 2014), our society seems to place increased weight on brain data compared with other kinds of data. A legal concern is that brain scans and other pieces of such information will somehow trump other evidence in legal proceedings (Gordijn and Giordano 2010, discussed in Bickle and Hardcastle 2012).

So, thinking back to my embracing answer "both!" at the beginning to the question: emancipatory materialism or handing ourselves over to men or robots in white coats? Must this "both!" bear the combined masks of the neuro-adviser to Tony Blair and that of the philosophers recommending that courts practice "neurolaw"? As you may guess, my answer is "no," or rather "niet," with Soviet accent.

Two Materialisms = Two Brain Theories

Brains are culturally sedimented, permeated in their material architecture by our culture, history, and social organization; and this sedimentation is itself reflected in cortical architecture, as first clearly argued perhaps by the brilliant Soviet neuropsychologist Lev Vygotsky in the early twentieth century. A major figure in fields including social psychology, developmental psychology and a kind of heretical Marxism (but one not afraid to invoke the brain), Vygotsky strongly emphasized the embeddedness of the brain in the social world, arguing that there may even be evidence of consequences in our central nervous system derived from early social interaction, so that past experience is embodied in synaptic modifications. As his younger collaborator Alexander Luria put it, "Social history ties the knots that produce new correlations between certain zones of the cerebral cortex" (Luria 2002, 22).[7] Less dramatically stated, in a recent summary by the cognitive archaeologist Lambros Malafouris: "Our minds and brains are (potentially) subject to constant change and alteration caused by our ordinary developmental engagement with cultural practices and the material world" (Malafouris 2010): a good definition of cultural-cerebral plasticity. Notice that this is materialism *sensu stricto*, as it is a description of the properties of brains; but it is not on the restrictively naturalist side of the Churchland-type neurophilosophical program (naturalism is a fairly open-ended set of programs, some of which are more open onto the social than others). In this more restrictive picture, naturalism begins to resemble scientism, in the sense that the promise is made for science to replace philosophy:

> It would seem that the long reign of the philosopher as the professional in charge of the mind-body problem is finally coming to its end. Just as has happened in the lifetime of most of us in the case of the origins of the universe which used to be a theological problem and is now an astronomical

7   Iriki 2009 is a recent comparable illustration of this.

one, so the mind-body problem is about to pass from the grasp of the philosopher into that of the neuropsychologist. (Place 1997, 16)

Instead, the mind-brain materialism of Vygotsky is both less passive and less mechanistic. For him, "History, changing the human type, depends on the cortex; the new socialist man will be created through the cortex; upbringing is in general an influence upon the cortex."[8] In this sense it is not a *scientism* or a denial of the symbolic and valuative dimensions of life. Following the helpful and suggestive response of John Sutton and Lyn Tribble to Hawkes' claims that materialism will destroy the symbolic, valuative, representational content in literature, materialism need not claim that "only matter exists," but that it is instead "firmly pluralist" in its ontologies.

> Even if all the things that exist supervene on or are realized in matter, the materialist can still ascribe full-blown reality to tables and trees and tendons and toenails and tangos and tendencies"; an account including the brain need not exclude "memories, affects, beliefs, imaginings, dreams, decisions, and the whole array of psychological phenomena of interest to literary, cultural, and historical theorists. (Sutton and Tribble 2011)

The materialism of the "cultured brain" (as in Vygotsky or recent work in cognitive archaeology on tools and cognition, Iriki 2009) is very much of this sort: it integrates the brain and the affects, cerebral architecture, and our aptitude to produce fictions, etc. But notice that it is not enough to rebut these visions of a cold, dead materialism seizing living value, sentiment and meaning in its embrace and reducing them to piles of inert matter. For just as there is bad neuronormativity and a more positive sense of the social brain, we must be careful to separate the cultured brain concept from "neuro-aesthetics" which claims to integrate materialism, brain science and art but in the flattest way:

> I picture a future for writing that dispenses with mystery wherever it can, that embraces the astounding strides in thought-organ research. Ideally, a future where neuroimaging both miniaturizes and becomes widespread, augmenting the craft of authors, critics, agents and publishing houses. (Walter 2012)

Note that I have slipped into discussion of forms of materialism (and their relation to brains), perhaps unconsciously adopting the posture of the philosopher. A different but complementary way of evaluating the more restrictive version of the neurophilosophical claims would be to look at precisely their *twenty-first century* outcomes, namely, claims from cognitive neuroscience and its extensions to deal with new areas like ethics, the law and the rest of

8   Vygotsky, *Pedologija Podrotska*. Moscow, 1929. Quoted in van der Veer and Valsiner 1991, 320. Further discussion in Wolfe 2010.

"neurohumanities." This is what "critical neuroscience" does (see Choudhury and Slaby 2012).

As its name indicates, the critical neuroscience program aims in part to criticize current developments, particularly in cognitive neuroscience (Choud-hury, Nagel, and Slaby 2009, 73). This can include the already-familiar social critique of our fascination with brain imaging (fMRI, etc.), the newer critique of "brain-centric" explanations of personhood, agency, and moral life, and also, scientifically informed challenges to exaggerated, perhaps even ideological reports of neuroscientific findings in popular media (including in the neuropo-litical sphere, as discussed below), but also in fields such as the "neurohuman-ities." Just as we are often confronted with bogus neuroscientific explanations in political decision-making or religious belief, similarly, certain current forms of neuro-aesthetic discourse will seek to augment literary scholarship by tell-ing us that in reading literary prose, "the line 'he had leathery hands' has just stimulated your sensory cortex in a way 'he had rough hands' can never hope to" (Walter 2012).

Conclusion

We have witnessed a series of tensions, most classically between a kind of Marx-Heidegger humanism and a purported brain science, and more interest-ingly, between two visions of socially embedded, plastic brains, namely that of Tony Blair's advisor versus the Vygotskian "socialist cortex," i.e., the brain as potential Communist *caisse de résonance*. Similar but not identical to the latter opposition would be that between current discourses of neuronormativity, and the Vygotsky-Negri line in which brain science is not merely facilitating a state of socio-political status quo, but is potentially destabilizing.

The same applies to the opposition between types of materialism, in which the latter, more plastic variety also embraces "cultured brain" materialism. One can think of the Baldwin effect (in which cultural/linguistic evolution com-bines with Darwinian evolution). The Baldwin effect is very close, in fact, to the promise of the social brain, namely, that "the human cerebral cortex [is] an organ of civilization in which are hidden boundless possibilities" (Luria 2002, 22)[9] and of course also to Deleuze's "neuroaesthetic" vision in which "creating new circuits in art means creating them in the brain" (1995, 60). This Baldwin-Vygotsky-Deleuze vision is tantamount to saying, to use Negri's words, that "*Geist* is the brain." Negri is deliberately being provocative with regard to the

9   Luria is glossing on Vygotsky (1997), whose last, posthumously published work, "Psy-chology and the Localization of Mental Functions" explicitly aimed to investigate the functional organization of the brain as the organ of consciousness (Luria 2002, 23). The development of new "functional organs" occurs through the development of new *functional systems*, which is a means for the unlimited development of cerebral activity (Luria 2002 19, 22).

German "hermeneutical" tradition, although his interests lie less in the realm of the social brain, and more towards a politics of affects (Negri 1995, 98). That properties of *Geist* such as its interpretive capacity, its social and intersubjective dimension, are in fact properties of the brain means—and I wish to insist on this point—that these are not just accounts of *interaction* between two *distinct* entities or fields of activity (e.g., brain and society, brain and symbolic relations, nature and freedom, etc.), nor an insistence that what matters is strictly the world of language in which we live, irreducible to the brain understood as a passive machine.

A question left unspoken, but somehow present here, is: does the "social brain" materialist have to grant special ontological status to the brain? Does she have to hold, in the terms of "brain theorists" Thomas Metzinger and Vittorio Gallese (2003, 549) that "the brain possesses an ontology too"? In the sense that, just as a theorist of cultural plasticity integrates more levels of analysis than a theorist of plasticity of the neural networks of the young rat, similarly, the social-brain materialist might allow for a richer account of what is specific about the brain in a materialist universe, compared to a mechanistic materialist or other, flatter forms of ontology, where there can be no "special zones." For materialism *sensu* the identity theorist Place (1997) or his colleague Smart (1959), the brain does not have an ontology. There is physics, and anything above (both biology and neuroscience) is like a special kind of radio engineering (Smart 1959, 142). In contrast, in Sutton's (2011) fluidity of animal spirits or Diderot's description of the brain as "the book which reads itself," it does. But how can materialism maintain that the brain has an ontology without reintroducing "kingdoms within kingdoms" (in Spinoza's celebrated way of describing the belief he challenged, that there were special laws and properties of human nature, different from the laws of nature as a whole)? One eloquent statement of how an interest in such plasticity can support an occasionally excessive claim for a kind of special ontological status is Victoria Pitts-Taylor's critique of such a "wonder tissue" vision of the brain, as transcendental *potentia* or biopolitical monster (to use a phrase of Negri's):

> The brain not only appears to us (through neuroscientific revelations) to be ontologically open to shaping, but (if the theory is right) it is always already actively shaped and shaping. Thus plasticity cannot be seen as an ontological condition captured, or not, by capital, or as a biological fact to be freed from social and cultural ones. (Pitts-Taylor 2010, 648)[10]

10   Pitts-Taylor's more general observation about the appeal of the concept of plasticity is worth citing: "For a number of scholars in a range of fields, plasticity offers the possibility of taking up the biological matter of the body while defying biological determinism. For sociologists of the body and medicine who have been looking for ways to overcome the limitations of social constructionism, brain plasticity appears to present the material body in a way that opens up, rather than closes down, sociocultural accounts of embodied subjectivity. In psychology, plasticity may offer those opposed to materialist views

If we over-ontologise the brain in order to not be mystical dualists or knee-jerk anti-scientists, we may also run the risk of reconfiguring humanity as just "a cerebral crystallization" (Deleuze and Guattari 1991, 197),[11] not unlike the way recent continental mystagogies of the brain in which "the frontier between the empirical and the transcendental is "deconstructed" within the materiality of the brain" (Williams 2013).

The other remaining question, which I have mentioned several times, is: if brain and politics are not two opposed spheres, does this have an emancipatory potential? The brain's *potentia* against the rule-concept of *potestas* (the immanent and constitutive essence of a living being that desires what is good for its being, versus power as the transcendent power of command assumed by rulers). In similar tones Pasquinelli (2014, 298) approvingly cites Metzinger's neuropedagogy and Consciousness Revolution as the "response of contemporary living labor to the regime of cognitive capitalism." In fact, I like the sobering way Lazzarato puts it: art and culture are "neither more nor less integrated" into the society of control and security than any other activity, and they have "the same potential and ambiguities as any other activity" (2008, 174). There is little to be gained by investing either a substance (brain, frontal cortex, organism) or a potentiality with an absolute *saving power*. This, however, does not change the way in which a Spinozist politics of brain and affects (Wolfe 2014) is an improvement over those planifications which lay out a blueprint for action, with a hierarchy of actors assigned to their unmoving roles, *à la* DIAMAT and the dictatorship of the proletariat.

So, again: navigating between the Charybdis of apolitical neuronormativity, where Churchland becomes Philip K. Dick (. . . neurolegal attempts to identify psychopaths before they commit crimes), and the Scylla of comfortable Marxist anti-naturalism, I find support in Negri's provocative affirmation, *Geist* is the brain. But which brain? Neither the brain of forceps or MRI-wielding "men in white coats," nor the brain of the bad neuro-aesthetic theorization of the experience of reading literary prose, which we saw with Walter above.

Against static materialism I oppose the combined fervor of the Bolshevik invocation of the socialist cortex—as if, contrary to present, tedious attacks on the "dangerous naturalism" of thinkers like Virno, the true radical Marxism

---

of both normative development and psychic suffering a way to account for physiological aspects of both without endorsing evolutionary or hard-wired views. For postmodernists, poststructuralists, and others interested not only in displacing the liberal subject but also in productive alternatives, plasticity seems to offer positive chaos, creativity, and multisubjectivity. For those pursuing posthumanism at various levels, plasticity renders the world as an infinite source of "wideware" for the brain, and positions the individual brain as inherently connected to others—things, artifacts, other brains" (Pitts-Taylor 2010, 647).

11   In response to the phenomenologist Erwin Straus's "humanist" statement that "It is man who thinks, not the brain" (in Straus 1935, 183).

was in the brain (Wolfe 2010, Pasquinelli 2014)—and Negri's incantatory assertion that "the brain is the biopolitical monster" (cit. in Wolfe 2008). Granted,
we might take a dose of deflationary realism towards such utopias; yet they
are infinitely more sympathetic than the melancholy cynicism of the *déraciné*
architecture theorists, the gleeful naïveté of metaphysicians of the prosthesis,
or (again) the reactive, fearful anti-naturalisms, anti-cerebralisms of some our
fellow-travelers.

Acknowledgments: Thanks to Matteo Pasquinelli and Pieter Present for their comments.

References

Alač, M. 2008. "Working with Brain Scans: Digital Images and Gestural Interaction in a fMRI
Laboratory." *Social Studies of Science* 38: 483–508.

Bickle, J. and V. Gray Hardcastle. 2012. "Philosophy of Neuroscience." *eLS*. http://www.els.net.
doi: 10.1002/9780470015902.a0024144.

Changeux, Jean-Pierre, and Paul Ricoeur. 2002. *What Makes us Think? A Neuroscientist and a
Philosopher Argue about Ethics, Human Nature, and the Brain*. Translated by M.B. DeBevoise.
Princeton: Princeton University Press.

Choudhury, Suparna, and Jan Slaby, eds. 2012. *Critical Neuroscience: A Handbook of the Social and
Cultural Contexts of Neuroscience*. Chichester: Wiley-Blackwell.

Churchland, Patricia Smith. 1986. *Neurophilosophy: Towards a Unified Science of the Mind/Brain*.
Cambridge, MA: MIT Press.

Churchland, Patricia Smith. 2002. *Brain-Wise: Studies in Neurophilosophy*. Cambridge, MA: MIT
Press.

Deleuze, Gilles. 1995. "On *The Time-Image*." In *Negotiations 1972-1990*. Translated by M. Joughin,
57–61. New York: Columbia University Press.

Deleuze, Gilles, and Felix Guattari. 1991. *Qu'est-ce que la philosophie?* Paris: Minuit.

De Vos, Jan. 2014. "The Death and the Resurrection of (Psy)critique: The Case of Neuroeduca-
tion." *Foundations of Science* (October): 1–17.

De Vos, Jan. "The transcendental-psychological spectre haunting Catherine Malabou's philosophy of plasticity." Manuscript.

Dumit, Joseph. 2003. *Picturing Personhood: Brain Scans and Biomedical Identity*. Princeton, NJ:
Princeton University Press.

Farah, Martha J. 2005. "Neuroethics: The practical and the philosophical." *Trends in Cognitive
Science* 9 (1): 34–40.

Fine, Cordelia. 2010. *Delusions of Gender: How Our Minds, Society, and Neurosexism Create Difference*. New York: Norton.

Guattari, Félix. 2011. "On Contemporary Art (1992 interview)." In *The Guattari Effect*, edited by Éric
Alliez and Andrew Goffey, 40–53. London: Continuum.

Hardt, Michael, and Antonio Negri. 2000. *Empire*. Cambridge, MA: Harvard University Press.

Hawkes, David. 2011. "Against Materialism in Literary Theory." *Early Modern Culture* 9. http://emc.
eserver.org/Hawkes.pdf.

Hirstein, William, and Katrina Sifferd. 2014. "Ethics and the Brains of Psychopaths: The Significance of Psychopaths for Ethical and Legal Reasoning." In *Brain Theory*, edited by Chares T.
Wolfe, 149–70. London: Palgrave MacMillan.

Iriki, Atsushi. 2009. "Using Tools: The Moment When Mind, Language, and Humanity Emerged."
RIKEN Research Report 4 (5). http://www.rikenresearch.riken.jp/eng/frontline/5850

Lazzarato, Maurizio. 2008. "The Aesthetic Paradigm." In *Deleuze, Guattari, and the Production of
the New*, edited by Simon O'Sullivan and Stephen Zepke 173–83. London: Continuum.

Luria, Alexander. (1966) 1978. "L.S. Vygotsky and the Problem of Functional Localization." In *The Selected Writings of A.R. Luria*, edited by Michael Cole, 273–81. New York: M.E. Sharpe. Also In *Journal of Russian and East European Psychology* 40 (1) 2002: 17–25.

Lynch, Zack. 2004. "Neurotechnology and Society (2010–2060)." *Annals of the New York Academy of Science* 1013: 229–233.

Malafouris, Lambros. 2010. "The Brain–Artefact Interface (BAI): A Challenge for Archaeology and Cultural Neuroscience." *Social Cognitive and Affective Neuroscience* 5 (2–3): 264–73. doi:10.1093/scan/nsp057.

Marx, Karl. 1973. *Grundrisse: Foundations of the Critique of Political Economy*. Harmondsworth: Penguin.

Metzinger, Thomas, and Vittorio Gallese. 2003. "The Emergence of a Shared Action Ontology. Building Blocks for a Theory." *Consciousness and Cognition* 12 (4): 549–71.

Negri, Antonio. 1995. "On *A Thousand Plateaus*." Translated by Charles T. Wolfe. *Graduate Faculty Philosophy Journal* 18 (1): 93–109. Translation of "Sur *Mille Plateaux*," *Chimères* 17 (1992): 71–93. https://antonionegriinenglish.files.wordpress.com/2010/09/4002-on_gilles_deleuze_and1.pdf.

Negri, Antonio. 2000. *Kairos, Alma Venus, Multitudo. Nove lezioni impartite a me stesso*. Rome: Manifestolibri.

Ortega, Francisco, and Fernando Vidal, eds. 2011. *Neurocultures: Glimpses into an Expanding Universe*. Frankfurt: Peter Lang.

Pasquinelli, Matteo. 2014. "The Power of Abstraction and Its Antagonism: On Some Problems Common to Contemporary Neuroscience and the Theory of Cognitive Capitalism." In *Psychopathologies of Cognitive Capitalism II*, edited by Warren Neidich, 275–92. Berlin: ArchiveBooks.

Pitts-Taylor, Victoria. 2010. "The Plastic Brain: Neoliberalism and the Neuronal Self." *Health* 14 (6): 635–52.

Place, Ullin T. 1997. "We needed the Analytic-Synthetic Distinction to formulate Mind-Brain Identity then: We Still Do." Symposium 40 Years of Australian Materialism, Dept. of Philosophy, University of Leeds.

Schmitz, Sigrid. 2014. "Feminist Approaches to Neurocultures." In *Brain Theory*, edited by Chares T. Wolfe, 195–216. London: Palgrave MacMillan.

Slaby, Jan, and Shaun Gallagher. 2014. "Critical neuroscience and socially extended minds." Manuscript. http://janslaby.com/downloads/gallslaby13critneuro_draftweb.pdf.

Smart, J.J.C. 1959. "Sensations and brain processes." *Philosophical Review* 68 (2): 141–56.

Straus, Erwin. (1935) 1989. *Du sens des sens*. Grenoble: J. Millon.

Sutton, John, and Evelyn B. Tribble. 2011. "Materialists are not merchants of vanishing. Commentary on David Hawkes, 'Against Materialism in Literary Theory.'" *Early Modern Culture* 9. http://emc.eserver.org/1-9/sutton_tribble.html.

Taylor, Matthew. 2009. "Left brain, Right Brain." *Prospect* 46 (September). http://www.prospect-magazine.co.uk/magazine/left-brain-right-brain/#.UmWAmfm-2Po.

Terranova, Tiziana. 2013. "Ordinary Psychopathologies of Cognitive Capitalism." In *The Psychopathologies of Cognitive Capitalism II*, edited by Arne de Boever and Warren Neidich, 45–68. Berlin: Archive Books.

Tiqqun (anon.). 2001. "L'Hypothèse cybernétique." *Tiqqun* 2: 40–83. English translation https://cybernet.jottit.com.

van der Veer, Rene, and Jaan Valsiner. 1991. *Understanding Vygotsky: A Quest for Synthesis*. London: Blackwell.

Virno, Paolo. 2001. "Multitude et principe d'individuation." *Multitudes* 7: 103–17. http://www.multitudes.net/Multitude-et-principe-d

Vygotsky, Lev. 1997. "Psychology and the Localization of Mental Functions." In *The Collected Works of L.S. Vygotsky. Vol. 3: Problems of Theory and Method in Psychology*, edited by. R.S. Rieber and J. Wollock, translated by R. van der Vee, 139–144. New York: Plenum Press.

Walter, Damien G. 2012. "What Neuroscience Tells Us about the Art of Fiction." http://damieng-walter.com/2012/06/10/what-neuroscience-tells-us-about-the-art-of-fiction/.

Williams, Tyler. 2013. "Plasticity, in Retrospect: Changing the Future of the Humanities." *Diacritics* 41 (1): 6–25.

Wolfe, Charles T. 2008. "L'anomalie du vivant. Réflexions sur le pouvoir messianique du monstre." *Multitudes* 33: 53–62. http://www.multitudes.net/l-anomalie-du-vivant-reflexions/.

Wolfe, Charles T. 2010. "From Spinoza to the Socialist Cortex: Steps toward the Social Brain. In *Cognitive Architecture: From Bio-Politics to Noo-Politics*, edited by Deborah Hauptmann and Warren Neidich, 184–206. Rotterdam: 010 Publishers, Delft School of Design Series.

Wolfe, Charles T. 2014. "Cultured Brains and the Production of Subjectivity: The Politics of Affect(s) as an Unfinished Project. In *Psychopathologies of Cognitive Capitalism II*, edited by Warren Neidich, 245–67. Berlin: ArchiveBooks.

TRAUMA

FREUD

LACAN

ŽIŽEK

[11]

Post-Trauma: Towards a New Definition?

Catherine Malabou

According to Žižek, contemporary approaches to trauma disregard Lacan's most fundamental statement: trauma has always already occurred. To state that trauma has already occurred means that it cannot occur by chance, that every empirical accident or shock impairs an already or a previously wounded subject. In this text, I want to chance a thought that would definitely escape the always already's authority, which would give chance a chance. The chapter goes on to compare the Freudian/Lacanian view of brain trauma versus psychic trauma with contemporary neurobiological and socio-political views on trauma.

In *Alleys of Your Mind: Augmented Intellligence and Its Traumas,* edited by Matteo Pasquinelli, 187–98. Lüneburg: meson press, 2015.
DOI: 10.14619/014

In his article "Descartes and the Post-Traumatic Subject," Slavoj Žižek (2009) develops a very insightful critique of the current neurobiological and neuro-psychoanalytic approach of trauma.1 He challenges the way in which these approaches tend to substitute for the Freudian and Lacanian definitions of psychic wounds. Žižek's critique may be summarized in the following terms: While developing its own critique of psychoanalysis, namely of Freud and Lacan, neurobiology would not have been aware of the fact that Lacan, precisely, has already said what they thought he has not said. They would thus be ventriloquized by Lacan at the very moment they thought they were speaking from another point of view, one other than Lacanian psychoanalysis.

Why is that? How is it possible to cite Lacan without knowing about it? According to Žižek, contemporary approaches to trauma would remain unaware—out of disavowal or of desire—of Lacan's most fundamental statement: trauma has always already occurred. A specific trauma, this or that empirical shock, may happen only because a more profound and originary trauma, understood as the real or as the "transcendental" trauma, has always already occurred. Trauma had always already happened. Already always already. Lacan had already said always already. The new approach to trauma would only be a confirmation, and not a destitution, of the always-already. It would be a mere repetition of what has already occurred and been said.

To state that trauma has already occurred means that it cannot occur by chance, that every empirical accident or shock impairs an already or a previously wounded subject. There is an obvious rejection of chance in Freud and Lacan. Beyond the always-already principle. Something that Lacan had never said, to the extent that I want to chance a thought that would definitely escape the always already's authority, which would give chance a chance.

Before I focus on the notion of chance, I want to state that the possibility of such a beyond is opened by current neurobiology and its redefinition of both the unconscious (named neural unconscious or neural psyche) and the trauma, and consequently the post-traumatic subjectivity (this is the central thesis of Malabou 2007). Neurobiology and neuropsychoanalysis challenge the Freudian conception of the psychic accident understood as a meeting point between two meanings of the event: the event conceived as an internal immanent determination (*Erlebnis*) and an encounter that occurs from outside (*Ereignis*). In order for an accident to become a proper psychic event, it has to trigger the subject's psychic history and determinism. The *Ereignis* has to unite with the *Erlebnis*. The most obvious example of such a definition of the psychic event is the example, often proposed by Freud, of the war wound. When a soldier on the front is traumatized by being wounded, or merely the fear of being wounded, it appears that the current real conflict he is involved

---

1   Žižek's article is a review of Malabou 2007.

in is a repetition of an internal conflict. Shock is always a reminder of a previ-ous shock. Freud would then have considered PTSD as the expression of the always-already character of the conflict or trauma.

Neurobiologists hold, on the contrary, that severe trauma is, first, fundamen-tally an *Ereignis* and as such something that happens by mere chance from the outside. Second, they thus maintain this dismantles the *Ereignis/Erlebnis* distinction to the extent that it disconnects the subject from her reserves of memory and from the presence of the past. After severe brain damage, which always produces a series of severed connections and gaps within the neural network, a new subject emerges with no reference to the past or to her previ-ous identity. A neural disconnection does not trigger any previous conflict. Instead, the post-traumatized subject disconnects the structure of the always-already. The post-traumatized subject is the *nevermore* of the always-already.

We can then state that a neural disconnection cannot belong to either of the three terms that form the Lacanian triad of the imaginary, the symbolic, and the real, to the extent that this triad is rooted in the transcendental principle of the always-already. We propose to entertain a fourth dimension, a dimen-sion that might be called the material. From a neurobiological point of view, the trauma would be taken to be a material, empirical, biological, and mean-ingless interruption of the transcendental itself. This is why post-traumatic subjects are *living examples of the death drive* and of the dimension *beyond the pleasure principle* that Freud and Lacan both fail to locate or to expose. Beyond the always-already principle is the true beyond-the-pleasure principle.

Žižek (2009) affords a certain credulity to these ideas but rejects them out of hand for three main reasons:
1. These statements are seemingly ignorant of the Lacanian distinction between pleasure (*plaisir*) and enjoyment (*jouissance*). Enjoyment in itself is precisely beyond pleasure. It is this painful surplus of pleasure that resists being contained within the framework of the pleasure principle. Enjoy-ment is the always-already confronting us with death, and without which we would be trapped in pleasure only. In other words, neurological trauma cannot be but a form of enjoyment. Lacan has always already said that dis-connection, separation from the past, loss of memory, and indifference are modalities or occurrences of enjoyment. The unconscious is always already ready for its own destruction: "What is beyond the pleasure principle is enjoyment itself, it is drive as such" (Žižek 2009, 136).
2. The second objection concerns destruction itself understood as the pres-ence of what Lacan calls "the Thing" (la Chose). The Thing is the threat of death. Without this threat, which mainly appears to the subject as the threat of castration, any empirical objective danger or hazard would remain meaningless to the psyche. Here comes the always-already again: "Castration is not only a threat-horizon, a not yet/always to come, but,

simultaneously, something that always already happens: the subject is not only under a threat of separation, it is the effect of separation (from substance)" (Žižek 2009, 141).

3. This last sentence expresses the main objection: according to Žižek, the subject is, since Descartes, a post-traumatic subject, a subject structured in such a way that it has to constantly erase the traces of its past in order to be a subject. Thus, and once again, the experience of being cut off from oneself is a very old one. Neurobiology does not teach us anything new on that point, according to Žižek it rather confirms the very essence of the subject: "The empty frame of death drive is the formal-transcendental condition" (2009, 27) of subjectivity: "What remains after the violent traumatic intrusion onto a human subject that erases all his substantial content is the pure form of subjectivity, the form that already must have been there" (2009, 144). Further: "If one wants to get an idea of cogito at its purest, its 'degree zero,' one has to take a look at autistic monsters (the new wounded), a gaze that is very painful and disturbing" (2009, 146).

From Descartes to Damasio via Lacan, there would be, once again, one and only one principle: *trauma has always already happened.*

To answer these objections one may insist that the motif of chance and thought, elaborated in a certain way, deconstructs the always-already, which appears to be a barrier to what it is supposed to be—that is, a barrier to destruction. If destruction has always already happened, if there is anything such as a transcendental destruction, then destruction is indestructible. This is what, in Freud and in Lacan, remains extremely problematic: Destruction remains for them a structure, the repetition of the originary trauma. What if the always-already might explode? What if the always-already were self-destructive and able to disappear as the so-called fundamental law of the psyche?

In order to address these issues more specifically, let us concentrate on the status of chance in a dream that Freud analyzes in chapter 7 of *The Interpretation of Dreams* and that Lacan comments in turn with his seminar XI *The Four Fundamental Concepts of Psychoanalysis* in chapters 5 "*Tuché* and *Automaton*" and 6 "The Split between the Eye and the Gaze." Freud writes:

A father had been watching beside his child's sick bed for days and nights on end. After the child had died, he went into the next room to lie down, but left the door open so he could see from his bedroom into the room in which the child's body was laid out, with tall candles standing round it. An old man has been engaged to keep watch over it, and sat beside the body murmuring prayers. After a few hours sleep, the father had a dream that his child was standing beside his bed, caught him by the arm and whispered to him reproachfully: 'Father, don't you see I'm burning?' He woke up, noticed a bright glare of light from the next room, hurried into it and found that the old watchman had dropped out to sleep and that the wrappings and one of the arms of the beloved child's dead body had been burned by a candle that had fallen on them. (1964, 5: 547–48)

The issue immediately addressed by Freud is to know whether we can consider such a dream as a wish fulfillment. On the contrary, is it not an objection, a counter example to the theory of dreams as wish fulfillment?

Let us consider Lacan's answer to this issue. First of all, after having reminded us of this dream, Lacan posits that psychoanalysis is "an encounter, an essential encounter—an appointment to which we are always called with a real that eludes us" (1978, 53). This essential missed encounter, or misencounter, with the real is the encounter with the trauma. According to Lacan, this dream stages such an encounter. The Freudian question comes back at that point: If this dream stages the encounter with the trauma, how can we consider it as wish fulfillment, as fulfillment of a desire?

We need to understand more precisely what the very notion of "encounter with the real" means. The analysis of this formula—"encounter with the real"—forms the content of Freud's chapters 5 and 6. This formula is contradictory to the extent that "encounter" for Freud refers to something contingent, accidental, to something that may or may not happen. For Lacan "real," on the other hand, designates the necessary and determined mechanism of repetition, the always-already of the trauma. How then can we encounter—contingently—the necessity of trauma? Here, the notion of chance is emerging. How can we encounter—by chance—the necessity of the trauma, which has been always already here?

It is on this point that Lacan refers to Aristotle, who in his *Physics* distinguishes two regimes of events or of causality. First to the mode of *"tuché"*: which means fortune, contingency; then to the mode of *"automaton,"* the blind necessity of the repetition mechanism, the compulsion to repeat as such. With those to modes, we have chance on the one hand, determinism on the other. Furthermore, according to Aristotle, everything that comes to pass is due to one of these two modes of temporality: *Tuché* will decide if you will meet by chance a friend on the agora today; *automaton* governs the cycle of sunset and sunrise, or the seasons cycle, etc. Lacan comments on these two modes: *"Tuché,* he says, is good or bad fortune" (1978, 69). *"Automaton* is the Greek version of the compulsion to repeat" (67). Even if this encounter between two regimes of events and two modes of causality is said to be a missed encounter, it is nonetheless an encounter. Again, how is this possible?

Here is where the analysis of the dream of the father and his dead child can begin. But what belongs to *automaton* and what to *tuché* in this dream? Or as

Lacan puts it: "Where is the reality in this accident?" (1978, 58) and where is the accident in this reality?

Obviously, what belongs to *tuché* is the falling of the candle and the burning of the child's arm. This is the reality, Lacan says, but not the real. The real is the unreal "resurrection" of the child and the words: "Father, can't you see I am burning?" Here, Lacan starts to analyze *tuché* as a secondary kind of causality or reality. The child's burned arm is not the real accident in this dream, it is not the real. The real comes with the speech, the son's address to his father. *Tuché* has no autonomy; it is in fact only a means for the real or the *automaton* to emerge. Accordingly, there would only be one mode of happening, that of *automaton*, with a disguised version of it, a mask, *tuché*.

Chance, or fortune, is only an appearance, an "as if." What happens as if by chance is in fact always the automatism of repetition, the primary trauma: "What is repeated, in fact, is always something that occurs *as if by chance*," states Lacan (1978, 54). Moreover, Lacan asks what is genuinely burning in the dream. Is it the child's arm, or the sentence uttered by the child: "Father, can't you see that I'm burning?" Lacan explicates:

> Does not this sentence, said in relation to fever suggest to you what, in one of my recent lectures, I called the cause of fever? . . . What encounter can there be with that forever inert being—even now being devoured by the flames—if not the encounter that occurs precisely at the moment when, by accident, as if by chance, the flames come to meet him? Where is the reality in this accident, if not that it repeats something more fatal *by means* of reality, a reality in which the person who was supposed to be watching over the body still remains asleep, even when the father reemerges after having woken up? (1978, 58)

It is clear that if contingent reality is always a means for the real to come to light, it is then always secondary. When Lacan asks what is the reality in this accident, he means that there is something other, in the accident, than the accident: "Is there no more reality in this message than in the noise by which the father also identifies the strange reality of what is happening in the room next door?" (1978, 58).

The contingent external encounter of reality (the candle collapses and ignites the cloth covering the dead child, the smell of the smoke disturbs the father) triggers the true real, the unbearable fantasy-apparition of the child reproaching his father. Again, what burns are the words, not the arm. "Father, can't you see I'm burning? This sentence is itself a fire-brand—or itself it brings fire where it falls," writes Lacan (1978, 69) Further: the veiled meaning is the true reality, that of the "primal scene." In other words, there is a split between reality and the real.

Now is the moment for approaching the problem of wish fulfillment. Lacan writes: "It is not that, in the dream, the father persuades himself that the son is still alive. But the terrible version of the dead son taking the father by the arm designates a beyond that makes itself heard in the dream. Desire manifests itself in the dream by the loss expressed in an image at the cruel point of the object. It is only in the dream that this truly unique encounter can occur. Only a rite, an endlessly repeated act, can commemorate this . . . encounter" (1978, 59).

This dream would then be a kind of fulfillment to the extent that it would render the encounter with jouissance, enjoyment, possible. The fulfillment is not always linked with pleasure, says Lacan, but it can be linked with jouissance. We remember that jouissance as defined by Žižek is the beyond of the pleasure principle, the excess or surplus of pleasure. It transforms itself in a kind of suffering which is the very expression of the death drive. Read in this way, the dream is, a wish fulfillment, because we can only encounter jouissance in dreams.

Is it not properly inadmissible, the way in which Lacan distinguishes two kinds of realities in this dream, a true one and a secondary one? Can we not think that the accident of the candle falling on the child's arm is traumatizing per se, and as such does not necessarily trigger the repetition mechanism of a more ancient trauma? Then, this accident would be as real as the words it provokes.

If there is a beyond the pleasure principle, can we still understand it as a beyond chance, beyond the accident or beyond contingency? This is precisely what is no longer possible. When the victims of traumas are "burning," we certainly do not have a right to ask: Where is the reality in these accidents? We certainly do not have a right to suspect contingency for hiding a more profound kind of event, for being the veiled face of the compulsion to repeat. We do not have a right to split reality from the real, contingency from necessity, the transcendental from the empirical, good or bad fortune (*tuché*) from necessity (*automaton*). Reading this Lacanian interpretation, we cannot help but visualize the psychoanalyst as a fireman looking at the catastrophe and saying: "There must be something more urgent, I must take care of a more originary emergency."

The accident never hides anything, never reveals anything but itself. We need to think of a destructive plasticity, which is a capacity to explode, and cannot, by any means, be assimilated by the psyche, even in dreams. The answer we can give to the second objection, concerning castration as something which has always already occurred, is that the threat of castration is what helps Lacan to always see, even if he says the contrary, the symbolic at work within the real.

While for Freud castration is the phenomenal form of the threat of death, because it means separation, it gives death a figurative content, Lacan declares about separation: "We must recognize in this sentence ['Father can't you see I'm burning ?'] what perpetuates for the father those words forever separated from the dead child that are said to him" (1978, 58). Here, we find the motive of separation: the child's death, the separation from the child is the trauma, the *automaton*. But since this separation can be expressed by another separation, that of words—words separating from the body—then the trauma encounters the symbolic and never escapes it. The real is separated from itself thanks to words, thanks to the symbolic.

What challenges the idea that castration or separation has always already happened is precisely the fact that this always already is the presence of the symbolic in the real, consequently also a kind of erasure of the trauma. There is no "pure" real.

What brain damage allows us to see is that the violence of the traumatizing lesions is consistent with the way they cut the subject from his or her reserves of memory, as we have already seen. The traumatized victim's speech does not have any revelatory meaning. His or her illness does not constitute a kind of truth with regard to their ancient history. There is no possibility for the subject to be present to their own fragmentation or to their own wound. In contrast to castration, there is no representation, no phenomenon, no example of separation, which would allow the subject to anticipate, to wait for, to fantasize what can be a break in cerebral connections. One cannot even dream about it. There is no scene for this Thing. There are no words.

We do not believe in the possibility of responding to the absence of meaning by reintroducing some kind of hidden repetition of the real. On the contrary, we have to admit that something like a total absence of meaning is the meaning of our time. There is a global uniformity of neuropsychological reactions to traumas, be it political, natural, or pathological traumas. Žižek, among others, considers this new uniformed face of violence:

> First, there is the brutal external physical violence: terror attacks like 9/11, street violence, rapes, etc., second, natural catastrophes, earthquakes, tsunamis, etc.; then, there is the "irrational" (meaningless) destruc- tion of the material base of our inner reality (brain tumors, Alzheimer's disease, organic cerebral lesions, PTSD, etc.), which can utterly change, destroy even, the victim's personality. We would not be able to distinguish between natural, political and socio-symbolic violence. We are dealing today with a heterogeneous mixture of nature and politics, in which poli- tics cancels itself as such and takes the appearance of nature, and nature disappears in order to assume the mask of politics. (2009, 125)

What Žižek does not seem to admit is that with this a new form of violence is emerging today, which is implying a new articulation of the concept of the real—we might also say the concept of what is burning, a concept that would give chance its chance, a chance that would never be an "as if," an "as if by chance."

Let us turn to the third and last objection. We remember that for Žižek, post-traumatic subjectivity is nothing other than the classical Cartesian form of subjectivity. The subject is an instance capable of erasing all substantial content in order always to be new and present to itself and to the world. This is as true as the whole history of metaphysics.

But while this might be true, it is difficult to believe that traumatic erasure can occur without forming each time a new subject, unaware of the previous one. Repetition is plastic, it gives form to what it destroys. We have to think of a form created by destruction, the form of a new person, which is not the transcendental subject, but what undermines it, as the threat of its explosion. The plasticity of contingency has the power to bestow its own form on the subjects that it shocks. A subject that burns, and which urges us to see, at long last, that it is *really* burning.

~

What is a shock? A trauma? Are they the result of a blow, of something that cannot, by any means, be anticipated, something sudden that comes from outside and knocks us down, whoever we are? Or are they, on the contrary, always predestined encounters? Are they something which would force us to erase the "whoever you are" from the previous sentence, to the extent that an encounter presupposes a destination, a predestination, something which happens to you, to you proper, and to nobody else? According to this second approach, a shock or a trauma would always result, as Freud states, from a meeting between the blow itself and a preexisting psychic destiny.

Is this Freudian conception still accurate to characterize current global psychic violence? Do we not have to admit that blows, or shocks strike any of us without making any difference, erasing our personal histories, destroying the very notion of psychic destiny, of childhood, of the past, even of the unconscious itself? For Freud and for Lacan, it seems clear that every external trauma is "sublated," internalized. Even the most violent intrusions of the external real owe their traumatic effect to the resonance they find in primary psychic conflicts.

When it comes to war neuroses, Freud declares in his introduction to *Psycho-analysis and the War Neuroses* that the external accident, which causes the trauma, is not the genuine cause of it. It acts as a shock, or a blow, which awakens an old "conflict in the ego." The genuine enemy is always an "internal enemy" (Freud 1964, 17:210).

According to Freud, there is only one possible kind of "neurosis aetiology": the sexual one. Some passages from "Sexuality" and from "My Views on the Part Played by Sexuality" in *The Aetiology Of The Neuroses* are clear in this respect. In the first, Freud states: "The true aetiology of the psychoneuroses does not lie in precipitating causes" (1964, 7:250). In the second text, Freud sums up his whole theory of infantile trauma and recapitulates all the changes he has brought to it. He says that he was forced to give up the importance of the part played by the "accidental influences" in the causation of trauma (1964, 7:275). Traumas are not caused by effective events or accidents, but by phantasms:

> Accidental influences derived from experience having receded into the background, the factors of constitution and heredity necessarily gained the upper hand once more. (Freud 1964, 3:250)

For Freud, brain injuries and brain lesions cannot have a real causal power since they are regarded as merely external. In the course of our psychic life and in the constitution of our subjectivity the brain has no responsibility. It is not responsible, which also means that in general it cannot bring a proper response to the questions of danger, fragility, and exposure. It is exposed to accidents but not to the symbolic and/or psychic meaning of accidents. For Freud, sexuality appears to be, first of all, not only the "sexual life," but also a new specific kind of cause, which alone is able to explain the constitution of our personal identity, our history, and our destiny. There is a wide gap between external and internal traumatic events, even if the frontier between inside and outside is being constantly redrawn by Freud. Nevertheless, it is clear that none of the determinant events of our psychic life has an organic or physiological cause. In a certain sense, such events never come from the outside. Properly speaking, there are no sexual accidents.

In *Beyond the Pleasure Principle*, Freud goes so far as to state that the emergence of a neurosis and the occurrence of a physical lesion are antithetic and incompatible:

> In the case of the ordinary traumatic neuroses two characteristics emerge prominently: first, that the chief weight in their causation seems to rest upon the factor of surprise, of fright; and secondly, that a wound or injury inflicted simultaneously works as a rule *against* the development of a neurosis. (1964, 18:12)

Here, Freud recognizes the importance of surprise and terror, and he seems to admit the power of chance and the absence of anticipation. However, this power either causes a physical wound or a psychic wound. In the first case, there is a narcissistic bodily investment that takes care of the wound, as if organic injuries were able to cure themselves without any help from psychic therapy. It is as if physical and psychic wounds have nothing in common, unless the first can be translated into the language of the second to be considered as "symptoms." This means that for Freud people suffering from brain diseases do not belong within psychoanalytic jurisdiction. And that is why, perhaps, we do not encounter any kind of despondency in Freud's clinical studies. But we then emerge with the idea that the psychic life is indestructible:

> The primitive mind is, in the fullest meaning of the word, imperishable. What are called mental diseases inevitably produce an impression in the layman that intellectual and mental life have been destroyed. In reality, the destruction only applies to later acquisitions and developments. The essence of mental disease lies in a return to earlier states of affective life and functioning. An excellent example of the plasticity of mental life is afforded by the state of sleep, which is our goal every night. Since we have learnt to interpret even absurd and confused dreams, we know that whenever we go to sleep we throw out our hard-won morality like a garment, and put it on again the next morning. (Freud 1964, 24:285–6)

Even if Lacan displaces many Freudian statements, he also shares many on the indestructibility of psychic life, which is another name for the always-already. Neurobiology puts the so-called psychic immortality into question. Our socio-political reality imposes multiple versions of external intrusions, traumas, which are just meaningless brutal interruptions that destroy the symbolic texture of the subject's identity and render all kinds of internalization/interiorization impossible, as well as the accident's re-appropriation or resubjectivation, because some regions of the brain have been destroyed. Nothing, in psychic life, is indestructible.

At some point in his review, Žižek evokes the possibility that neurobiologists would only project their own desire, in their account of neurobiological victims and meaningless trauma, without mentioning it: do they "not forget to include [themselves], [their] own desire, in the observed phenomenon (of autistic subjects)?" (2009, 137).

Here comes desire again! But of course, we might reverse the objection: Does not Žižek omit to include his own desire for the always-already? Even if he is one of the most accurate and generous readers of current neurobiology, as becomes manifest in his great text, we might interpret the meaning of such a desire as a fear of the trauma of being definitely separated from Lacan.

Acknowledgments: This text is a response to Slavoj Žižek's review (2009) of Catherine Malabou's book Les Nouveaux Blessés (2007). It has been previously published in the Open Access anthology: Tom Cohen (ed.) Telemorphosis: Theory in the Era of Climate Change. Ann Arbor, MI: Open Humanities Press, 2012.

Bibliography

Freud, Sigmund. 1964. *The Standard Edition of the Complete Psychological Works of Sigmund Freud.* 24 vols, 1956–1974. London: Hogarth Press.

Lacan, Jacques. 1978. *The Four Fundamental Concepts of Psychoanalysis.* Translated by Alan Sheridan. New York: W.W. Norton.

Malabou, Catherine. 2007. *Les Nouveaux Blessés: de Freud a la neurologie: penser les traumatismes contemporains.* Paris: Bayard. English translation: *The New Wounded: From Neurosis to Brain Damage.* New York: Fordham University Press, 2012.

Žižek, Slavoj. 2009. "Descartes and the Post-Traumatic Subject: On Catherine Malabou's *Les nouveaux blessés* and Other Autistic Monsters." *Qui Parle* 17 (2): 123–47.

APPENDIX

Keyword: Augmented Intelligence

Matteo Pasquinelli

Augmented intelligence is an umbrella-term used in media theory, cognitive sciences, neurosciences, philosophy of mind, and political philosophy to cover the complex relation between human intelligence on one side, and mnemo-techniques and computational machines on the other—both understood to be an expansion (also to a social and political degree) of human cognitive faculties.

Main Synonyms

Synonyms include: augmented human intellect, machine augmented intelligence, and intelligence amplification. Specifically, extended mind, extended cognition, externalism, distributed cognition, and the social brain are concepts of cognitive sciences and philosophy of mind that do not necessarily involve technology (Clark and Chalmers 1998). Augmented reality, virtual reality, and teleoperation can be framed as a form of augmented intelligence, moreover, for their novel influence on cognition. Brain-computer interfaces directly record electromagnetic impulses of neural substrates to control, for instance, external devices like a robotic arm, and raise issues of the *exo-self* and *exo-body*. Augmented intelligence must be distinguished from artificial intelligence, which implies a complete autonomy of machine intelligence from human intelligence despite sharing a logical and technological ground; and from swarm intelligence, which describes decentralized and spontaneous forms of organization in animals, humans, and algorithmic bots (Beni and Wang 1989). In the field of neuropharmacology, nootropics refers to drugs that improve mental functions such as memory, motivation, and attention. Like artificial and augmented intelligence, the idea of collective intelligence also bred (especially in science fiction) a family of visionary terms that is not possible to summarize here (for example Stapledon 1930).

History: Engelbart and Bootstrapping

The relation between cognitive faculties, labor, and computation was already present in the pioneering work of Charles Babbage (1832). The "division of mental labor" was the managerial notion at the basis of his famous calculating engines, which aimed to improve industrial production. The concept of augmented intelligence itself was first introduced in cybernetics by Engelbart

(1962), who was influenced by the works of Bush (1945) on *the Memex*, Ashby (1956) on *intelligence amplification*, Licklider (1960) on *man-computer symbiosis*, and Ramo (1961) on *intellectronics*, among others. In his seminal paper, "Augmenting Human Intellect: A Conceptual Framework," Engelbart (1962) provides a definition of augmented intelligence specifically oriented to problem solving:

> By "augmenting human intellect" we mean increasing the capability of a man to approach a complex problem situation, to gain comprehension to suit his particular needs, and to derive solutions to problems. Increased capability in this respect is taken to mean a mixture of the following: more-rapid comprehension, better comprehension, the possibility of gaining a useful degree of comprehension in a situation that previously was too complex, speedier solutions, better solutions, and the possibility of finding solutions to problems that before seemed insoluble. And by "complex situations" we include the professional problems of diplomats, executives, social scientists, life scientists, physical scientists, attorneys, designers—whether the problem situation exists for twenty minutes or twenty years. (1962, 1)

Engelbart was a pioneer of graphic user interfaces and network technologies, inventor of the computer mouse and founder of the Augmentation Research Center at Stanford University. The methodology called *bootstrapping* was the guiding principle of his research laboratory and aimed to establish a recursive improvement in the interaction between human intelligence and computer design (the term has also been adopted in the discourse on artificial intelligence to describe a hypothetical system which learns how to improve itself recursively, that is by observing itself learning; as yet such a system has not been successfully designed). Engelbart's vision was eminently political and progressive: Any form of augmentation of individual intelligence would immediately result in an augmentation of the collective and political intelligence of humankind. Despite the fact that Engelbart does not account for possible risks, social frictions, and cognitive traumas due to the introduction of augmented intelligence technologies, his combined technological and political definition can be useful to draw a conceptual map of augmented intelligence.

Conceptual Axes of Augmentation

The conceptual field of augmented intelligence can be illustrated along two main axes: a technological axis (that describes the degree of complexity from traditional mnemo-techniques to the most sophisticated knowledge machines) and a political axis (that describes the scale of intellectual augmentation from the individual to a social dimension).

- *Technological axis.* Any technique of external memory (such as the alphabet or numbers) has always represented an extension of human cognition.

McLuhan (1962) underlined how innovations such as the printing press and electronic media have caused a further expansion of our senses on a global scale, affecting cognitive organization and, therefore, social organization. According to McLuhan, it is possible to periodize the history of augmented intelligence in four epistemic periods according to the medium of cognitive augmentation: *sign* (alphabet, numbers, symbolic forms), *information* (radio, TV, communication networks), *algorithm* (data mining, computer modeling, simulation and forecasting), and *artificial intelligence* (expert systems and self-learning agents: as a hypothetical limit). The interaction between the human mind and techniques of augmentation is recursive (as Engelbart would register), since humankind has always continued improving upon them.

– *Political axis.* The political consequences of augmented intelligence are immediately manifested as soon as a large scale of interaction and computation is achieved. Indeed, Engelbart's project was conceived to help problem solving on a global scale of complexity: The collective scale cannot be severed by any definition of augmented intelligence. A vast tradition of thought has already underlined the collective intellect as an autonomous agent not necessarily embodied in technological apparatuses (Wolfe 2010). See the notions of: *general intellect* (Marx), *noosphere* (Teilhard de Chardin), *extra-cortical organization* (Vygotsky), *world brain* (Wells), *cultural capital* (Bourdieu), *mass intellectuality* (Virno), *collective intelligence* (Levy). Across this tradition, "the autonomy of the general intellect" (Virno 1996) has been proposed by autonomist Marxism as the novel political composition emerging out of post-Fordism. The project of such a *political singularity* mirrors perfectly the a-political model of *technological singularity*.

The combination (and antagonism) of the technological and political axes describes a trajectory toward augmented social intelligence. According to this definition, however, political conflicts, on one side, and the computational aporias, on the other, go unresolved. Deleuze and Guattari's notion of the machinic (1972, 1980)—also inspired by the idea of mechanology by Simondon (1958)—was a similar attempt to describe, in conjunction, the technological and political composition of society without falling either into fatalism or into utopianism. Among the notions of augmentation, moreover, it is worth recalling their concepts of machinic surplus value and code surplus value (Deleuze and Guattari 1972, 232–237).

Criticism and Limits

Any optimistic endorsement of new technologies for human augmentation regularly encounters different forms of criticism. "Artificial intelligence winters," for instance, are those periods of reduced funding and fall of institutional interest, also due to public skepticism. A first example of popular

criticism directed toward augmented intelligence in the modern age would
be the Venetian editor Hieronimo Squarciafico. After working for years with
Aldus Manuntius's pioneering press, he stated in an aphorism, an "abundance
of books makes men less studious" (Lowry 1979: 31). The essay "The Question
Concerning Technology" by Heidegger (1954) is considered a main reference
for technological critique in continental philosophy. Heidegger influenced
a specific tradition of technoskepticism: Stiegler (2010), for instance, has
developed the idea that any external mnemo-technique produces a general
grammatization and, therefore, a *proletarization* of the collective mind with
a consequent loss of knowledge and *savoir-vivre*. Berardi (2009) has repeatedly remarked upon the de-erotization of the collective body produced by
digital technologies and the regime of contemporary *semio-capitalism*. The
physical and temporal limits of human cognition when interacting with a
pervasive mediascape is generally addressed by the debate on the attention
economy (Davenport and Beck 2001). The discipline of neuropedagogy has
been acclaimed as a response to widespread techniques of cognitive enhance-
ment and a pervasive mediascape (Metzinger 2009). Specifically dedicated to
the impact of the Internet on quality of reading, learning, and memory, the
controversial essay "Is Google Making Us Stupid?" by Carr is also relevant in
this context. The thesis of the nefarious effect of digital technologies on the
human brain has been contested by neuroscientists. Carr's political analysis,
interestingly, aligns him with the continental philosophers just mentioned:
"What Taylor did for the work of the hand, Google is doing for the work of the
mind" (Carr 2008). A more consistent and less fatalistic critique of the relation
between digital technologies and human knowledge addresses the primacy of
sensation and embodiment (Hansen 2013) and the role of the "nonconscious"
in distributed cognition (Hayes 2014). In neomaterialist philosophy, it is femi-
nism, in particular, that has underlined how the extended or augmented mind
is always embodied and situated (Braidotti, Grosz, Haraway).

Augmented Futures

Along the lineage of French technovitalism, yet turned into a neo-reactionary
vision, Land (2011) has propagated the idea of capitalism itself as a form of
alien and autonomous intelligence. The recent "Manifesto for an Accelerationist Politics" (Srnicek and Williams 2013) has responded to this fatalist scenario
by proposing to challenge such a level of complexity and abstraction: The idea
is to repurpose capitalism's infrastructures of computation (usually controlled
by corporations and oligopolies) to augment collective political intelligence.
The Cybersyn project sponsored by the Chilean government in 1971 set out to
control the national economy via a supercomputer; this is usually mentioned
as a first rudimentary example of such *revolutionary cybernetics* (Dyer-Witheford 2013). More recently, Negarestani (2014) has advocated for a functional

linearity between the philosophy of reason, the political project of social intelligence, and the design of the next computational machine, where the logical distinction between augmented intelligence and artificial intelligence would no longer make any sense. The definition of augmented intelligence, however, will always be bound to an empirical foundation that is useful to sound out the consistency of any political or technological dream to come.

Acknowledgments: This keyword is part of the Critical Keywords for the Digital Humanities project, a series to be published by meson press 2016 that was realized with Leuphana University of Lüneburg. Available at: http://cdckeywords.leuphana.com/augmented_intelligence

References

Ashby, William Ross. 1956. *An Introduction to Cybernetics*, London: Chapman & Hall.

Babbage, Charles. 1832. "On the Division of Mental Labour." In *On the Economy of Machinery and Manufactures*, 241–47. London: Charles Knight.

Beni, Gerardo, and Jin Wang. 1989. "Swarm Intelligence in Cellular Robotic Systems." *Proceed. NATO Advanced Workshop on Robots and Biological Systems*, Tuscany, Italy, 26–30 June 1989.

Berardi, Franco. 2009. *The Soul at Work: From Alienation to Autonomy*. Translated by Francesca Cadel and Giuseppina Mecchia, Los Angeles: Semiotext(e).

Bush, Vannegar. 1945. "As We May Think." In *The Atlantic*, July.

Carr, Nicholas. 2008. "Is Google Making Us Stupid?" In *The Atlantic*, July.

Chalmers, David. 2010. "The Singularity: A Philosophical Analysis." In *Journal of Consciousness Studies* 17 (9–10): 7–65.

Clark, Andrew, and David Chalmers. 1998. "The Extended Mind." In *Analysis* 58 (1): 7–19.

Davenport, Thomas and Christopher Beck. 2001. *The Attention Economy: Understanding the New Currency of Business*, Harvard Business School Press.

Dyer-Witheford, Nick. 2013. "Red Plenty Platforms." In *Culture Machine* 14. http://www.culture-machine.net/index.php/cm/issue/view/25.

Engelbart, Douglas. 1962. *Augmenting Human Intellect: A Conceptual Framework*. Summary Report AFOSR-3233. Stanford Research Institute, Menlo Park, California.

Hansen, Mark. 2006. *Bodies in Code: Interfaces with New Media*, New York: Routledge.

Hayles, N. Katherine. 2014. "Cognition Everywhere: The Rise of the Cognitive Nonconscious and the Costs of Consciousness." In *New Literary History* 45 (2): 199–220.

Heidegger, Martin. (1954) 1977. "The Question Concerning Technology." In *The Question Concerning Technology and Other Essays*, translated by William Lovitt, 3–35. New York: Harper and Row.

Land, Nick. 2011. *Fanged Noumena: Collected Writings 1987–2007*. Falmouth, UK: Urbanomic.

Licklider, Joseph. 1960. "Man-Computer Symbiosis." *IRE Transactions on Human Factors in Electronics* 1: 4-11.

McLuhan, Marshall. 1962. *The Gutenberg Galaxy: The Making of Typographic Man*. Toronto: University of Toronto Press.

Metzinger, Thomas. 2009. *The Ego Tunnel: The Science of the Mind and the Myth of the Self*. New York: Basic Books.

Negarestani, Reza. 2014. "The Revolution is Back." Paper, Incredible Machines Conference, 7–8 March, Vancouver, Canada.

Ramo, Simon. 1961. "The Scientific Extension of the Human Intellect." In *Computers and Automation* (February).

Simondon, Gilbert. (1958) 1980. *On the Mode of Existence of Technical Objects*, Ontario: University of Western Ontario.

Srnicek, Nick, and Alex Williams. 2013. "Manifesto for an Accelerationist Politics." In *Dark Trajectories: Politics of the Outside*, edited by Joshua Johnson et al., 135–55. Miami: Name.

Stapledon, Olaf. 1930. *Last and First Men*. London: Methuen.

Turing, Alan. 1950. "Computing Machinery and Intelligence." In *Mind* 59: 433–60.

Vinge, Vernor. 1993. "The Coming Technological Singularity: How to Survive in the Post-Human Era." In *Whole Earth Review* (Winter).

Virno, Paolo. 1996. "Notes on the General Intellect." In *Marxism beyond Marxism*, edited by Saree Makdisi et al., 265–272. New York: Routledge.

Wolfe, Charles. 2010. "From Spinoza to the Socialist Cortex: Steps Toward the Social Brain." In *Cognitive Architecture: From Biopolitics to Noopolitics*, edited by Deborah Hauptman and Warren Neidich, 185–207. Rotterdam: 010 Publishers.

Authors

Benjamin H. Bratton is Associate Professor of Visual Arts at the University of California, San Diego. His work is situated at the intersections of contemporary social and political theory, computational media and infrastructure, architectural and urban design, and the politics of synthetic ecologies and biologies. His forthcoming book *The Stack: On Software and Sovereignty* will be published by MIT Press January 2016.

Orit Halpern (PhD) is a historian of science whose work bridges histories of computing and the human sciences with design and art practice. Her most recent book *Beautiful Data: A History of Vision and Reason since 1945* (Duke Press 2014) is a genealogy of interactivity and our contemporary obsessions with "big" data and data visualization. She is currently working on the history and political economy of ubiquitous computing, logistical systems, and responsive environments. She has also published and created works for a variety of venues including The Journal of Visual Culture, Public Culture, Configurations, C-theory, and ZKM in Karlsruhe, Germany. You can learn more at: www. orithalpern.net.

Adrian Lahoud is Director of the M.Arch Urban Design and Reader at Bartlett School of Architecture UCL and lecturer at the Centre for Research Architecture, Goldsmiths. His research is situated between philosophy, architecture and digital design, and focuses on post-traumatic urbanism and forensic architecture among other topics. Recently his work has been published in *Forensis: The Architecture of Public Truth*, *The Journal of Architecture*, *Architecture and the Paradox of Dissidence*, *New Geographies*, and *Performing Trauma*.

Jon Lindblom is currently writing a thesis on the cultural implications of the scientific image of man, with a particular focus on the relationship between technology and cognition in the Visual Cultures Department at Goldsmiths, University of London. https://technihil.wordpress.com/.

Catherine Malabou is professor in the philosophy department at the centre for research in modern European philosophy (CRMEP) at Kingston University London. Her research has evolved around the term "plasticity" with regards to Hegel, medical science, stem cells, and neuroplasticity, among others. Her last book *Self and Emotional Life: Philosophy, Psychoanalysis, and Neuroscience* (Columbia University 2013) was published with Adrian Johnson. Her next book *Avant Demain, Epigenèse et rationalité* (Paris, 2014) wil be published with Polity Press in 2016.

Reza Negarestani is a philosopher. His current philosophical project is focused on rationalist universalism beginning with the evolution of the modern system of knowledge and advancing toward contemporary philosophies of rationalism.

Luciana Parisi is Reader in Cultural Theory, Chair of the PhD programme at the Centre for Cultural Studies, and co-director of the Digital Culture Unit, Goldsmiths University of London. Her research develops philosophical conceptions of matter and thought in the context of technocapitalist investments in artificial intelligence, biotechnology, nanotechnology. Currently she is working on the history of automation and the philosophical consequences of logical thinking in machines. Her last book was *Contagious Architecture. Computation, Aesthetics and Space* (MIT Press 2013).

Matteo Pasquinelli (PhD, London) is visiting Assistant Professor at the Department of Humanities and Media Studies of Pratt Institute, New York. He wrote the book *Animal Spirits: A Bestiary of the Commons* (Rotterdam: NAi, 2008) and edited the anthology *Gli algoritmi del capitale* (Verona: Ombrecorte, 2014) among others. He lectures frequently at the intersection of political philosophy, media theory and cognitive sciences in universities and art institutions. Together with Wietske Maas he wrote the Manifesto of Urban Cannibalism (2013). In 2014 at NGBK Berlin he co-curated the exhibition The Ultimate Capital is the Sun and the symposium The Metabolism of the Social Brain.

Ana Teixeira Pinto is a writer from Lisbon based in Berlin currently lecturing at UdK (Universität der Künste). Her work has been published in publications such as *e-flux Journal, Art-Agenda, Mousse, Frieze, Domus, Inaesthetics, The Manifesta Journal*, or *Text zur Kunst*.

Michael Wheeler is Professor of Philosophy at the University of Stirling. His primary research interests are in philosophy of science (especially cognitive science, psychology, biology and artificial intelligence) and philosophy of mind. His book, *Reconstructing the Cognitive World: The Next Step*, was published by MIT Press in 2005.

Charles T. Wolfe is a researcher at Ghent University, Belgium, working primarily in history and philosophy of the early modern life sciences, with a particular interest in materialism and vitalism. His edited volumes include *Monsters and Philosophy* (2005), *The Body as Object and Instrument of Knowledge* (2010, with O. Gal), *Vitalism and the scientific image in post-Enlightenment life-science* (2013, with S. Normandin) and *Brain Theory* (2014); he has papers in journals including *Multitudes, Progress in Biophysics and Molecular Biology* and others.

Ben Woodard is a PhD student in Theory and Criticism at Western University. His work focuses on the naturalism of FWJ von Schelling and the status of nature in contemporary philosophy. He is most recently the author of *On an Ungrounded Earth: Towards a New Geophilosophy* (Punctum, 2013).

www.ingramcontent.com/pod-product-compliance
Lightning Source LLC
LaVergne TN
LVHW042123070326
832902LV00036B/558